Pits

A Pictorial History of Mining

This is the 'Ram-Jam' pit on Sackup Lane in an area known as Bloomhouse (Darton). It is believed the pit closed soon after 1900. *Loaned by the Hyde family*

Pits

A Pictorial History of Mining

A Combined Volume of Pits 1 & 2

John Threlkeld

Wharncliffe Books

First published as *Pits 1*, 1987 and *Pits 2*, 1989

Reprinted 2003 by
Wharncliffe Books
an imprint of
Pen and Sword Books Limited,
47 Church Street, Barnsley,
South Yorkshire. S70 2AS

For up-to-date information on other titles produced under the
Wharncliffe imprint, please telephone or write to:

> **Wharncliffe Books**
> **FREEPOST**
> **47 Church Street**
> **Barnsley**
> **South Yorkshire S70 2BR**
> **Telephone (24 hours): 01226 - 734555**

ISBN: 1-903425-50-6

A CIP catalogue record of this book is available from the
British Library

Printed and bound in Singapore by
Kyodo Printing Co (S'pore) Pte Ltd

Contents

Acknowledgements

My thanks to Helen Williams, the family of Frank Ashton, Ian Harley, Carolyn Thorpe, June Walton, Paul Greenam, Josie Clark, Jim Marsden, George Beedan, Rosemary Preece, Mr and Mrs R Firth, John Goodchild, Mr F Williamson, Mr J Gill, Mrs R Hirst, Roni Wilkinson, Wes Hobson, Jenny Wood, Don Oakes, Alan Billingham, Lord Mason, Mr J McKenning, Doncaster Borough Council, Barnsley Library (Local Studies), Ruth Vyse, Sheffield Library (Archives) Department, British Coal Public Relations Department and the Yorkshire NUM (Phil Thompson and Tom Bellamy).

Bibliography

Ten Year Stint, A Robens.
The Miners (series), R Page Arnot.
Historical Directory of Trade Unions, Arthur Marsh and Vicitoria Ryan.
The Yorkshire Miners, Frank Machin.
Coals from Barnsley, John Goodchild.
The Changing Role of the Miners Rescue Team, G V Jollife.
Report of Mining in Silkstone, 1901, G H Teasdale.
Report on the explosion at Wharncliffe Woodmoor 1/2/3, Government Mines Department.
Report on the explosion at Barnsley Main, Ministry of Fuel and Power.
Scargill and the Miners, Michael Crick.
The Coal Scuttle, Joseph Jones.
Scargill: The Unauthorized Biography, Paul Routledge.
Barnsley Record and *Barnsley Chronicle* files.

Grimethorpe Colliery.

Miners starting to undercut the coal. *Yorkshire Mining Museum/Leeds City Museum*

Introduction

It is sixteen years since the first *Pits* book was published. At that time the once mighty coal industry was reeling from the 1984/85 Miners' Strike and from the subsequent run down of the Barnsley coalfield but the town was still rich in working class culture and coal dust.

Since then there has been a transformation in lifestyles, the environment and in working lives; I am told children sometimes ask their parents and teachers: *'What is coal?'* Instead the growth industry at Manvers – once the home of the South Yorkshire coalfield – has more to do with call centres than digging coal.

Pits 2 was first published in 1989 and was followed by a new and enlarged version of *Pits 1* in 1993. Earlier this year we came to the conclusion that the merger of the two books would help to create a permanent record of the history of coal mining in the Barnsley coalfield. The twentieth anniversary of the start of the 1984/85 Miners' Strike is also approaching and we believe this will lead to people wanting to learn more about their mining roots.

This hardback book has been published to enable the present and future generations to relish what life was like in the days when pit headgear, spoil heaps and miners with bible black faces dominated the area and when mines were regarded as permanent features in the landscape. How wrong we were.

Unfortunately not all the words or photographs from the earlier books have been included in the new version. For instance, there were more than 400 photographs and illustrations, and it would have been impossible to make room for all of them. Instead the best have been carefully selected to give the publication maximum impact.

Wombwell Main shortly before closure. *R Firth*

Chapter 1

Pre 1900

Growth and Brass

Barnsley was one of the crude and growing towns in the early Victorian era. It was a jumble of smoking hills and hollows, haphazard development and ugly pits, all sandwiched between the wind-swept moors at Penistone and what was described as the rich and beautiful countryside at Wombwell and Worsbrough.

As the nation underwent one of its spasmodic convulsions in the mid nineteenth century, changing from a society based on agriculture to one concentrating on industry, the thick coal seams in Barnsley were exploited and then towards the end of the century the even larger and deeper reserves in the Dearne Valley. Urban sprawl, the decline of farming and a life rich in working class culture followed in the footsteps of the shaft sinkers as they moved across Barnsley and then through Wombwell, a pastoral village, and into the farming villages of the Dearne.

These men, a rare breed with a thirst for perilous and filthy work and strong beer, dug shafts to the seams. The shafts were then widened, the headgear and surface buildings erected and finally the miners lowered in the cages to hew (cut) the coal in the seams.

In the early days there was coal mania as the shafts were randomly sunk without any apparent reason: some had a vague resemblance to modern mines, others were glorified holes with just two or three men running the operation. In later decades the pits became larger and more sophisticated as technology improved and the industry consolidated, with inefficient and exhausted mines being elbowed into the dustbin of history by the burgeoning coal companies.

Mining continued to expand as the demand for coal increased, the pits dominating the scene for the next 100 years and touching almost every family in Barnsley and in the surrounding small towns and villages. But how did it all start?

Mining is seen as a relatively modern industry with its roots in the Industrial Revolution, but in Silkstone mining was an old industry 200 years before the Norman Conquest. When the Abbot of Peterborough gave a grant of land for the digging of coal in 833 he probably thought he was one of a new breed of entrepreneurs who would blaze a new trail by exploiting this early version of a privatised coal mine; however, when the workers arrived on the scene they found the local inhabitants had been mining for years and there were outcrops all over the countryside: an example of local enterprise 833-style!

In 1370 several leases for coal working at Corkworth, near Wentworth, were awarded to the Fitzwilliam family at Wentworth Woodhouse, who later became one of the

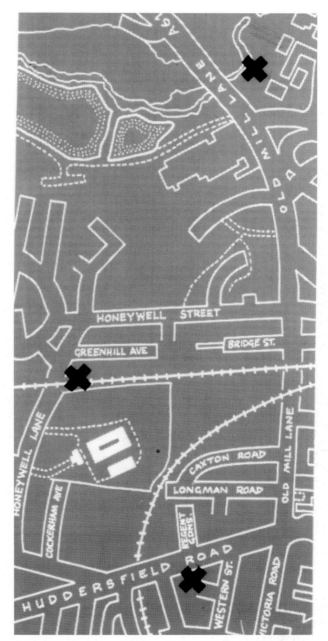

Approximate locations of Hopwood's Pit off Huddersfield Road; Honeywell near the railway line and Old Mill (part of Mount Osborne pit) near Old Mill Lane, which were worked in Barnsley in the early Victorian era.

major pit owners in Barnsley, running mines at Elsecar, Jump and Hemingfield. The Court Rolls of Wakefield contain an entry in 1308 that a licence was granted to dig

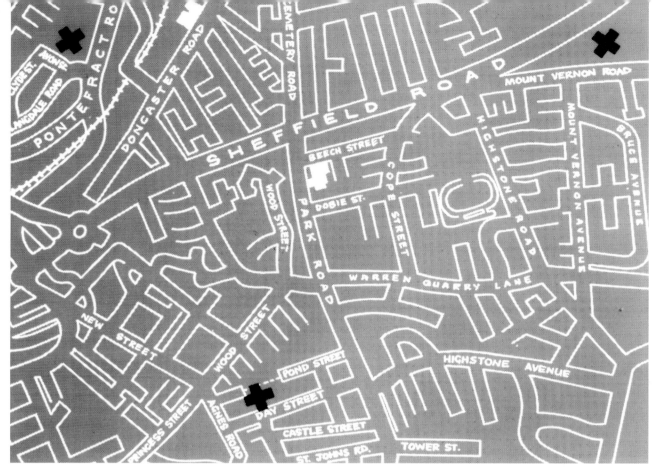

Approximate locations of Agnes Main, near Agnes Road; Mount Osborne off Pontefract Road and Bank Top off Sheffield Road (the location of Bank Top colliery should be further up Mount Vernon Road), which were worked in Barnsley during the 1850s and 1860s.

for coal at Hipperholme, near Wakefield, and by the beginning of the fifteenth century, coal mining was an established industry in Wakefield. Yorkshire coal was used for the burning of lime needed to build York Minster, and the Fabric Rolls show a payment in 1499 for the purchase of coal from Wakefield. At about the same time the Cluniac Monks of Pontefract acquired a coal pit at Barnsley for eight pounds, the estimated life of which was sixteen years and there was primitive mining in Gawber in the 1500s. But the industry did not expand until the middle of the seventeenth century, when coal came into general use. A local newspaper, speculating on the sluggish expansion of the industry in the sixteenth century, stated in the 1870s:

This was no doubt attributable to the plentiful supply of wood. Not that the inhabitants were so long ignorant of this mineral, but wood was easily procured, and our ancestors not having the advantages of the mechanised contrivances by which coal is now so readily won, we can at once excuse them from putting forth great efforts for its acquisition.

That was not the full story. Mining has always aroused controversy and until the mid-seventeenth century there were objections on the grounds of air pollution and public safety. In 1306, 650 years before the infamous London smogs of the 1950s and nearly 700 years before pollution and the greenhouse effect became fashionable, Parliament petitioned the King to try to prohibit the use of the fuel, as it polluted the air, and the authorities clamped

down on mining operations. One man was tried, convicted and hanged for burning coal. There was opposition in Barnsley as well. In 1413, five men were fined for extracting coal without permission at Darton. Two hundred years later, again at Darton, Michael Wentworth was fined because he had not covered up old coal pits on the common. Opposition subsided but even in 1659 no coal could be mined at Clayton West at haytime.

The first known pit explosion in Barnsley occurred in 1672, resulting in the death of James Townend, who lived in Silkstone. In 1693 Abraham Rock leased part of Keresforth Farm for coal getting, at an annual rent of seventeen pounds; four years later there were coal pits at Gawber Hall. In 1714, according to Thoresby's *History of Leeds*, the pits were '*now without number.*' South Yorkshire was described as '*black with coal pits and the smoke of fire engines, but with good land, and with many gentlemen's seats.*' Bell-pits, so called because on reaching coal the workings were widened in the form of a bell, were in use in 1728. Other developments: in 1776 John Curr, of Sheffield, who was the manager of the Duke of Norfolk's collieries, substituted trams running on cast-iron rails for the sledges then in use for transporting coals; the first shaft of any great depth in Barnsley was sunk by James Clarke about 1790, near Noblethorpe, the coal being brought out in baskets. Coal was consumed locally and went by land on the back of a pack horse or cart. It was still a small industry, heading in the right direction but without an efficient transport system to move the coal around the country. The industry expanded when the nation embarked on the industrial revolution.

There were three growth villages in Barnsley: Silkstone, Elsecar and Gawber, all dominated by families who worked alone: the Clarkes (Silkstone), the Fitzwilliams

(Elsecar) and the Thorps (Gawber). Such was the significance of Silkstone in the early development of mining in this area that a seam stretching from the outskirts of Leeds to Alfreton in Derbyshire derived its name from the village. In 1804, Mr Clarke was corresponding with captains of ships and London merchants with a view to sending coal to the capital. A cargo was delivered to London on 29 July 1805, via canals to Goole, where it was transhipped into a sloop but the costs were too high to establish trade at that time. Nothing could stop the formidable Clarkes when the railways arrived. In 1846 the Manchester and Sheffield line was opened for coal traffic, and Mrs Clarke sent the first train of coal through the Woodhead Tunnel from Oxspring to Tintwistle. The 1851 Exhibition in Hyde Park put Silkstone coal firmly on the map, the family having sent a three hundred weight lump of coal to the exhibition for display purposes and it caused a sensation, resulting in the family's coal becoming well-known in London and throughout the country. Three years later, the Worsbrough branch of the South Yorkshire Railway Company which went through the Dove Valley as far as Moorend Colliery, belonging to Mrs Clarke, was opened.

The Thorps were almost as resourceful as the Clarkes: they were selling coal in Barnsley between 1805 and 1809. Samuel Thorp, of Gawber Hall (demolished in the 1930s due to mining subsidence) and Banks Hall, Cawthorne, was the first man to work the Barnsley seam on a large scale, at Cobbler Hole Pit, and the family had at various stages pits at Stainborough, Honeywell and Willowbank. Gawber is still riddled with old mine workings. The third family, the Fitzwilliams, members of the landed gentry who boasted of close links with Royalty, monopolised coal mining in Elsecar, having taken advantage of the opening of the Dearne and Dove canal in 1805. At about that time it was said that the Elsecar pit was so clean and spacious that sometimes the ladies from Wentworth Woodhouse,

the largest country house in the nation, and owned by the Fitzwilliams, went down the pit to witness the operations. The Fitzwilliams were humane proprietors who provided decent housing and decent working conditions, although some pit managers grumbled that some of the employees expected jobs for life which, they said, was not conducive to healthy competition and business! With the growth of the railways, the most significant development in the opening up of the local coalfields, some of the leading pit proprietors formed a trading company under the title Silkstone and Elsecar Owners' Company. The spin of a coin gave Silkstone the right to appear first in the title of the company which included Mrs Clarke, Earl Fitzwilliam, Lord Wharncliffe and the Wombwell Main Company.

These families were important to the development of early mining but there were other major figures as well. Worsbrough was the home of a number of coal owners, one of the most notable being Joe Mitchell who as a child had bought and delivered coal. He was born at Brightside in 1807 where his father was manager of Brightside forge. Young Joe established Worsbrough Dale Foundry, manufacturing engines, boilers, machinery and railway bridges. He later became sole owner of a colliery at Worsbrough Bridge, after which he sunk Edmund's Main Colliery, in conjunction with Charles Bartholomew, engineer on the South Yorkshire Railway, and John Tyas, a solicitor. He also helped to sink nearby Swaithe Main. In 1870 Aldham coalfield, owned by Henry Garland and others, came on the market and in partnership with Mr Worms, the continental coal merchant of Paris, and Mr J. Josse, of Grimsby, he opened Mitchell Main at Aldham, Wombwell.

William Day was born in 1822, the son of a Shafton farmer. He owned the Mount Osborne Colliery, sunk in Pontefract Road, Barnsley, on a large farm belonging to the Duke of Leeds (the pub, *The Mount*, is near the site). The original owner was his uncle, Richard Day, of Monk Bretton, and John Twibell. After the death of Richard in 1844 William and Twibell opened the Old Mill shaft.

Edmund's Main Colliery, Worsbrough, a fine example of the small mine which flourished in Barnsley. *John Goodchild Collection, Wakefield*

Canal barges at Elsecar, pre 1900. Elsecar was one of the growth villages in South Yorkshire. *John Goodchild Collection*

Old workings at Elsecar, eighteenth or nineteenth century. The entrance to the workings can be seen near the *Market Inn*. *John Goodchild Collection*

Market Hill, the old quarter.

Twibell then retired and William opened Agnes Main Colliery near Agnes Road.

Robert Craik, born in 1803, was an assistant to a draper, started in business as a linen manufacturer and ran the bleach works at Old Mill before leasing more than 200 acres from Lord Wharncliffe and the trustees of Shrewsbury Hospital under the New Lodge estate in 1854. Other pit owners were Samuel Cooper, a member of Field, Cooper and Co., Worsbrough, which owned coal and iron works at Worsbrough and William Hopwood, who started as a clerk in Wentworth's Bank in Church Street, Barnsley, and who owned Hopwood's pit in Huddersfield Road. Hopwood's father had been the owner of a corn mill in Summer Lane. The coal owners met in Barnsley as early as 1819.

Most of these companies were small compared to the larger companies which dominated trade in the early part of the twentieth century. The big boys exploiting the latest technology would take over in the virgin coalfields of the Dearne Valley and in Doncaster, pushing the smaller companies out of the way – just as Messrs Mitchell and Day had shunted the small fry out of the way in their prime.

Meanwhile, in the 1850s Barnsley was staking its claim to be the coal capital of South Yorkshire. With the coming of the railway in 1850 coal owners began sinking shafts all over the town: 50 in that decade. In 1853 the Strafford Collieries, Stainborough, found the Flockton seam at a depth of 159 feet, in 1857 the Silkstone seam at 236 yards (five feet seven inches thick and all marketable coal), and in 1858 the Parkgate seam. This kind of operation was repeated all over Barnsley and the West Riding in that frantic decade: 374 pits in the riding produced nine million tons in 1855. While most mines were digging deeper to reach rich seams, some pits were working Silkstone seam coal a few yards below the ground: mines that would fit into your back garden. The Clarke family had worked, as well as large mines of course, the Little Pit (twenty yards) and Nopie (ten yards). There is an amusing story about Nopie Pit. Imagine the scene when a woman, Ann Paddle, fell down the ten yards-deep shaft. Luckily, she fell feet first and did not suffer any injury. On being helped out she said she would not have cared a damn if she had not split her NEW wooden clogs! According to documents published at the time, there were twelve seams or beds in the Yorkshire coalfield, ranging from the New Hill, Abdy Coal and the Whinmoor (all two feet thick) and the Parkgate, Silkstone and Kent's Thin (five feet) to the

The market pictured in the 1890s. The market was an ancient institution long before the boom in coal.

Grimethorpe Colliery. *Mr R D Watson, Higham*

Men at Wharncliffe Woodmoor in the 1890s. *Yorkshire Mining Museum, Caphouse Colliery*

prestigious Barnsley Bed (nine feet). Of these only the Barnsley Bed and Silkstone seams were said to be in quantities worth exporting. Barnsley also became a centre of trade and commerce, the railways drawing in shoppers from the neighbouring and newly established mining villages – on Wednesdays and Saturdays the town was said to double its population – as well as new industries to feed off the money supply generated by mining. But even in those days there were Jeremiahs. Just as today, experts are always predicting that the earth's resources will run out, or that some plant or animal species is on the point of extinction, the experts in the 1860s were saying that the reserves of coal would be exhausted. Jevon's *The Coal Question*, published in 1865, warned that the nation could not continue its rate of progress because there would be no coal left. He said soon the mines would need to be 4,000

feet deep! By 1878, however, *The Standard* declared:

> *To a nation like England coal is only another name for gold, and we may even say that the presence of gold in Kent would be of far less importance to London than the existence of coal.*

Between 1850 and 1880 Barnsley underwent extraordinary changes and much was due to mining and the underground savages, as miners were known. Barnsley had its old quarter, Market Hill, May Day Green and Shambles Street, each with a nearby labyrinth of yards, inns and crooked alleys but the rest of the centre had the look of a frontier town, the atmosphere of a frontier town without the gunsmoke. Early photographs

An unknown pit, pictured in the 1890s. *Photographed by Warner Gothard of Barnsley*

Houghton Main Colliery, 1890s. *Loaned by Mr W Milford, Cudworth*

look as if the owners had hurriedly erected buildings on the grounds that the coal boom would not last and that they had to make a killing as quickly as possible. There was something transitory about Barnsley, a town in flux, all bustle, grime and excitement, and it was a rough town according to the local police chiefs with a reputation that went beyond the borders of the Yorkshire coalfield. Development was haphazard with pits and terraced streets appearing almost overnight: in the early days there was certainly money to be made and there was a general air of 'stumbling vitality like a blind man on a spree,' words which were also used to describe the wild and burgeoning mining towns of Wales. Whereas the frontier towns in America, Australia and South Africa had their wilderness a few hundred yards beyond the town boundaries, Barnsley had its 'wilderness' hundreds of feet below ground in the honeycomb of galleries and tunnels where the conditions and environment were barren, hot and menacing. The core of this wilderness: the coal face where the miners hewed the coal and then shovelled it into tubs

for transportation back to the shafts. To some miners the coal face was the 'tigress,' which was as fickle and as ferocious as a wild animal and which claimed at least a life a week at most local pits; to some older miners the face was still controlled by primeval forces around which superstitions were spun.

Prosperity peaked in the early 1870s, during which it was thought prudent and fashionable to invest money in coal, a nice little earner for the owners of pit shares, as they would say today, and the coal owners, the big boys, came to the conclusion that sinking a shaft resulted in automatic riches. Coal was the new fuel – needed for steamships, trains, factories and gas works and a new phrase became popular: *'When you start working with coal, you soon stink of brass (money).'* As in any age, fortunes were made and lost. Coal miners in some cases earned a pound a day – which earned them the nickname of gold miners, a phrase which would reappear in the national newspapers during the coal boom years of the 1970s, and they came to the conclusion that the wages spiral would never end and that the days of poverty were behind them. Appearing before a Select Committee in

15

Oaks Colliery, one of Barnsley's major pits in the 1840s and 50s. The men claimed it was one of the most dangerous in England. Their predictions came true in 1866, when about 350 miners were killed in an explosion.

1873, John Dixon, secretary of the West Yorkshire Miners Association, said many miners had been thrifty and had accumulated large bank accounts. Miners' homes were said to have *'good chairs, china, bright brass candlesticks, chimney ornaments and mahogany chest of drawers.'* Like people today, miners expected their standard of living to rise each year and everyone declared with confidence that it was a new age, an age of full employment. Even the miners' union prospered, saving enough money to build the miners' offices in Huddersfield Road, an ostentatious and ornate building which demands attention. The design and construction was supposed to show to the outside world that the union was an institution as respectable as a bank or borough council, not a fly-by-night organisation like some of the other early unions: in many respects it was ahead of its time because the union was poised to hit the deck. As in modern property and share booms the coal mania ended in a big bang and by the mid 1870s and early 1880s the pits, the union and miners were on their knees. By 1880 few people wanted coal mines, the bottom having dropped out of the market. The owners and the miners, all bewildered by this sudden transformation in their fortunes, wondered what had happened to their world. Only the middle-aged and older men had known very hard times –

in their nonage – and the younger men in the 1880s had not been programmed to handle such upheaval. In 1880 South Kirkby Colliery was offered for sale at the *King's Head*, Barnsley, but not a single offer was made; in 1882 Mitchell's Main Colliery, Wombwell, was offered for sale at the hotel but withdrawn at £2,000. Mitchell's was a new pit, opened in the 1870s in a blaze of publicity with the French tricolour flying from the pithead, one of the original backers being a French businessman.

Although coal mining was in the throes of a depression, at least one business connected with the industry was prospering. John Gillott and Son, of Summer Lane, are now largely forgotten but in the Victorian era their coal-cutting machines were ahead of their time. John Gillott, a former mechanical engineer to Newton Chambers and Company, of Thorncliffe, took out the first patent on the well-known Gillott and Copley machine in 1868. The patent consisted of a disc with cutting tools assembled on its circumference, driven by a pair of cylinders which oscillated. Later the

This photograph was taken, probably in Nottinghamshire, at the beginning of the twentieth century when the use of electricity was slowly expanding. Vast improvements were made between 1860 and 1910 but life down a mine was still harsh. Many pit ponies spent their lives underground and only saw daylight during a prolonged strike and on retirement. Pit lads developed close working relationships with their ponies but there were cases where miners, whose wages depended on production, would deliberately create an accident to kill what they thought was a lazy pony. But the culprits had to be clever, for pit managers thought ponies were more valuable than men.

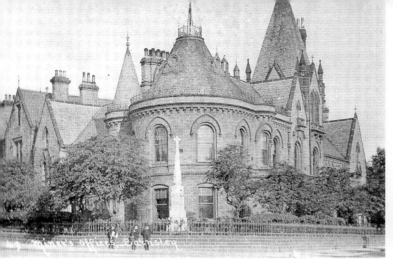

The miners' offices in Barnsley were designed to give the impression the union was a respectable organisation.

Gillott coal cutting machine.

machine was altered to the form which became in common use – two cylinders side by side. Mr Gillott did not claim to be the originator of the idea of a disc: his machine was an improvement on the machines of the type that were then in use. The company was awarded a silver medal at a mining exhibition in 1885. By then John Gillott and Company were well established in Barnsley, at their Lancaster Works, the Dominion Works coming later. Both works, near the Summer Lane railway station, employed hundreds of men. The company prospered throughout the 1890s and by 1904 John's son, Joseph William, had bought the first car in Barnsley, a Norfolk, later owned by Eyre Bros.

In the 1890s, during which Barnsley settled down to become a carbon copy town with the banks, hotels and railway stations resembling their counterparts in other industrial towns in the north, the coal markets improved. The owners' resistance in the 1893 miners' strike collapsed when the demand for coal reached a new peak and the price went through the roof in London, the lucrative market for domestic as well as industrial coal. As a consequence new pits were sunk but the growth spots were Grimethorpe and the Dearne Valley rather than Barnsley and Silkstone. The first sod was cut at Grimethorpe Colliery on 13 October 1894, the *Barnsley Chronicle* reporting:

Instances are common enough hereabouts of sleepy, out-of-the-way villages being suddenly transformed into busy centres of population through the sinking of a new mine. Such a change, there is every reason to believe, will shortly be experienced in the village of Grimethorpe.

One of the speakers, Mr C G Tyas, made a jocular reference to the fact that the best part of the Badsworth Hunt country had been taken by the mining company, and the runs some of them had enjoyed for so long would soon be impossible. Mr Joseph Mitchell, of Bolton Hall, who was the managing director, said the new pit would be capable of drawing 2,500 tons per day, more than one million tons per year. As they got deeper with their sinkings, more machines would become necessary and more skilled men needed to work them, and he hoped that

miners would feel they had something more to do than dog-racing and pigeon-racing. It was expected that the Barnsley Seam would be reached at a depth of 500 yards and the total area of the new coalfield would be 3,000 acres, he said.

Grimethorpe was a sign of things to come. It was a large colliery with massive reserves. The Doncaster pits developed in the twentieth century – the titans of the industry in Yorkshire – would resemble Grimethorpe more than the small Barnsley pits sunk in the 1850s and 1860s and which had been seen as the pinnacle of technological achievement in their day.

Depths of Collieries in South Yorkshire.
SPECIALLY COMPILED FOR "LODGE'S ALMANACK."
The following list shows the depths of Collieries in South Yorkshire:—

Name of Colliery.	When Won	Depth of Shaft. Yards.
Thorne, Barnsley Seam	(Boring Test) 1909	920
Yorkshire Main, Edlington Barnsley Bed	July, 1911	905
Maltby, Barnsley Bed	1910	818
Cadeby	1892	750
Silverwood, Barnsley Bed	December, 1903	740
Dinnington, Barnsley Bed	August, 1904	667
Frickley, Barnsley Bed	May, 1905	661
South Kirkby	August, 1878	635
Bentley Colliery	April 3, 1908	624
Brodsworth Colliery, Brodsworth	Oct. 21, 1907	595
Grimethorpe	1899	586
Askern Main, Barnsley Bed	Sept. 13th, 1912	568
Glass Houghton, Silkstone Seam	January, 1902	550
" Haigh Moor		347
Hickleton Main	June, 1894	540
Houghton Main	February 1, 1878	530
Ackton Hall, Silkstone Seam	1894	575
" Haigh Moor	1894	402
" Warren House	1887	330
Ackworth, Haigh Moor Seam	February 1913	540
New Sharlstone		511
Hoyland Silkstone	February, 1876	501
Wombwell Main, Barnsley Seam	October, 1854	223
" Parkgate Seam	April 26, 1893	502
Prince of Wales, Pontefract		496
Barrow, Silkstone Seam	1875	481
" Thorncliffe Seam	1886	420
Thorncliffe, Silkstone		481
Kiveton Park	December 1867	401
Earl Fitzwilliam Colliery, Elsecar, Parkgate Seam	February, 1908	
Darfield Main	July, 1860	350
New Oaks	July, 1870	337
Mitchell Main	September, 1875	336
Monk Bretton	August, 1870	307
Carlton Main, Barnsley Seam	1877	300
Old Oaks		298
Whitwood Main, Stanley Seam	August, 1879	295
Thrybergh Hall		288½
Charlesworth's, Swinton		288
Strafford Main, Silkstone Seam	July 12, 1857	237
" Rob Royd	January 26, 1897	235
Corton Wood	March, 1875	237
Swaithe Main		232
Lundhill		230
Dodworth, Silkstone		214
Higham, Silkstone		210
Mount Osborne		210
Edmunds Main		196
Elsecar		180
Darley Main		154
North Gawber		130
Ryhill Main		108
Victoria Main, Barnsley, Haigh Moor Seam	March, 1874	55
		60

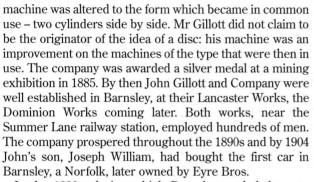

The Barnsley Bed seam, included in the adjoining list of pits, was ten feet in the neighbourhood of Barnsley, but near Sheffield it was only half that thickness. In Derbyshire it was known as Top Hard coal, an excellent quality product. It has been worked continuously from Nottingham to Barnsley. Towards the north the Barnsley Bed splits up and takes the name of Warren House, and was only a second-class seam. Other important seams are the Parkgate and Silkstone, the former being the Deep Hard and the latter the Blackshale of Derbyshire. The 'hards' were best steam coal, whilst the 'softs' were often sold as a gas or house coal. House coal should take fire readily, be clean and free from white ash, and give a bright fire with little smoke.

Women worked underground until the early 1840s. At Silkstone they were expected to dig coal like men but at most pits they were used to pull or push coal tubs. The withdrawal of women underground led to protests from some coal owners, who thought a labour shortage would hit the mines, and from some miners who wanted their daughters to have highly paid jobs. *Courtesy of the Fellows of Triniity College, Cambridge*

Postcards of Lancashire women were popular during the nineteenth century. The middle classes, who bought the postcards were fascinated by the sight of women dressed in men's clothes. Tourists often turned up at the pits to peep at the women and management at one mine had to ban the curious onlookers because they were a nuisance. *Courtesy of the Wigan Record Office*

Women were treated like galley slaves – sometimes they were harnessed like dogs to a cart, 'crawling on their hands and feet, pulling heavy tubs behind them.'

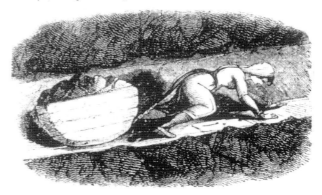

Women and children were used to pull or push tubs from the coal face to the shaft. The youngest children however, wre employed to open and close the ventilation doors. As Samuel Hirst, aged nine of Jump pit commented: 'I sit by myself; I never have a light. I sit still all day and do nothing but open and close doors.'

Women and Children

When colliers walked through the streets of Barnsley in the 1830s and early 1840s, all grime and muscle, wearing trousers and shirts and thick wooden clogs, the onlookers could not distinguish to which sex they belonged. For years women had worked at the older pits at Silkstone where some were expected to hew coal like men; now, with the coalfield moving eastwards, they were becoming a familiar sight on Barnsley streets.

With perseverance, the local population believed they could tolerate the uncouth and swarthy male miners but the middle classes, both in Barnsley and beyond, could not come to terms with pit women. According to one Victorian writer, women were supposed to be angels, not animals like men. So pit women were seen either as innocent victims of a brutal industrial system, 'sacrificed to the shameless indecencies of working underground,' according to the Children's Employment Commission, or as liberated creatures endowed with too many unseemly male characteristics, incapable of performing the duties imposed on women in Victorian society. The reformist and missionary zeal of the nation's middle classes was just waiting to be released.

The women and children aged up to 17 or 18, all known as hurriers, were used to take coal from the coal face to the shaft, sometimes harnessed like dogs to a cart, crawling on their hands and feet, pulling heavy tubs behind them. The coal hewers, self employed men, hired and paid them; the proprietors were responsible for discipline. In 1840 the Children's Employment Commission set up to investigate the mental and moral conditions of the mines, particularly in respect of children, revealed that there were 22 adult women for every 1,000 men in the pits; 36 girls aged between 13 and 18 for every 246 boys of the same age; and 41 girls under 13 for every 246 boys of that age group. The commission, some people believed, had been set up too late to deal with the problem of women, the use of them in the mines having started to decline in the late eighteenth century when proprietors found horses were cheaper and stronger in the newly developed thicker seams. Some proprietors, like the Fitzwilliams, who owned pits in Elsecar, Jump and Hemingfield, did not permit women to work underground in the nineteenth century. But the sub-commissioner said *'oppressively hard work was performed by young females at other Barnsley pits,'* and added: *'were they galley-slaves their work would not be so oppressive.'* Elizabeth Day, aged seventeen, who worked at Hopwood's Pit, Barnsley, told the sub-commissioner she had to push or pull corves (carriages for carrying coal) up slopes, adding:

I have been nearly nine years at the pit. I trapped two years and have been a hurrier ever since. When I riddle, I hold the riddle, shake it to remove the slack and then throw the rest into the corve. I work naked to the waist.

Ann Eggley, aged eighteen, who worked at Thorp's Pit, said:

The work is very hard. The sweat runs all over sometimes. Father said last night it was both a shame and a disgrace for girls to work as we do but there was

This photograph from Wigan, shows women sorting coal in the early part of the twentieth century.

nowt else for us to do. Sometimes we get home at night and we haven't the power to wash ourselves. We work twelve hours per day. We wear trousers and great big boots, clinkered and nailed. The girls at our pit do not work naked to the waist.

Her father, James Eggley, aged forty-five, said he had six girls, and a boy who was not old enough to work down the pit and the girls had to go underground to earn money.

According to the sub-commissioner, labour was distributed indifferently among both sexes except that it was rare for both men and women to hew coal. Men worked naked, assisted by females of all ages, from girls of six to women of twenty-one, with females naked to the waist. He wrote:

One of the most disgusting sights I have ever seen was of young females, dressed like boys in trousers, crawling on all fours, with belts round the waists and chains passing between their legs, in pits near Holmfirth and New Mill. Two of the girls had worn large holes in their trousers and any sight more disgusting or revolting can scarcely be imagined than these girls at work – no brothel can beat it.

On descending Hopwood's Pit, Barnsley, he found sitting round a fire a group of girls, some of whom were at the age of puberty, the girls as well as the boys naked to the waist.

Their sex was only recognisable by their breasts. I had some difficulty on occasions pointing out which were girls and which were boys and that caused a great deal of laughter and joking.

Edward Newman, a solicitor of Barnsley, displayed all the double standards of the Victorian age. He abhorred the sight of half-naked girls – but he could not resist peering into their homes when they were washing.

There are a great many girls at Silkstone who work in the pits and I have seen them washing much below the waists as I passed their doors and as they are doing that they will be chatting and talking with any man who happens to be there. Men, young and old, are washing in the same place at the same time. They dress so well after their work, and on Sundays, that it is impossible to recognise them. They wear ear-rings even whilst at work and I have seen them with ear-rings nearly two inches long. There is a great deal of loud talk and slang between the lads and girls as they pass along the streets from work and I believe they would behave more decorously were it not for the dress and disguise it affords. I have never heard similar language pass between people respectably dressed in Barnsley.

Matthew Lindley, who worked at a Barnsley pit owned by Day and Twibell:

I wish the Government would expel all girls and women from the mines. I can give proof that they are immoral, and I am certain that the girls are worse than the men as far as morals are concerned, and use far more indecent language. It unbecomes them in every way; there is not one out of ten of them who knows how to cut out a shirt, or make one, and they learn neither to sew nor knit. I have known of a case myself where a married miner and a girl who hurried for him had sexual intercourse on the bank where they worked.

George Armitage, a thirty-five year old Hoyland teacher, and a collier until he was twenty-two, said no doubt debauchery took place and added: *'I think it is scarcely possible for girls to remain modest, regularly mixing with such company and hearing such language.'*

A Silkstone woman: *'I am informed that in some pits scenes pass which are as bad as in a house of ill fame; this I have been told by young men who work in the pits.'*

Michael Thomas Sadler, a surgeon of Barnsley:

The female character is destroyed by the mines. I see the greatest differences in the homes of those colliers whose wives do not go down the mines in cleanliness and good management. The pit women neither discharge their duties as wives nor mothers.

John Thorneley, described as a JP in the county of York: *'The young of both sexes work in a half naked state and passions are excited.'*

John Cawthra, a collier at Messrs. Wilson's Pit, Barnsley: *'I do not think it is a good system to bring girls down the pit; they get bold and it tends to make the girls have bastards.'*

Matthew Fountain, underground steward at Darton Pit, owned by Thomas Wilson, believed that sexual intercourse took place and added: *'Girls work as well as boys but they can't make a shirt.'*

Joseph Ellison, of Leeds, said he knew of the case of a girl, employed as a hurrier by her father-in-law, who refused to go down the mines again because he tried to ravish her.

A vivid account of similar working lives underground in French pits is contained in Emile Zola's book, *Germinal,* in which he refers to girls who could move tubs as well as grown women, *'in spite of doll-like arms,'* and of young women who *'could take on two pit boys together.'*

He wrote:

...but the voice of the receiver shouted up orders to dispatch – doubtless some deputy was on the prowl down there. Movement began again on all nine levels, and nothing could be heard but the regular calls of the boys and snorting of the haulage girls as they reached the incline, all steaming like overloaded mares. It was at times like this that one of the waves of bestiality ran through the mine, the sudden lust of the male that came over the miner when they met one of the girls.

All kinds of arguments were put forward to try to stop the withdrawal of women from the pits. Coal proprietor John Hopwood said there could be labour shortages in Barnsley. But the loudest protest came from some colliers who were more concerned about finding jobs for their daughters than morals. However, there were exceptions. In the late 1830s a large gathering of miners in Barnsley passed a resolution urging the withdrawal on the grounds that the use of women was a shameful practice.

Children

Members of the commission were told that children of three and four were frequently taken down the mines. One collier said he took his child of three underground with him and it was made to follow him into the workings. The child held a candle and when exhausted with fatigue was cradled on the coals until the collier returned home at night.

Edward Ellis, surgeon, of Silkstone, said: *'I have 25 professional years' service among colliers. The children round here go down the pits at five.'*

The Reverend Richard Morton, a curate at Dodworth,

The Husker monument at Silkstone.

Before 1842, young children were employed in the pits.

said parents got their children into the pits as soon as they could do the task. Matthew Lindley, collier: *'Children are sometimes brought to the pit at the age of six, and are taken out of their beds between 4 a.m. and 5 a.m. throughout the year.'*

John Twibell, coal owner:

My opinion is that children should not be employed until the age of ten. We intend to direct our attention to this point with a view to it being made a rule of the pit. I am aware that some children are working as young as seven in some pits. I look on this as objectionable, both on the grounds of health and education.

The youngest children worked as trappers. They sat in a little hole with a length of string attached to an air-door; when they heard the approaching corves they pulled the string and opened the door. They worked twelve hours per day, sitting in the dark, often on a damp floor and exposed to draughts. The sub-commissioner wrote:

It is a most painful thing to contemplate the dungeon-like life these little creatures are doomed to spend, a life for the most part in solitude, damp and darkness. I found one boy who scooped out a hole in a great stone and having obtained a wick begged contributions of melted tallow from the candles of any Samaritan passer-by.

Samuel Hirst, aged nine, of Jump Pit: *'I sit by myself; I never have a light. I sit still all day and do nothing but open and close doors.'*

Mr. Armitage, the Hoyland teacher, said hurriers were often overworked, not only had they to push or pull corves but they also had to help fill them, and the slower a miner was the more the child had to help him.

Yet doctors told the commission that the children were healthy. Dr Sadler, the Barnsley surgeon, said they lived well and were robust. Dr Ellis, the Silkstone surgeon, said colliers and their families were great consumers of meat, milk, beer and ale, and the children were healthier than weavers' or farm labourers' children. The children as well as the adults had bread or milk or porridge for breakfast; huge lumps of bread and bits of cheese or bacon or fat for their lunch at the pit; a hot meal at home at 6 p.m. and bread and milk for supper. The doctors said the colliers

bought the best quality food from shops. However, there were exceptions. Mr Crooks, a surgeon of Barnsley, had been told that some parents sent their children to the pits without breakfast, although colliers often shared out food to a dinnerless child. Poor John Ibbetson, aged thirteen, said he couldn't *'lake with the other children'* because his parents couldn't afford to buy him clothes.

Severe beatings were rare. But the sub commissioner said the children had to be kept at work and therefore slight beatings occurred. Joseph Gledhill, underground steward at a Barnsley pit, said children were not hurt or ill used. The youngest generally got scolded and were 'given a bang or two'.

James Ibbitson said some hurriers were kept at work with sharp speaking and *'sometimes were disciplined with a pick shaft and anything else the collier could get his hands on.'* George Traviss, a Worsbrough coal master, said children were not overworked so as to hurt themselves. They always appeared to be cheerful and ran and played about when they came out of the pits. Another coal master, Robert C Clarke, of Silkstone, agreed: *'The children run home when they come out of the pit and they get up to all kinds of mischief.'*

The Ban

In 1842, after considering the Commission's Report, Parliament approved legislation banning females underground and children under the age of ten from pits. Women were still working at the pithead in Yorkshire and Lincolnshire in 1878. In his annual report, the Mines Inspector said five females aged between ten and thirteen worked on the surface; three between thirteen and sixteen and eleven above sixteen. At about that time pit women were becoming a tourist attraction in Wigan and at least one pit banned tourists because they were becoming a nuisance. When there was a move to ban pit women in the 1880s, a contingent from Lancashire, dressed in their Sunday best, organised a protest demonstration in London. The middle classes had a curious fascination for these women who worked in men's clothes and thousands of post cards were sold to satisfy their whims. The problem of women working in Yorkshire did not reappear until 1914, when the Yorkshire miners heard a complaint that women were working on the surface at Sharlston Colliery, because boys would not do the work. The last pit woman retired, in Cumbria, in the early 1970s.

The Mines Inspector in his 1878 report disclosed that boys aged between ten and twelve were still working underground in Leeds, Bradford and Halifax, where the seams were too thin to permit older boys and men to work. At least the figure was on the decrease: in 1873, 837 such boys were employed; in 1877, the figure was 74.

The Colliers

Colliers were in a minority in Barnsley until the middle of the nineteenth century, the linen trade having monopolised the labour market for decades. According to the Children's Employment Commission, the contrast between the two types of workers was striking:

> *The collier of fifty is usually an aged man; or if he is not aged looking he looks overstrained by labour,'* wrote the sub-commissioner. The weaver was *puny and pallid* and *wore a dirty apron and a feminine look.*

As Barnsley expanded (the population rose from under 2,000 in 1750 to nearly 18,000 in 1861), the linen industry and later mining sucked in workers from all over the country, often resulting in acute labour shortages in rural areas. The decline of the linen industry coincided with the growth of mining and weavers' sons were soon breaking family traditions by going down the mine. Old and new Barnsley met near New Street in the 1860s: Wilson's Piece, a collection of fifteen streets inhabited by weavers' families, represented the old; the nearby Agnes Main Colliery the new.

Between 1850 and 1860 more than fifty shafts were sunk in Barnsley and thick-set men of medium build and enormous strength became the norm rather than the exception on Barnsley streets. If the immigrant workers, or the sons of weavers, were puny, they soon changed their physique when they went underground. *'It is only by having a well developed, muscular body that we can earn a living at all,'* wrote a Barnsley miner decades later. Miners were a new breed of man, not unlike the railway navvies

The Collier, 1814.

who built the railways in this country and in some parts of France and who terrorised the local populous in their spare time. Miners, like navvies, were wild and unpredictable, had gargantuan strength and worked in hazardous conditions. Unlike the navvies, who never

The cage, an example of the harsh conditions underground in the nineteenth century. *British Coal*

The Barnsley Record stated in the early 1860s, that conditions underground were so bad that only miners could endure them. Working in narrow seams led to injury and premature death. A Lancashire colliery manager noted more than 100 years ago: '*I have known men constitutionally old and finished at thirty-four because they worked in the worst areas in the pits. Besides the extra labour in this class of work, there is a certain amount of oppressiveness owing to the small and confined space in which the work is performed. So confined is it that the men not only breathe again the same air, but inhale a great amount of coal dust, so much so that their discharges are as black as coal itself.*' Robert Leigh, Thorneley Arms, Dodworth

Pitmen playing quoits in 1836. A painting by Henry Perlee Parker. *Loaned by the Laing Art Gallery, Tyne and Wear County Council Museums*

'Knur and spell', dangerous in Locke Park, but safe, it seems, at *The Sun Inn,* Monk Bretton.

The miner often worked in dangerous condiitons. Note the candle to the right of the hewer. *Courtesy of Beamish, North of England Open Air Museum*

stayed in one place very long, miners became rooted in closely-knit communities, developing their own social rules over several generations.

Miners had their own sports: 'knur and spell', miners' golf, was popular throughout the nineteenth century. Henry Bromley, a well-known knur and spell player, was charged under Section 17 of the *Barnsley Local Board Act*, 1862, with playing the game in Locke Park, contrary to the by-laws. It was the first case taken under the new laws. A report in a local newspaper stated:

Last July printed notices were put up, stating that any person who played knur and spell would be liable to a penalty of 40s. On the day the notices appeared the defendant persisted in playing, as well as on July 3rd, 5th and the 14th.

Bromley was fined 1s, plus costs of 11s 6d, or, in default, fourteen days imprisonment. The by-laws were introduced because the game was considered to be dangerous to passers-by – the small, hard missiles struck by a burly miner with an implement similar to a golf club could have killed someone. Elsewhere, under proper supervision, the sport drew large crowds and generous prize money and created local celebrities, like Bromley. In Wigan, miners had an unusual game. They stripped naked, put on clogs with steel caps and then, to use the local parlance, clogged each other. It was known as 'purring'. Miners developed their own dialect and jargon (tramming, play day, main gate).

According to Mr Trevor J Lodge, of Sheffield, many UK mining terms originate in the mining areas of Mediaeval Europe. The terms were introduced to this country from the sixteenth century, when Queen Elizabeth encouraged working class artisans, including wire drawers and miners from Germany. In a letter to the *Barnsley Chronicle* in 1989, he wrote:

The word 'ruhe' or 'druhe' was used in Germany to describe the box or container in which coal was brought from the coal face. This seems to have been distorted to drug, one of the many English terms describing small coal tubs. The ancient German word for a metal tub carrying metal ore was 'hund' – literally dog – and said to be derived from the growling noise it made running along underground roadways.

These were the conditions that miners faced underground in the 1890s. *Yorkshire Mining Museum/Leeds City Museum*

Miners had to have a muscular body to survive, a Barnsley miner said in the 1800s. After working a few years many were broken men. This miner was photographed in the north-east. *Courtesy of Beamish, North of England Open Air Museum*

Whilst we do not use the literal translation directly, some words seem likely to derive from it. In Yorkshire and Nottinghamshire, for example, 'dog-belt' was used to describe the leather strap worn round the hurrier's waist which was clipped on to the coal tub he was pulling. Other areas used the terms 'dogger-on' and 'dogger-off' for the attaching and detaching of coal tubs from a wire rope haulage system. Main gate and Tail gate – the main underground roadways in a mine – are derived

from the German 'gang', meaning a path or roadway.
He said the confusion surrounding mining folklore was widespread.

Snow White and the Seven Dwarfs was probably the most famous mining fable to have become distorted through the ages. The story originated in the old German empire as 'Snow White and the Seven Miners' but confusion arose between the German words for miners and dwarfs.

Walt Disney, outwardly a pure romancer, was in reality a stickler for detail and knew the true origin of the tale. The hooded costumes worn by dwarfs in his cartoon versions are identical copies of those worn by continental miners in the Middle Ages.

Colliers were independent characters and often enjoyed flaunting this trait. On Sundays and during holidays many miners discarded their work clothes and dressed in gaudy attire, showy waistcoats called posy vests because of gaudy pictures of flowers on them, breeches fastened at the knees with stockings adorned with 'clocks' and round hats which would be decorated with ribbons – it may have been a reaction against the drab clothes they wore underground and the bleak environment in which they worked. John Wilson, a Durham miners' leader in the nineteenth century, stated in his book that miners at that time could be identified by 'the peculiarities of their dress'.

By the end of the century, however, things were changing, their clothes having become more conventional. Life was becoming more standardised following the introduction of free state education in the 1870s – D H Lawrence said the first generation of miners' children to be taught at school were beaten down by the cane – and growing conformity in the industrial age. In addition the new unions helped to enforce dress code and discipline at special events, such as at Yorkshire miners' galas, by stipulating what colliers could wear.

Miners developed their own superstitions. According to E and M Radford's *Encyclopaedia of Superstitions,* there was a widespread belief that the souls of the dead dwelt in the flowers of broad beans. Old colliers in the North and Midlands claimed that accidents occurred more frequently when they were in bloom. *The Leicester Chronicle* in March, 1855, claimed that a few days earlier a collier had been asked why he was not working that day. He replied that not only he but all his colleagues had heard *The Seven Whistlers*, the term given to certain birds whose cries were said to warn of a disaster.

In the 1870s, in some mines in Wales, miners thought there were

...a remarkably good-natured race of beings, closely allied to the fairies and known as knockers, whose business it is to point out by means of a peculiar kind of knocking a rich vein of ore or coal,

according to a colliery magazine printed at that time.

A colliery manager wrote in the 1870s:

I once knew a man who would not go down a shaft if he saw a white pigeon on his way to work, believing that if he went down after the 'warning' an accident would occur to him. If some miners saw a white bird hovering above the head-gear they believed it was a sign that an explosion of foul air was imminent.

In more recent times, a miner who saw a woman on his way to work would return home, believing it to be a bad omen, and there was a widespread belief that washing the back weakened it.

It was been claimed that in the 1850s and 1860s surnames had not been fully established in some parts of England, particularly in mining districts. This did not appear to be the case in Barnsley. In other coalfields, however, *'hereditary designations seem to be the exception rather than the rule,'* stated *Knight's Quarterly Magazine* in 1862. Clergymen in Staffordshire *'have been known to send home a wedding party in despair after a vain attempt to gain from the bride and bridegroom a sound by way of a name.'* The journalist added:

> *Every man in these colliery fields, it seems, bears a personal sobriquet, descriptive of some peculiarity, but scarcely any person has a family name, either known to himself or others. In one case an old miner's name, though he was a man of substance and had legal battles to fight (a solicitor's clerk was trying to trace him), was not known to his daughter.*

Although surnames were established in Barnsley, the town would have been regarded as uncivilised in that period. Wrongdoers were still put in the stocks in Market Hill until the early 1840s and there was at least one case of wife selling, at Wombwell, as late as the 1870s.

Between the 1850s and 1870s miners adopted

The Miners, by Albernus Antonius Houthuesen. *Courtesy of Sheffield Art Galleries*

contradictory public faces. To many people, they were men who led short and violent lives, who lived and worked hard and who drank too much.

The Barnsley Record in the 1860s said miners did not live long, pointing out that lives of twenty-seven years were not unusual, whereas agricultural workers could expect to live beyond forty. The amount of sickness in mining exceeded by sixty-seven per cent that of other workers. Edward A Rymer, a miner born in the 1830s, and who worked in pits in Durham and Lancashire as well as in Barnsley, wrote that he worked and lived in hell. Describing his early life in a book published in the 1890s, Rymer said there were coal cutting competitions underground.

> *Bill and I worked like horses, going home after a twelve hour shift with tired and sore bones. This kind of thing, which went on year after year, broke strong men. This slavish, ignorant, clumsy competition kept criminal passions predominant over the better half of miners. Scuffles broke out on pay day. At the office on Friday there used to be hundreds of men who rushed, yelled and forced their way like savages to receive their pay. It was seldom that anyone did not come away from the mob cut or bruised, or without leaving a cap behind.*

Life in the villages was no better. In Durham,

> *...a huge, fiery heap ran nearly the entire length of the village. Half a million tons of coal, broken wood and shale were burning day and night. In consequence of this, drinking, fighting, gambling and reckless pastimes were universal.*

In the 1860s *The Record* carried weekly reports of violence and drunkenness; together with the occasional case of

Portrait of John Evans, 1819. He was buried without food or light for twelve days and nights in a mine near Wrexham. *The National Museum of Wales*

27

rape and highway robbery. In 1862 crime rose by forty-two per cent in the West Riding, although miners could not be blamed entirely for such a large rise.

Yet others painted a different picture. To a few people, miners were God-fearing, home-loving men, as the Reverend C Marshall discovered in 1863. His Manchester flock were aghast to hear that he planned to visit 'Black Barnsley'. After a tour of the town, however, he told *The Record* that Barnsley should be renamed 'Bible Barnsley' or 'Blessed Barnsley', adding: *'There is not an angel in heaven who would not rejoice in such a place.'* It seems extraordinary that a city not more than thirty-four miles from Barnsley should view the town in such a poor light, for Manchester was no stranger to social unrest, inter union violence and an ugly environment but the Pennines must have been an effective barrier despite the railways.

The remoteness of towns like Barnsley exaggerated the darker side of miners. In London, where few people ventured north, Barnsley was known as 'The King of Pandemonium.' National newspapers in the 1850s and 1860s rarely carried stories about miners or mining except to chronicle the disasters and the violent strikes and lock-outs. A journalist who accompanied Charles Dickens to Barnsley in 1857, and who referred to the Pandemonium tag, was surprised to find it clean and respectable.

After the troubles of the 1860s, a short spell of prosperity led to dramatic changes in miners' lives. In the early 1870s, when the nation enjoyed its only period of full employment in the nineteenth century, and when miners were seen as elite workers, Rymer, who was living at the time in Pogmoor, wrote:

Coal flew up in price and miners boasted of earning one pound a day. Even public cadgers complained when they received coppers from Yorkshire miners. Tons of new furniture, clothing, pianos, organs, jewellery and pictures were freely accumulated. Houses could not be had for love nor money, yet thousands flocked to Yorkshire.

The roving reporter of the *Manchester Guardian* arrived in Barnsley in 1873 to find local miners were the best paid in the country. He wrote:

The miners live in a land where the hills seem softer in outline, the woodlands richer in colour, the hedgerows fuller of beauty and the grass a more lovely green than anywhere else in England. Instead of the loud hum of machinery making the air vibrate with sound, only the lowing of the cattle, the bleating of the sheep, the singing of the birds, the soughing of the wind in the trees are heard in the sylvan villages, deep in the Yorkshire vales. Barnsley miners lead the worthiest of lives. The physical and moral contamination of the town seem far removed. They are free from the temptation to dissipation which seems to beset the urban workers at every street corner. The half mining, half pastoral villages of Wombwell and Dodworth are distinguished by sobriety and industry. The miners enjoy Colliers' Monday, when they work in the gardens attached to their homes but through the rest of the week, they work with some semblance of regularity.

Some miners had bought their homes for £20. That did not seem to surprise the journalist but when he found a piano in a miner's home he was shaken. He wrote:

I asked the miner's wife whether she could play the piano and she replied: 'I cannot. He bought it when we were married and he is now taking lessons.' I have no doubt that the story of a collier taking piano lessons will try the credulity of many a cynic; but there the piano is and I will give the name and the address of the collier to whom it belongs to any doubter if he so wishes.

The journalist discovered that pit lads were great buyers of concertinas and harmoniums and that colliers had formed their own choral society at Worsbrough Dale; that butchers sold their best joints to the working man and that miners were great consumers of tobacco: after a recent pay rise, they were opting for 3d instead of 2d cigars. He wrote:

Another luxury in which miners are indulging is marriage. In church and chapel the number has increased but the most marked rise is at the register office. As a rule, miners, like curates, have large families and marry young.

In the 1880s, in marked contrast to the previous decade, miners found themselves short of money and living standards dropped as a result of a deepening trade depression. The union, powerful in the previous decade, was now on its knees. Joseph Knowles was a miner and music teacher who lived in Hemingfield and who kept a diary for six months in 1886. At the end of December, 1885, he wrote:

Thursday, another play day [the pit was closed]. *Fitting end to the worst year I have ever known. It started in April when the coal masters wanted a ten per cent reduction in wages. We were out* [on strike] *for five weeks. Since the dispute we have worked about four days* [out of six] *per week. The Tory Commission investigating the trade depression says that it has agitated the political miner.*

The problems had started in the late 1870s when the Fitzwilliams, the owners of pits at Elsecar, Hemingfield and Jump, and hitherto regarded as progressive owners, had withdrawn home coals and had introduced the notorious Billy Fairplay riddles which separated coal from slack and which the men claimed had reduced their wages. Because there was no home coal, Knowles had to burn slack and he said the men were aggrieved that men at collieries owned by other companies still retained the perk. In a letter to the miners, Earl Fitzwilliam claimed that if he restored concessionary coal, his land workers would demand the same concession.

1886 did not see any improvement in the lot of the miners; in fact, things got worse. During the first eight days of January there were three play days and a Sunday, although the nearby Lundhill Colliery, owned by another company, was working normally. The men thought their pit management were closing the pit deliberately to punish them for raising their grievances with the Earl at Wentworth Woodhouse. The truth was that pits were facing a slump and the Fitzwilliams were finding it difficult to compete with the bigger, more modern pits that had

A Welsh miner with his pick, before the First World War. D H Lawrence wrote at that time: 'The great fallacy is to pity the men. A collier didn't dream of pitying himself till agitators and sentimentalists taught him to. He was happy, or more than happy, he was fulfilled.' *F Burgin*

opened during the coal boom in the previous decade.

The men found themselves in a new ball game and therefore looked for scapegoats. The pit management, the Fitzwilliams' front men, were at the top of the complaints league, according to Knowles' diary, closely followed by the union leaders and then the Earl. An odd line-up. One would have thought the Earl, the owner, would have been at the top of the list. The men poked fun at the Earl behind his back but they had a naive belief he could solve the problem of short time working, or at least relieve the distress in the villages.

When the Earl's daughters were canvassing for votes for their brother who was contesting the Parliamentary constituency in the general election, Knowles said the men *laughed up their sleeves,'* adding:

Why didn't you come sooner to remedy these local abuses which are eating up all the great respect we had for the honoured house and then we may remedy the national abuses?'

He believed,

the general movement of the upper classes is to provide the working classes with better or more comfortable homes and what would make a working man's home more comfortable than a good cheap fire.

In January, he heard that the miners' leader, Ben Pickard, had been given a salary of £500 per year. Referring to the union, he wrote:

I should think they were all going off their heads to think of paying such a sum; it ought to be cut in two. Here we are struggling to live on 15s per week and we are expected to contribute a small sum to allow Mr Pickard £500. Some will refuse to make one of their own class a prince.

Knowles was probably better off than most miners. He taught music in the evenings and on occasions played the piano at *The Albion* public house in Hemingfield, earning in one week as much from the piano – 5s. – as he drew from the pit. He had some savings and during the 1885 strike had spent a week with a pal in London. On occasions he and his wife enjoyed the luxury of a Turkish bath at Wombwell, even mackerel for breakfast! From his comments in the diary, he may appear to have been a moaner; but the hungry 1880s had come as a shock to him, for his union leaders in the 1870s had boasted that they would never allow wages to fall again. There was widespread distress in Hemingfield and Elsecar, families could not afford the necessities of life and he believed the Earl was unaware of the poverty, isolated as he was at Wentworth.

Knowles was a branch official of the union, or at least a member of the branch committee and worked to help to co-ordinate the efforts of miners at all the Fitzwilliam pits to try to persuade management to reintroduce home coals and get rid of the 'Billy' riddles, often writing letters to the Sheffield newspapers to put the miners' case, or to put into perspective a letter written by the manager to the editor. He helped to organise fund raising efforts for an ex-miner called Guest who would never work again. When a friend,

Ben Hough, and a man called Hicks, together with other men from Hemingfield pit and Simon Wood Colliery (opposite the Reform Row, Elsecar), received their notices, he was heartbroken. Hough believed it was because they had played a crucial part in the long strike.

Poor Ben seems dreadfully put out. He has a wife and five children all looking to him for support. And with every pit overcrowded with men, what will he do?

After the death of a mate, James 'Boxer' Swift in a pit accident, in the summer of 1886, his attitude to the Fitzwilliams changed. It was now obvious that, after months of short time working, the Earl did not have a magic wand. In almost despair, Knowles wrote:

They pay us a small price for our labours. It is only by having a well developed, muscular body that we can earn a living at all. We run so many risks at work that we grow indifferent to them. I wish all mine owners could be forced to work a year as miners and then they would have some sympathy for us.

The diary ended abruptly that summer. Having moved house, he was spending more time cultivating the garden, to help the family budget, as well as learning first aid, attending Liberal Party meetings and acting as special constable during an exhibition week at Elsecar.

The 1880s and 1890s were hard years. In some respects miners had not seen much improvement in the fifty years since the formation of the mining communities in Barnsley. Poverty had returned on a vast scale. Working conditions were still hazardous and both management and men took risks, although the days of titanic disasters with long casualty lists had gone. In other respects, there had been vast improvements. Rymer, whose story was probably ghost written, belonged to an uneducated world, harsher and more violent than that of Knowles, almost impossible for the modern mind to grasp. Rymer had seen women hauling canal barges in Lancashire; young boys shackled to coal tubs; doctors vaccinating children without their parents' consent on the streets of Pontefract; and families using water from the canal at Wombwell because there was no piped supply. Knowles, only thirty years younger than Rymer, would not have understood that world. Reading Knowles' diary, one realises he was in the mould of modern man – he belonged more to the twentieth century than to the nineteenth. He was literate, an avid newspaper reader and he had wide horizons for a working man. His description of a day trip from Elsecar to Liverpool, and his tour of *The Great Eastern* ship and the Mersey Railway tunnel, is a product of a searching mind.

The improvements in the early twentieth century, in living and working conditions, were due as much to men like Knowles as to miners' leaders or politicians. Like thousands of other young miners of his age, he had a profound faith in collective action and solidarity to achieve a better life.

Chapter 2

Pre 1900

Ugly Pits and Disasters

Mines have never conjured up beautiful images and most writers have usually likened them to beasts or man-eating monsters. Emile Zola, the French writer describing the descent of miners into the shaft, wrote that *'the pit gulped down mouthfuls of twenty or thirty men and did not seem to notice them going down.'* The pit cage resembling *'some nocturnal beast, with its four decks each containing two tubs, leapt noiselessly up and down in the darkness.'* In *Sons and Lovers,* D H Lawrence wrote that *'one of the pits waved its plumes of white steam, coughed and rattled hoarsely.'* Almost everything about a mine was seen as ugly and dehumanizing, from the spoil heaps (in *How*

Green Was My Valley they were likened to the backs of monsters emerging out of the shaft) and the pit chimneys to the conditions the miners endured underground.

In one memorable but morbid passage in *How Green Was My Valley* the writer refers to peering at the *'shining black strip in the orange light of the candles,'* believing it to be the *'mourning band of the earth,'* and wondering whether they were committing an offence against nature, *'and us taking it away to burn and she looking at us with half shut eyes, waiting for her reckoning.'* The author, Richard Llewellyn, said that miners working underground were rarely free of the fear of the coal face; a mixture of nervous tension, claustrophobia and the darkness played tricks on the mind and sometimes they thought they could

The explosion at Lundhill Colliery, 1857. *Photograph: John Goodchild Collection*

Lundhill Colliery, Wombwell, shortly after the disaster. Note the tourists. Today the site is a golf course.

see faces in the shining coal, images created by the weak and distorted reflections of lamp light, and hear voices above the noise of the machines (stories about the knockers, the little spirits said to inhabit the mines, particularly in Wales, probably originated from such experiences). Jack Lawson, the ex-miner, MP and writer, had a different line of approach and did not mention beasts, saying instead that the bad and fickle moods of the pit were similar to those of a woman, 'a she devil' who got her revenge in human lives: sometimes she was reluctant to let them go and the mine became the cemetery where miners were entombed.

These graphic but bleak descriptions of mines and life in the underground galleries illustrate the hazardous and almost barbarous nature of the job. Not only had miners to work in eternal darkness but they had to face water, gas explosions and falls of rock as well as inhale dust. Apart from sailors, miners in the nineteenth century had the most perilous jobs in the country. In the 1840s accidents were so frequent that the Children's Employment Commission were unable to publish accurate figures. Until 1850 fatal accidents were not always reported and some managers could neither read nor write. But the perils of early mining were chronicled by local newspapers. In the 1850s and 1860s accidents were almost weekly occurrences. During a week in 1861, for example, Edward Frost was killed at Low Valley pit; John Tomlinson, of Baker Street, was crushed at Oaks Colliery;

a Mr Spink, of Ardsley, injured in a roof fall at Darfield Main; and George Clapham, of Market Street, severely injured at Old Mill Colliery. There were accidents at East Gawber, Mount Osborne and Agnes Main collieries during a week in 1863 (both weeks were chosen at random from copies of local newspapers). At the latter pit Messrs Simmons and Edge, of Barebones, were severely burnt while using candles. Not all the accidents were underground. In October, 1863, a fifty-five-year-old man and a seven-year-old boy were on a cart crossing a tramway belonging to Vizard's pit, Jump, when a convoy of coal wagons travelling down an incline en route to the canal at Elsecar ran into the cart. The man's horse was killed on the spot and the man and the boy died a few minutes later. These news items were often relegated to the depths of the newspaper columns indicating that in the view of the editor, they were frequent and minor incidents.

There were the big explosions which could blow out the headgear, with flames and debris roaring up the shaft, often illuminating the night and attracting onlookers to the scene like moths to a light. The ground rumbled and the underground roof timbers collapsed like ninepins, and on the surface the noise of the falling roof sounded like the repeated firing of a distant artillery battery; if the wooden props withstood the blast and the flames they still became encrusted with cinders and soot, as did the bodies of the victims. Not only did the roof fall in, the floor was capable of rising when the earth moved as in the Barnburgh disaster, the pit tubs becoming embedded in the roof! No wonder pits were described as 'beasts' and as 'she-devils'.

The 'she-devils' had voracious appetites in Barnsley.

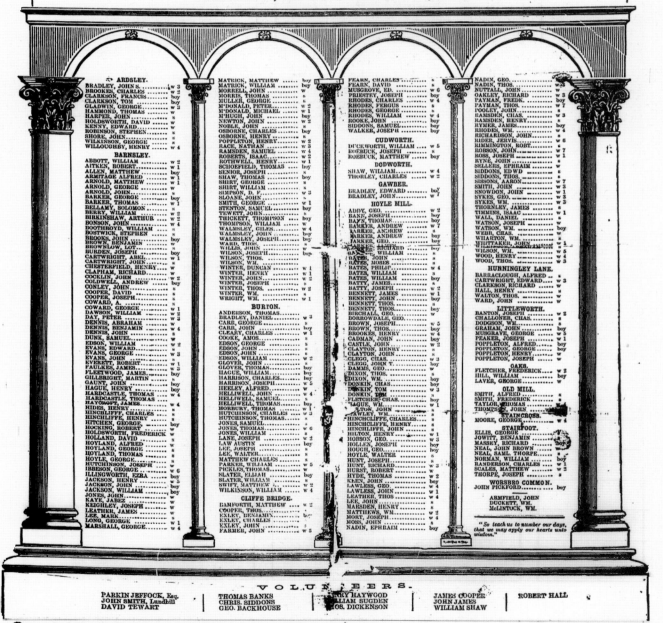

There were discrepancies in the Oaks death toll figures. The *Barnsley Chronicle* in 1867 referred to 341, the Remembrance Card to 'upwards of 350' and a newspaper report ten years later stated 361. In 1966 the *Chronicle* mentioned 365.

The Oaks memorial to the Oaks Rescue Team erected in 1913.

Between 1841 and 1857, 450 men and boys perished in firedamp explosions in Barnsley pits, said to be the most gassy and dangerous in Britain, and the figures did not include deaths from other accidents. The biggest disaster was at the Oaks Colliery in 1866 when 350 men and boys died. At Lundhill Colliery, Wombwell, nine years earlier, 189 men were killed in an explosion. About 200 men from both pits were entombed. The casualty lists from both disasters read like those in the local newspapers after the titanic battles of the First World War or a tragedy at sea. The mass funerals were on a scale never seen before in Barnsley. Victorian society was accustomed to unexpected death, for almost every family had experienced at least one case of infant mortality and cholera could wipe out all the inhabitants in a city slum street in a few days, but disease is as old as mankind and the working classes saw it as yet another cross to bear, a cross handed down from one generation to another. What happened in mining in Barnsley was different: the industry was still relatively new and when disaster struck it struck without warning and on a mass scale. It seemed, as in war, that the world was going mad, that there was no sense in all the carnage. Catastrophe followed catastrophe with perplexing and sickening regularity between the late 1830s and the 1870s: Husker, Mount Osborne (14 killed), Darley Main (75), Oaks (78, 1847), Lundhill, Old Oaks and Swaithe (143, 1875) and it took time for science to come to terms with nature and to produce the measures required to make the underground scene as safe as possible. In addition, miners and management appeared to be incapable of becoming safety conscious, with men using naked lights rather than safety lamps because they provided better light and pit managers, some of whom in the early days could neither read nor write, turning a blind eye to certain perilous situations to try to produce more coal. It is difficult to visualise how unsophisticated miners were when it came to safety, but we have forgotten that since the Victorian era a new industry, complete with its own propaganda machine and its own way of doing things, has evolved to try to make people more safety conscious. Today all firms seem to have safety officers and posters festoon every office notice board. Back in the nineteenth century all workers appeared to be as bad as each other; for example during the construction of the Tay bridge men working on their small platforms attached to lofty positions on the superstructure would forget that below them were more men standing on similar platforms and hammers and other heavy tools repeatedly cascaded on to the lower levels, inflicting all kinds of injuries. Despite warnings from other workmen and management, the problem did not go away and careless workers continued to allow their tools to fall on workers who had to keep a watchful eye on the platforms above. Whereas the construction of a large bridge would involve the deaths of a few men, miners worked on the edge of a precarious world and human error underground or a quirk of nature sent them hurtling over the edge en mass. It was an ultra anxious and turbulent period during which families lived with the perpetual fear that fathers, sons, brothers and uncles would not return from the pit. The clatter of clogs in the back yard at the end of a shift was a reassuring sound to any family and all families felt uneasy when the father failed to arrive home on time.

It was one of the smaller disasters that changed the course of history. The 1838 Husker Disaster at Silkstone brought to the public eye the working conditions experienced in mining communities. The fact that children were the victims touched the heart of a nation, and this was a nation which treated its young in an uncivilised manner. Once the national conscience had been troubled, however, there was no stopping the reformist zeal. A monument in Silkstone cemetery commemorates the disaster in which twenty-six children died in a flash flood. A very hot morning resulted in a violent thunderstorm in the afternoon with the stream running alongside the pit in Moorend Lane becoming a torrent which put out the surface furnace fires and made

The Remembrance Card

In Remembrance of the
UNFORTUNATE SUFFERERS,
WHO
LOST THEIR LIVES
IN THE OAKS COLLIERY EXPLOSION,
BARNSLEY,
DECEMBER 12, 1866,
WHEN UPWARDS OF
350 Souls were Launched into Eternity.

The Angel of Death spread his wings on the blast,
And the eyes of the sleepers wax'd deadly and chill,
In the face of the miner he breatned as he pass'd ;
And their hearts but once heav'd, and for ever grew still.
"Prepare to meet thy God."

Swaithe Colliery, Worsbrough, and right, a commemoration plate to mark the Swaithe explosion.

the Moorend Lane shaft inoperable. On attempting to escape via the old Husker (House Carr) drift and having negotiated the air doors, the children found themselves trapped against the doors as water broke into the drift. The water subsided quickly but claimed twenty-six children. Later they were buried in seven graves, the girls at the feet of the boys: the youngest was seven, the eldest seventeen. With public feeling running high, Queen Victoria sent a deputation to hold an inquiry into the mental and moral conditions in the pits. They found that women and girls wore trousers, worked naked to the waist and some women were expected to hew coal like men.

Adolescent girls were employed alongside men who worked naked. After considering the report, Parliament in 1842 banned the employment in mines of children under ten. The longest living survivor of the tragedy, Elizabeth Pashley, was still alive in 1903 and lived at the old cottages at Hillside, Silkstone.

Nearly 200 men and boys were killed at Lundhill on 19 February 1857, when a firedamp explosion ripped through the underground workings. Ninety women were widowed,

The scene after an explosion at Wharncliffe Carlton Colliery in 1883 in which twenty men died. *Photograph: John Goodchild Collection*

The tragic scene at a pit top. *Published by permission of* The Illustrated London News

NOTABLE COLLIERY EXPLOSIONS AND MINING DISASTERS IN YORKSHIRE SINCE 1672.

AT the request of a number of our patrons we have reproduced the local colliery explosions in a somewhat more extended form, and have added short notices of the most serious disasters which have unfortunately occurred from time to time in connection with the working of coal in the county, which can be traced back to early in the fourteenth century. Unfortunately the Barnsley district, owing to the fiery nature of some of the seams, has at times been the scene of some very sad disasters. The Rev. W. Thorp, B.A., vicar of Misson, Notts., in a pamphlet on "The Causes of the Explosions in the Barnsley, or Thick Coal of Yorkshire," states that from 1841 to 1857, when his pamphlet was printed, 450 persons perished by fire damp in the pits in the Barnsley districts alone. There were also at one time many serious outbursts of gas, chiefly in the Silkstone seam, of which little is now heard, and the district for some time has been happily free from serious disaster. The most serious mishaps are as under :—

1672, July 11. Colliery explosion at Barnsley, when a miner named James Townend was killed.

1755, May 2nd. Explosion at Mr. Boden's pit, Genne Lane, when John Tasker, Thos. Horsforth, and Geo. Burdett were killed by fire damp. The register of Worsbro' Church contains an entry of these men's deaths.

1797. Explosion at a Rothwell Haigh colliery, thirteen men and boys killed. Amongst those who perished was a father and four sons.

1805. A terrific explosion occurred at the Barmby Furnace Colliery, which was sunk by the Low Moor Company about 1802, on land leased from the late Walter Spencer Stanhope, of Cannon Hall, between 28 to 30 persons lost their lives.

1805, August 19th. Explosion at Barmby Furnace Colliery, which resulted in the death of seven men, including John and Mark Teasdale (brothers), who had come to sink the shafts from the north of England. The explosion was caused by the gas coming in contact with the naked light.

1809, June 30. A lamentable accident occurred at Messrs. Lee, Watson, and Company's colliery, East Ardsley, near Wakefield, owing to an immense body of water rushing out of some old workings. Ten men and boys were drowned, four were rescued after being entombed three days and nights.

1821, May 23. Serious accident at Norcroft Colliery in the township of Cawthorne. Eleven persons were ascending the shaft when the chain broke and they were precipitated to the bottom, a depth of nearly sixty yards. Seven were killed and two died afterwards. Nine lives lost.

1822, July. Five men were killed by fire damp in a colliery near Sheffield.

1825, January 12. Explosion at the Garforth Colliery, Middleton, near Leeds. Twenty-five men and boys perished.

Extracts reproduced from Lodge's Almanac in chronological order.

220 children orphaned and the Kellett family lost seven sons. Two hundred and fourteen men and boys descended the 660 feet deep shaft at the two year old colliery at 6 a.m. At twenty minutes past twelve a loud report and shock was heard and felt up to two miles from the mine. Writing in the *Barnsley Record,* a reporter said he arrived at the colliery to find *'the wild alarm, half-stifled enquiry and the almost maddened stare of the women and children at the pithead baffled all description.'* On descending the pit a team of rescuers found they could not move in a southerly direction because the coal was on fire and therefore abandoned the operation, having realised their own lives were in danger. After the team left the pit a large volume of fire rushed to the mouth, the cupola becoming a mass of flames which illuminated the countryside. A stream had to be diverted to flood the galleries and the 185 bodies (four men were never traced) were not recovered for several months.

The *Barnsley Record* observed:

It will be remembered by many that the day preceding this explosion, February 18, was a dense, foggy day, with a lack of oxygen in the air. It is remarkable that previous disasters have been preceded by similar days.

The writer recommended a 'meteorological observance' to see if there was a connection. Today miners are still evacuated from a mine when there is a sudden and dramatic fall in atmospheric pressure which affects methane gas. The subsequent inquiry into the disaster

declared there had been 'criminal negligence, but the explosion was accidental.

On the Sunday following the disaster the mood at the pithead was one of laughter. A London reporter observed:

The level ground and the steep slope between Wombwell and Lundhill Colliery was crowded, and when the decision was made known to close the pit it staggered the hopeful and appalled to silence those who had dared to hope that yet many human beings might be got up alive. This measure showed that hope was abandoned. It was felt that no further search could be made while the fire raged, and that no-one could get through the fire to the shaft.

As is not unusual on these occasions the behaviour of the masses was not exemplary. Every train today [there was a platform at Lundhill on the South Yorkshire Coal Railway] has brought a large number of excursionists who by their conduct seemed bound to a fair or country fete rather than the scene of a frightful calamity. Every road leading to the colliery was covered with throngs of people dotting the highway for miles in every direction. The immediate neighbourhood of the colliery could only be compared with Greenwich Hill on a summer day. At two o'clock this afternoon there were from 10,000 to 15,000 persons at the spot, and few indeed were there who appeared to realise they were standing over the bodies of nearly 200 human beings hurled without a moment's notice to eternity. In the dense crowd the loud laugh and jeer were heard

Notable Colliery Explosions and Disasters.

1833, May 30. Explosion at Lindley Top Colliery, near Huddersfield. Five killed.

1836, August 22. Explosion at Worsbro' Park Colliery, near Barnsley. Three killed.

1836, December 13. Explosion at the Bog Pit, near Wakefield. Thirteen men and six boys were badly burnt, and several died from the effects of the injuries.

1838, February 16. Explosion at the Robin Hood Colliery, near Wakefield, belonging to Messrs. Charlesworth. Several killed.

1838, July 4. During a terrific storm of thunder and hail the valley on the south-west side of Dodworth was inundated. The water rose to such a height that it reached a coal pit on the hill side, belonging to the late Mr. R. C. Clarke, of Noblethorpe, called the Moor Side pit, and twenty-six persons were drowned, eleven of them being females. Fourteen of the largest escaped by getting into the old slit ends. Those drowned were from seven to seventeen years of age. A monument was erected in Silkstone church yard as a reminder of the sad event.

1839, May 29. Three brothers named Jaggar and another miner named John Robinson were killed at Worsbro' Park pit by an accident.

1841, November 21. About six o'clock this morning an explosion occurred at Mount Osborne Colliery, Barnsley, when four miners and eleven hurriers were killed, and a man named Edward Walton lost his life whilst descending the shaft in a corf.

1842, February 21st. Explosion at Hopwood's Colliery, Cookerham Road, Barnsley. Killed : Fanny Day, fifteen years ; Ann Mallinson, sixteen years ; Martha Mallinson, fifteen years. Mallinsons' father had died three weeks before the explosion. There were two explosions.

1843, April 14. Explosion at Darley Main Colliery, Worsbro' Dale, one life lost.

1845, June 11. Explosion at the Oaks Colliery, which then belonged to Messrs. Firth, Barber, & Co. Three killed.

1847, January 29. Six men lost their lives at Darley Main Colliery by choke damp from the ignition of gas in blasting coal with gunpowder. Five of the men were married and one single. They were interred in one grave in Worsbro' Churchyard.

1847, March 5. Explosion at the Oaks Colliery, near Barnsley. Ninety-seven men were in the workings, 73 of whom were killed. The explosion, which was a terrific one, originated in an old break or abandoned working. Though the shafts were 283 yards deep, the explosion was so violent that the noise of it was heard at a distance of several miles. The verdict of the jury was "Accidental Death," but the jury were of opinion that efficient regulations were not enforced in the district to prevent the use of naked lights in those parts of the mine in which inflammable gas was known to exist. Forty-six of the victims were interred in the St. Mary's Burial Ground, Barnsley ; thirteen at Ardsley ; and the rest in different parishes. Twenty-five of those killed were married men and left twenty-three widows and sixty-three children. Only five of the married victims were over forty, and only two of the forty-eight single men were thirty years of age. A subscription was set on foot which raised about £1,000.

1847, May 15. Explosion at Beeston Main Colliery, near Leeds. Nine lives lost.

1847, August. Another explosion at Darley Main Colliery. Two killed.

37

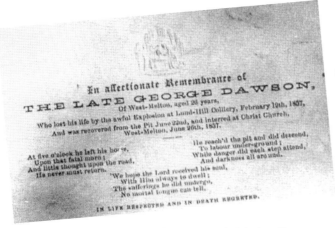

A card published 'In affectionate Remembrance' of the late George Dawson, aged 26, of West Melton, who died in the Lundhill disaster in 1857.

incessantly. The larger part of the crowd were neighbouring pitmen and their wives. It is difficult to understand the callousness of their behaviour with those of whose voices were raised occasionally in hymns.

A year later a man was killed in a firedamp explosion at Wombwell Main Colliery, a mile from Lundhill. According to the H M Inspector's Report, candles used by surveyors caused the accident and he wrote:

Soon after the Lundhill explosion, I advised the principal agent at Wombwell Main to abandon naked lights and adopt the use of safety lamps. I regret the suggestion was not acted upon. About seventy lamps had been introduced in certain parts of the mine but candles were permitted elsewhere. My belief is that the existing powers of the inspectors are not strong enough to subdue the reprehensible prejudice entertained by some employers [chiefly for economic reasons] against the use of the most efficient instrument yet for protecting their mining servants in the presence of gas.

It was not just the fault of management. Conditions underground were primitive and men took risks. Although Davy lamps were invented in 1815 some miners still preferred candles because they provided a brighter light. Ventilation was poor, resulting in all kinds of ailments and not many miners worked beyond the age of forty or fifty. The industry needed a shake-up, tough legislation and more inspectors.

On 8 December 1862, disaster struck at a colliery three miles from Lundhill. Fifty-nine miners were killed in an explosion at Edmund's Main, Worsbrough Dale. The colliery, owned by Mitchell, Bartholomew and Tyas, was situated near the South Yorkshire Coal Line and the Dearne and Dove Canal. The workings at the nine year old pit had been extended 1,800 yards to form a connection with the new Swaithe shaft. More than 300 men and boys worked in the nine foot thick seams, and most of them were working round the clock; it was later said that the reckless pursuit of coal and bonus payments was one of the factors in the cause of the explosion. The explosion

Extracts reproduced from Lodge's Almanac in chronological order.

was caused by a fire in the workings near the Swaithe shaft. Gas was ignited and a seam of coal caught fire. More gas followed the explosion and the survivors told how they stumbled over the dead and dying, and there was confusion and panic at the main shaft because the cages were packed. A survivor, George Stubbs, said he had to stuff his cotton cap into his mouth to keep out the gas. The passages filled with gas and there was a danger of another explosion, so management decided to flood the mine. This led to trouble at the pithead on the surface where young miners threatened to riot on the grounds that they thought there should be another rescue attempt. When water was poured down the mine the cupola spewed out smoke, revealing that the fire was still burning underground.

Again the disaster caused a sensation. The 20 December issue of the *Barnsley Chronicle* disclosed that thousands of spectators arrived from all parts of the country. A crowd surged up Sheffield Road and between 2 p.m. and 3 p.m. fourteen thousand went through Barnsley Toll Bar. Another explosion occurred a few days later, obscuring the pit and houses in a cloud of dense smoke. So violent was the explosion that the timber which covered the shaft mouth was hurled into the headgear. The door of the engine house was blown off its hinges and the room was filled with smoke. An artist from the *Illustrated London Times,* who was sketching a group of men when the explosion occurred, swiftly took flight. An expert said a blast of gunpowder had fired the gas four days before the explosion and again was fired by a candle on 6 December.

Notable Colliery Explosions and Disasters.

1849, January 24. Another explosion took place at Darley Main Colliery, Worsbro' Dale. Over 100 men and boys were in the pit, of whom 75 lost their lives, leaving 31 widows and 55 children. The verdict of the jury was "Accidental Death." Most of the poor fellows were interred in five large graves in the Church yard at Worsbro', on January 27. A relief fund was started, towards which the company subscribed £200; F. W. T. V. Wentworth, Esq., £100 ; John Jeffcock, Esq., £50 ; Earl Fitzwilliam, £50 : and Joseph Locke, Esq., £50.

1850, April 30. A large body of earth fell into an air pit, which was being sunk at the Oaks Colliery, which caused the drawing shaft, 200 yards in depth, to be filled up and a fresh one having to be sunk.

1850, June 9. An explosion took place in the downcast shaft at the Oaks Colliery, which killed three men.

1851, June 7. A fourth explosion occurred at Darley Main Colliery killing three persons.

1851, July 20. Three men were killed by a fall down the shaft of the Worsbro' Park Colliery, and subsequently ten men by an explosion.

1851, December 20. Explosion at Warren Vale Colliery, Rawmarsh, near Rotherham, worked by Messrs. Charlesworth. Seventy-three persons were at work at the time of whom fifty-two perished. Smoke and flames burst out of the shaft.

1851, December 21. Explosion at the Elsecar Colliery, belonging to Earl Fitzwilliam ; nine killed.

1852, December 22. Explosion at the Elsecar Colliery when five persons lost their lives, and several were severely injured. Explosion caused by a man named Stenton taking off the top of his lamp.

1854, June 2. Explosion at Warren Vale, one killed.

1854, August 22. Explosion at Lundhill Colliery. Six men were killed by being blown out of the shaft whilst engaged in sinking operations. Their names were Noah Ely, 52, wife and four children ; James Batty, 32, banksman ; Wm. Hulse, 30; Wm. Davis, 50, married; Matthew Thompson, 50 ; and Thos. Jackson, 48.

1855, June 12. Explosion at Skiers Spring Colliery, two killed.

1855, July 18. Explosion at Strafford Colliery, one killed.

1857, February 19. Explosion at the Lundhill Colliery belonging to Messrs. Taylor & Co. The Barnsley seam of coal, which was 200 yards from the surface, was won after two years sinking on April 14, 1855. The explosion which occurred about noon ignited the coal, and by evening the flames had obtained such a hold that the cupola appeared one mass of flame. In order to subdue the fire it was found necessary to turn water into the pit, so that several months elapsed before the bodies could be recovered. In some instances the entire male members of families were swept away. One family, named Kellett, lost seven sons. The verdict of the jury was " That it was criminal neglect, but accidental." Two hundred and fourteen persons were at work, of whom 24 were rescued, 189 being killed. There were 90 widows, and 220 orphans left. One hundred and eighty-five corpses were recovered, four bodies not being found. Relief fund raised nearly £8,000 Estimated loss to owners £20,000. One hundred and forty-nine of those who perished were interred at Darfield Parish Church in four graves, a monument marking the place. The last body recovered was that of Matthew Broadhead on July 16, 1857. By the end of March, 1860, 46 of the widows had re-married.

THE EXPLOSION ON WEDNESDAY WEEK AT EDMUND'S MAIN COLLIERY, BARNSLEY.—SEE NEXT PAGE.

Scene at Edmund's Colliery, Worsbrough. *Published by permission of* The Illustrated London News

A letter in a local newspaper, published in January, stated *'I doubt whether in the annals of colliery atrocities a blacker case is recorded than Edmund's Main.'* It was the third great Barnsley pit disaster which had been caused by the use of naked candles. *'Safety lamps should have been used,'* declared the writer. *'Coal mining is becoming more dangerous as pits get deeper and unless naked lights are excluded there will be frequent explosions.'*

Barnsley's worst mining disaster was the Oaks explosion in 1866, believed to have been Britain's largest peace-time disaster since the Fire of London. It claimed the lives of more than 350 men and boys and forty pit ponies. The bodies of more than 100 men remain entombed to this day. The force of the early afternoon explosion on 12 December was such that the cage of No. 1 shaft was damaged. Leased from Mr R Micklethwaite of Ardsley, the pit was run by Messrs. Firth, Barber and Company and was sometimes called Ardsley Main. At the time, 350 men and boys were underground and 18 were

found alive by a rescue team led by Mr T Dymock, the managing director, who descended after hasty repairs to the cage. All the rescued men were badly affected by afterdamp and only six lived to the New Year. Later members of the rescue team, still underground, noticed that the air was being drawn from them into the lower part of the workings. The under-deputy, William Sugden, ascended the shaft to warn another party of men, led by Derby mining engineer, Parkin Jeffcock, of the danger. Ignoring the advice the second team, including Sugden, descended the shaft and then a second explosion ripped through the workings. The cage was sent down again but came back empty. Then a third explosion sent the cage roaring up the shaft into the headgear. To the astonishment and relief of the onlookers, one man had survived. Early the following morning the signal bell was heard, then a voice. With the cage and headgear out of action, a bottle of brandy and water was lowered on a piece of wire. After a makeshift cage was made a youth called Embleton and a colliery official were lowered down the shaft. It was a courageous act for the pit winder baulked at the responsibility of his task. Drenched with water from burst water pipes they found Sam Brown sitting at the

39

Scenes above ground at Swaithe Main following the disaster. *Published by permission of* The Illustrated London News

bottom of the shaft. The scene resembled hell with tubs of burning coal and the mangled bodies of the rescue team scattered in the roadways. Brown had been very lucky. The second explosion had knocked him unconscious and therefore missed the blast of the third. At last the Government Inspector decided that further journeys down the mine were too dangerous and he was proved right – a fourth explosion sent clouds of gas up the shaft the following day and there were further explosions over the next few days. The fire was eventually put out by stopping up the shafts to starve the flames of oxygen.

A year later there were still 260 bodies underground. About 160 were reclaimed over the next three years but more than 100 were never recovered. The inquest heard that the pit had one upcast shaft ventilated with a large furnace and two downcast shafts. Gunpowder was not used for blasting coal but had to be used to get through the hard stone underground. It was in use on the day of the first explosion. After a thirteen day hearing, the jury returned a verdict that Richard Hunt and others were killed by an explosion of firedamp but there was not

sufficient evidence to prove where and how it was ignited. A second hearing, held in respect of the rescue workers, came to a similar conclusion but added that rescue parties should be limited in number and work in relays once it had been ascertained that there were no persons alive in the workings. It was decided to site the new Oaks Colliery half a mile away. The new pit – the junction into the old workings took place on the fourth anniversary of the explosion – saw naked lights banned and Clannylamps and Stephenson lamps take their place.

At Edmund Main's 'sister' pit, Swaithe Main, 143 men and boys were killed in 1875. Blacksmith, George Miller, who was working on the surface, was startled by a blast like the sound of a cannon; a deputy said it felt as if he had been struck on the neck by an iron bar. A local newspaper referred to *'a dull rumbling underground resembling the sound of distant thunder, followed by a heavy boom'* in a populous valley known as *'t dale'*. The rescue teams who went down the pit on 8 December – almost thirteen years to the day since the Edmund's disaster – found that the force of the explosion had blown one of the heavy cages a few yards up the shaft. The rescuers discovered George

Scenes below ground at Swaithe Main following the disaster. *Published by permission of* The Illustrated London News

Notable Colliery Explosions and Disasters.

1866, December 12 and 13. Explosion at the Old Oaks Colliery, near Barnsley, owned by Messrs. Barber and Co. Three hundred and forty men and boys descended the shaft on December 12, of whom 320 were killed, and the remainder were rescued, but 14 afterwards succumbed, making a total of 334 deaths. After the first explosion 198 persons, forming rescue parties descended the mine, of whom 27 lost their lives owing to subsequent explosions, the total being 361 deaths. When operations were finally suspended there were 386 bodies in the pit. A relief fund was started, and the total subscriptions from all sources ultimately reached £48,747 3s. Her Majesty, the Queen, contributed £200, and amongst other subscribers were "A. Z" £1,000, Earl Fitzwilliam £500, whilst the amount forwarded through the Mansion House Committee was £11,697. Chargeable to the fund were 68 men, 248 women, and 374 children, a total of 690 persons.

1867, May 6. Explosion at Outwood Colliery, near Bingley. Three men, named Benjamin Devenport. Richard Howarth, and Robert Seddon, killed.

1867, October 1; 1870, August 31; 1877, January 30. Serious outbursts of gas in the Silkstone seam of the Strafford Main Colliery, near Barnsley.

1870, April 7. Two men were suffocated at the West Redford Colliery, near Sheffield, by inhaling a quantity of carburetted hydrogen. Four others had narrow escapes.

1870, August 29. Explosion at Newbiggin Colliery, Thorncliffe, caused by two men named Edmund Arthur and Hira Shires who were going to examine the place where they formerly worked with a naked light. The two men, who only commenced work on the day of the accident, had been locked out since the previous March. They were seriously injured and died a few days afterwards.

1870, December 2. Two men killed at the Agnes Colliery, Barnsley, by a fall from the roof. One of the men was one of the last survivors from the explosion at the Old Oaks Colliery in 1866.

1871, January 16. Inundation at Wheatley Hill Colliery. Seven lost, fourteen others had a very narrow escape.

1871, May 3. Two men killed by a fall of roof at the Orgreave Colliery near Rotherham ; their names were Alexander Renshaw, 29, and W. Gee, 24

1871, November 25. Explosion at Tankersley Colliery, two lives lost.

1872, October 7. Explosion at the Morley Main Colliery, belonging to Messrs. W. Ackroyd Bros., when 34 persons were killed. The jury expressed the opinion that there had been carelessness on the part of some persons in charge of the workings.

1872, October 13. A most disastrous fire took place at the Darfield Main Colliery, by which 45 horses and ponies were burnt or suffocated. The horses killed were valued at £1,500. The fire was caused by the bursting of the tubbing, which reversed the air current driving the fire from the furnace.

1873, January 4. Three men, named William Leatherland, David Taylor, and George Robinson were killed at the Woolley Colliery by the breaking of a capstan rope, which supported a scaffold on which they were standing.

1873, January 5. Boiler explosion at Smithy Bridge pit, near Barnsley, when a boatman named John Spendler, who was wheeling some slack to the boilers, was killed, his body being blown across the canal a distance of 84 yards, and shattered to pieces.

1873, January 14. Explosion at the Black Flat pit, Clifton. near Brighouse, belonging to the Low Moor Iron Company. Four men were killed and five injured.

Extracts reproduced from *Lodge's Almanac* in chronological order.

Linford from Worsbrough Dale, alive and wedged in a sump where he had been hurled by the blast. A few minutes later they came across an eerie sight – three lamps were burning as if nothing had happened – and then they found a horse on its side with the arms of a dead boy around its neck. The animal was still alive and was brought to the surface, dazed and still suffering from the after effects of the after damp gas. As the teams made their way to the 'dips', half way between the Swaithe and Edmund's Main shafts, where the explosion occurred, they came across more bodies including those of a man and a boy who were running when they were overcome by the gas or the explosion.

At first the cause of the explosion was thought to have been shot firing but, as the bodies began to arrive on the surface, tobacco and matches were found in some of the pockets and it was known that some miners hid their pipes underground.

The sight, wrote a reporter, *was truly ghastly. There were some whose features were as composed as if death had overtaken them in their sleep. Other faces were distorted by terror, their glassy eyeballs staring out of their sockets and their hands clasped in agony. In some cases every bone in the body had been broken.*

Many bodies were mutilated but there was often a patch on the trousers that a mother or daughter could identify as her own, or perhaps there was something unusual about the clogs. The jury could not agree on the cause of the explosion, although later some experts thought the ignition

Extracts reproduced from *Lodge's Almanac* in chronological order.

---

of coal dust was the culprit. Experimental work was soon carried out into the explosibility of this kind of dust.

But by the turn of the century tragedies involving large scale slaughter in Barnsley were almost over, safety having become the preoccupation of men, owners and government. Average death rates fell from more than 4 per 1,000 per annum around 1850 to 2.2 in the 1870s. But it was still a dangerous trade and almost every week the local newspapers carried stories with the headline 'Fatal accident at local pit.' By the turn of the century roof falls had become the most common cause of death, although the occasional spectacular disaster still shook the nation: the worst was at Senghenydd in 1913 when 439 men lost their lives. In the peak years of the industry, between 1900 and 1913, one in ten workers in this country was employed in the mines and up to 1,000 were killed every year.

Stark statistics fail to illustrate the drama behind an accident. One of the most graphic descriptions of a pit mourning the death of a miner was written by Lewis Jones, a miner who had witnessed similar scenes on countless occasions:

The whole pit seemed to hold its breath, and the usual clamour was still. Yet as if the warm air had whispered the news in every ear, everyone knew what had happened in the pit, and in the pit bottom everything was in readiness.

On the day of the funeral:

...though the pit hooter blasted the air as usual, no one answered its hysterical screams. It kept blowing and bellowing like an animal robbed of its food, and still no one answered, until at last its shrieks faded and died out. The men had determined not to go to the pit on the day of the funeral.

Notable Colliery Explosions and Disasters.

1886, December 30. Ten men killed at the Houghton Main Colliery, Darfield, owing to being dashed to the bottom whilst ascending in the cage. All were members of the West Riding Miners' Permanent Relief Fund. Seven of them belonged to three families. Two widows and one child were left. The names of the men killed were Joseph Walker, miner, Darfield Bridge, widower ; Samuel Walker, and Charles Walker, sons of the above, trammers ; James Hardcastle, 48, Snape Hill, Darfield, miner, left widow and one child ; Alvin Hardcastle, 18, son of the above, trammer ; Joseph Pearson, Snape Hill, miner, married ; Joseph Pearson, 18, son of the above, trammer ; Edward Baxter, 28, Low Valley, single ; William Manning, Low Valley, trammer ; and William Burton, Low Valley, trammer. Berresford, The engineman, was tried for manslaughter and acquitted A monument to the victims was erected in Darfield Churchyard.

1887, December 7. Fire at Monk Bretton Colliery, £2,000 damages.

1893, July 4. Explosion at Combs Colliery, Thornhill, near Dewsbury, belonging to Mr. E. J. Ingham, Mirfield, when 139 persons perished.

1895, April 18. Alarming outburst of gas at Mitchell Main Colliery, Wombwell.

1896, February 26. Alarming inrush of water at Wharncliffe Silkstone Colliery, Birdwell ; 300 men withdrawn.

1896, April 30. Explosion at Heckfield Colliery, belonging to the Micklefield Coal & Lime Co., at Micklefield. Sixty-eight men and boys were killed.

1897, December 20. Accident at South Hiendley Colliery, belonging to Messrs. Musgrave, when three men, viz. : John Whitworth, 46 ; David Wood, 31 ; and Oliver Buffin, 17, were killed by fall of a large stone 18 feet in length and four feet in thickness.

1907, November 15th. Cage Accident at the Barrow Colliery, Worsbro' seven men killed, viz., Walt. Lewis Goodchild, Byas Rooke, William Adams, Tom R. Cope, Frank Dobson, Thos. W. Jennings, and Isaac Farrar. Three men were severely injured

1907, November 23rd. Accident in the boiler house in the Parkgate Seam at the Hoyland Silkstone Colliery, Platts Common. Four lives lost. Greenwood Ogden, Arthur Cooke, Leonard Chandler, and Walter Sistern. Frank Chandler, deputy, whose son was fatally injured, was severely hurt but recovered and was awarded the "Edward" Medal, for bravery in trying to save Cooke.

1910, May 7th. Accident whilst sinking at Water Haigh Pit, Oulton. Six lives lost

1910, July 21. Explosion at the Rotherham Main Colliery, in the Parkgate Seam. Three deaths resulted

1910, November 17th. another accident at Water Haigh Pit, Oulton, two lives lost

1911, July 11th. Shocking accident at Grimethorpe Colliery. Frank Green, engineer, John Allen, enginewright, and Herbert Duckworth, foreman, Brightside, being killed by the bursting of a steam valve.

1912, July 6th. Explosion at Barnsley Main Colliery, Walter Jebson, deputy, Thomas Hunt, machineman, and Thomas Eltoft, machineman, killed

1912, July 9th. Terrible Disaster at the Cadeby Main Colliery, There were three explosions and 87 lives were lost. Mr. W. H. Pickering, H. M. Chief Inspector of Mines in Yorkshire, and other Inspectors and Colliery Officials being amongst the victims. The King and Queen visited the ill-fated colliery

Colliery officials, Tankersley Collieries, 1893. *Yorkshire Mining Museum*

Police were drafted into Barnsley during the 1893 dispute. Pit officials and East Riding Police pictured at Woolley Colliery.

The Strikes

The deeper one dips into the history of the miners, the more one realises that nothing changes. A few years ago a national newspaper claimed that *'flying pickets'* were invented by Yorkshire miners in the 1960s, a tactic that enabled the union to concentrate large numbers of miners at strategic points during strikes (if you stopped coal going into a power station then you were on your road to victory). Another writer said they appeared for the first time during the so-called stint strike at Grimethorpe Colliery in 1947. Not so said a writer to a newspaper a few days later. He said in 1740, when a strike had closed most of the Tyne collieries, a coal master talked of,

> *...a Newcastle mob of pit men, wagon-men and keel-men... and I expect disturbances around my boundaries from these oppressors, since men working at my collieries gave great offence because they would not join the strike.*

Court injunctions against miners, a familiar tactic during the 1984/85 Miners' Strike, had earlier roots. In 1619, the Whickham Grand Lease Owners asked for injunctions against pickets who halted their coal trade.

All the ingredients of a modern miners' strike – violence, 'black legs', police stationed at pits – can be traced to the 1850s and 1860s in Barnsley. As long ago as the 1850s, miners selected prosperous pits for strike action to enforce wage demands for all local miners. And, despite the miners' reputation for solidarity, there was always someone who was prepared to strike break. It is often forgotten that miners in those days were self employed and therefore sometimes acted like self-made men by displaying a maverick streak to all and sundry. 'Black sheep', as working miners in strikes were called in Victorian times, were ostracised and intimidated – much more so than in modern times. In the late 1850s striking miners used gunpowder to blow up a working miner's greenhouse at Birdwell and that was typical of what took place. Violence was common. In 1869 a pit manager's house was damaged and during the 1893 lockout pits were wrecked. Even novel ways of raising money for strike funds, common in the 1984/85 Miners' Strike, can be traced to the 1870s in Barnsley.

The early miners' unions found it difficult to put down roots. The 1841 Miners' Association of Great Britain had fleeting success when it reached a membership of 100,000 but, like other fledgling unions, collapsed in the face of the power of the coal owners. The South Yorkshire Miners' Association was formed at a meeting at the *White Bear* in Shambles Street, Barnsley, in April, 1858, when delegates agreed to set up branches. Membership fluctuated and by the mid-1860s the association had 2,000 members in eighteen lodges. In 1872 John Normansell, general secretary of the South Yorkshire miners, was the first miner to be elected on to a local authority, Barnsley Borough Council. At the 1873 miners' demonstration in Wakefield men carried sixty banners, many of which were nine feet by seven feet and made of pure silk, a sign that miners and the union – in this case the West Yorkshire Miners' Association – were becoming prosperous. About 30,000 were said to be present at the demonstration. By 1874 the South Yorkshire association and the North Derbyshire Union had substantial memberships and money in the bank which enabled them to open new offices in Huddersfield Road. But things changed. In 1877 the demonstration at Pontefract was said to be a mere shadow of those organised between 1872 and 1874. In 1875 there had been forty seven brass bands but two years later the number had dropped and only 8,000 people assembled in the park.

West Riding and Cheshire Police and pit officials at Wharncliffe Silkstone Colliery, Tankersley.

OFFICIALS CHESHIRE AND WEST RIDING CONSTABULARIES ON DUTY AT TANKERSLEY COLLIERIES DURING THE GREAT COAL STRIKE, OCTOBER 25th, 18..

Police and officials at Tankersley Pits. *Yorkshire Mining Museum*

In 1880 only 2,800 out of the 60,000 Yorkshire miners were organised and union funds had dwindled from £50,000 in 1876 to about £6,000. According to the former Barnsley journalist, Harold Bunting, writing in the *Sheffield Mail* in 1926, strikes in the 1870s and 1880s were sometimes declared by the men without consultation with the union leaders. In September 1879 a strike started at Monk Bretton Colliery which drained £1,500 from the association's funds. It lasted nearly twelve months. Such strikes, coupled with bad times, led to men drifting away from the union and in 1881 the South Yorkshire Association and the West Yorkshire Association merged. The year 1889 saw the formation of the Miners' Federation of Great Britain, covering all the inland coalfields and by 1899, Scotland and South Wales. By 1893 the federation had 300,000 members. Yet by 1900 only two thirds of the national workforce had been unionised. Membership had a tendency to rise when coal markets were robust and contract during slumps or depressions when the coal owners had the upper hand. On top of that hewers in the last century were basically self employed men who displayed all the attributes and flaws of such men: an independent frame of mind and streak of bloody-mindedness; they did not like being regimentated.

Some of the strikes in the nineteenth century left behind a trail of violence, evictions and hard poverty. The 1864 dispute was a good example. The stoppage started early in the year when the Coal Masters' Association closed Oaks, High Royd and other pits until the Oaks miners' demand for a wage rise was withdrawn. About 560 were members of the union and 3,000 non-union. At a meeting of the Barnsley Guardians, Mr U Corbett, one of the Inspectors said that miners with a wife and children would have to go into the workhouse when they ran out of money. On 21 April a meeting was held on May Day Green, attended by a large group of miners. According to *The Barnsley Record,*

Cheapside presented an animated appearance. A large number of miners with their wives and children then made off to the workhouse, where a number of policemen were on duty to prevent anyone going in save those who had orders.

In May the Masters' Association opened Oaks and High Royd pits to allow miners who wanted to work to return at the old rates. After a union meeting was held to warn miners not to go back, the *Record* reported that miners who broke the law by attacking 'black sheep' (black legs) would not receive a penny from the union. A Mr W Cartwright, stated the newspaper, said all the miners had seen what the union could do and he hoped that if they ever resumed work, they would join the union and pay to it like men. A Mr George Moore said he knew plenty of

Darton Cyclists' Club who attended a fancy dress parade at Ravensthorpe in aid of the miners' soup kitchens, September 1893. The photograph was taken outside the *Rose and Crown*, Darton. *Loaned by Mrs E Thompson, Darton*

A soup kitchen in the 1893 dispute. The landlady and landlord at *The Cock Inn*, Birdwell, gave miners breakfast. *Loaned by K and Mrs Burkinshaw, Birdwell*

An unofficial coal mine, Warren Quarry Lane, Barnsley, during the 1912 minimum wage strike. *John Goodchild Collection*

Wharncliffe Silkstone Colliery, Tankersley, one of the trouble spots in the nineteenth century.

men who had worked at the Oaks Colliery for three shillings a day, a low figure.

There was a whiff of gunpowder in the air three days later when *'a good deal of excitement was created in Barnsley by the arrival in the centre of some hundreds of colliers with a cart pulled by men.'* The cart contained a number of Oaks workmen with printed notices in their hats. It appeared that the men had been given notice to quit their colliery houses that afternoon, when *'there had been scenes of violence and riot.'* The tension turned to farce in July when Hannah Goodliffe and Mary Haigh appeared in court charged with assaulting Mr Thomas Ashirst and causing damage to his property to the amount of two shillings and sixpence. Walking to work Mr Ashirst said he was followed by a number of children who escorted him by playing tin cans. When a lad called Goodliffe threw a stone at him, he seized the boy and took him to the complainant's house. Ashirst had not been at home long when Mrs Goodliffe arrived and demanded the return of her son. Mrs Goodliffe must have been a formidable woman, for she struck Ashirst and then threw

stones at his windows. Mrs Haigh, the other defendant, was a little more direct – she broke down the door with a firm kick. She was fined 5s and Mrs Goodliffe 10s. The lad was ordered to be kept on bread and water for twenty-four hours.

On arriving in Barnsley in a cart on a shopping expedition, escorted by policemen, on 16 July, the wives of six 'black sheep' found themselves facing a large crowd shouting *'Baa, baa black sheep.'* The women went to a flour store and two grocery stores in Sheffield Road, but the traders, threatened by the crowd, refused to sell them anything. As the crowd became more threatening one of the workers' wives fainted several times. On the return journey along Doncaster Road the inhabitants turned out with frying pans, shovels and set-pot covers which they

Coal pickers during the 1893 lock-out. Location unknown. *E Tasker*

Weavers massed on May Day Green to air their grievances before Barnsley became a mining town. When the linen industry went into decline, the miners took over their meeting spot. This photograph was probably taken in 1893. The former *Cross Keys* pub and *The Red House* (left) can be seen in the background.

Map of May Day Green with its numerous taverns. Dates from the 1850s.

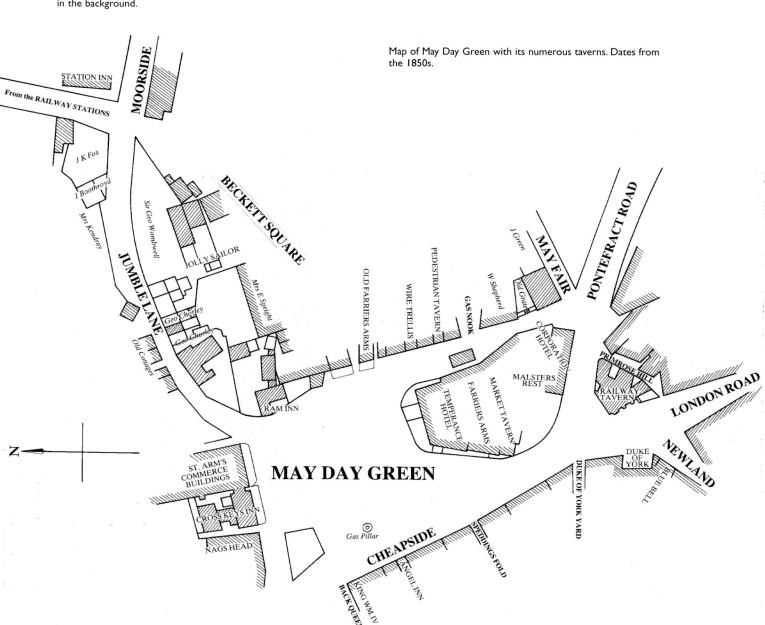

Three policemen at Houghton Main Colliery. The police and the military were brought in to quell riots. At Houghton there was a scare when there were rumours the pit manager had been shot.

beat all the way to the Oaks Colliery. Throughout the day and night large crowds assembled outside the pit and as the workers came out they were shouted at, and those who lived in Barnsley were escorted home by the police or chased by the mob. One man escorted to his home in New Street had to face the gauntlet of onlookers drumming tin cans and shouting.

At a meeting of miners, Mr Normansell, the chairman, said men at the High Royd Colliery had not received an increase in pay for eight years, although the price of coal had increased by two shillings and sixpence a ton during the same period. One man at the meeting claimed the owners at Silkstone had loaded a table with roast beef, pudding and other delicacies, and then sat down to eat it in the presence of starving miners. On 25 July the owners decided to end the lock-out, sending out circulars to customers announcing their intention to resume work in

John Normansell, South Yorkshire miners secretary, 1864-1875.

a few days. The men eventually drifted back to work at the old rates.

Victory followed defeat, in 1866, when miners at Edmunds Main and Swaithe Main achieved a five per cent rise in their wages as a result of a strike. This prompted the editor of the *Record* to declare:

A time has come when trade unions must be taken notice of, attended to with proper respect when right and put down when wrong. The association of miners are

strong and growing stronger every day, and the Association of Masters should be in the same position.

The strength of the miners in the 1870s is underlined by a report in a national newspaper which described a Yorkshire miners' gala in Barnsley, said to have been attended by 40,000 miners and their families. He said the few stone-paved streets in the town had been scrubbed until they looked like *'the quarter deck of a man o' war.'* The town was crowded with people in gay rosettes, sashes and rakish-looking billycock hats. From the Queen's Ground (near Oakwell soccer ground) he could see

...a whole district containing scores of world famous pits. Right in front, Worsbrough Dale exhibited a forest of chimney stacks which today, standing smokeless, only mark the site of prolific pits, or the scene of mining disasters. To the miner's eye every feature in the swarthy landscape is a memorial of sadness.

Only that morning the journalist had heard that one mine owner who had for years refused to have unions in his pits now found that unionists were easier to control and did better work *'than the dog-fighting scamps who mutinied or deserted whenever he* [the owner] *was in difficulty.'*
He added:

It may disturb some of our metropolitan conceptions formed from vivid pictures of colliers feeding on buttered beef steaks and wearing 20 guinea gold rings on Sundays, but if there is anything that a genuine Yorkshire collier hates, it is the loafer who discredits his order. His proud boast is to be the hardest working, soberest living and most peacefully disposed man in England. The gala day which has been celebrated in Barnsley proves that he might claim also to be the most rational, orderly Englishman in the locality.

Within two years that journalist would have changed his mind about the industry, for the coal boom did not last. The Great Depression arrived and the cycle of strikes and lock-outs started all over again. In April 1876 the coalfield was at a standstill with the owners demanding a fifteen per cent reduction in wages. Large outdoor meetings of miners were held at the top of Station Road, Wombwell, and at Church Fields, Barnsley, where Thomas Haigh of Pindar Oaks said eighteen years earlier they had stood out against a fifteen per cent cut in wages, and he wanted to know why the coal owners wanted to pull down the common man who went to work with his life in one hand and his livelihood in the other. During the strike a group of sixty miners adopted a novel way of raising money for the hardship fund. The men hauled a large dray from Dillington, Worsbrough Common, to Kingstone Place where families handed out bread, sugar and tea. At a small mine owned by Sam Brown they were allowed to load a ton of coal. The dray was then hauled down Racecommon Road to The Vine Tavern where the load was deposited and in return the men received 10s (50p) for the coal and 15s (75p) for what was called the leading (delivery). Later another load of coal was collected from Mr Brown's pit and taken to *The Travellers Rest*. A ton of coal supplied free at Richard Brown's pit on Keresforth Hill was hauled to the Dillington Park Hotel. In the same week 500 loaves were handed out to striking miners' families. (One hundred years later, miners were still raising money for hardship funds by organising unusual events).

Strike breakers were nothing new in that era, either. In 1877 the management of Dodworth Colliery brought in thirty-five Welshmen while miners were on strike. Arriving at Dodworth Railway Station from Manchester, one of them said he was surprised to see a policeman on the platform.

We were offered 6s to 10s per day and thought we would come over to Yorkshire. We soon realised we had been misled when we arrived at the pit and the manager pointed out a pile of stones for our protection and a place where we could play marbles.

The 1870s and 1880s were riddled with disputes but none could compare with the 1893 lock-out during which youths roamed the outskirts of the town demanding tolls and mobs wrecked pit premises. Such was the violence that the authorities were compelled to call in the army – about 200 soldiers – and an extra 300 policemen from the East Riding, Cheshire and London. It all started when, having refused to accept a twenty-five per cent reduction in wages, the Miners Federation of Great Britain found their members were locked-out in July. Within five weeks the iron trade was suspended in some parts of the country and the price of coal began to rise, a significant development which resulted in the owners' resolve cracking a few months later. Trouble must have been brewing when Mr Ben Pickard, MP, and president of the Miners Federation, said in September that any miner causing a disturbance outside the law would be a traitor to his cause. Four days later, when some men lodging in Heelis Street were suspected of working at Barrow Colliery, a nasty incident occurred. After the men had entered the *Shoulder of Mutton* pub a crowd gathered outside and then hurled stones and other missiles through the windows. The balloon went up the following day when 400 young men descended on Rylands Colliery, Stairfoot, and smashed windows. With rumours spreading that men were working at Mitchell's Main, Wombwell, a large crowd gathered on the canal bridge leading to the pit; some deputies who were working at the pit were treated roughly and the police were called. James Theaker, of Station Road, Wombwell (in June 2003 his grandson was still living in the same yard), had worked throughout the lockout with the permission of his union branch but one day he was met by a mob of 300. He was struck on the head by a man called Beck before the under manager Mr Neville could intervene. Beck was fined £2 and sent to prison for a month. The cases against two other men, Henry Lisle and William West, were dismissed. Three women were convicted in connection with a riot at Simon Wood Colliery, Elsecar. The women claimed they had not not taken part in the trouble but witnesses said they had incited youths to damage the premises. Down the road 2,000 people met in the market place at Wombwell, the speakers demanding that men be withdrawn from Mitchell's and that work cease on a stack at Hoyland Silkstone pit, Platts Common. Marching to Hoyland, 700

men descended on Hoyland Silkstone from four directions, forcing labourers to flee the pit yard. Struck by a cudgel, the pit manager had to be protected from further injury by some of his workmen. To round-off the visit someone blew a whistle and stones, bricks and bolts were hurled at the premises. Rockingham Colliery at Hoyland Common was the next target. On the way the men met a drayman with a load of ginger beer. *'Entering into the humour of the situation,'* according to the *Barnsley Chronicle*, the drayman said they were welcome to all he had provided they did not smash the bottles. At Rockingham the premises were wrecked and the stables burned down. Assuming that they would be the next target, management at Barrow Colliery telegraphed for more policemen and when the mob saw one of the newly arrived policemen they changed direction, heading towards Blacker Hill. Marching past Hoyland Silkstone Colliery, now in the hands of the police, the mob moved on to Elsecar and headed for Simon Wood Colliery in front of Reform Row, where policemen on the canal bank were pelted with stones. At Hemingfield pit, ten minutes walk from Simon Wood, the strikers amused themselves by pushing pit tubs down an incline; then they pushed each other into the canal! Returning to Simon Wood they destroyed a cabin and 500 miners' lamps.

It was too much for the authorities to stomach. On 6 September, a detachment of between fifty and sixty men of the 6th Dragoons came to the town from York, to be followed by the Dublin Fusiliers who were stationed at Wombwell Main Colliery. Also drafted in were 100 men from the Royal Scots and 300 policemen. Meanwhile, gangs were roaming the roads demanding tolls. Faced with men armed with sticks, Mr J Kaye, a JP, and a police superintendent who were in a hansom cab near Hoyland

Simon Wood Colliery, Elsecar, scene of violent incidents in the 1893 dispute. Ten years later the pit closed. Elsecar Main Colliery was then sunk in the wood behind Simon Wood. *Photograph: Alan Stevenson, Elsecar*

The big dispute of the nineteenth century – the lock out of 1893. Policemen pictured with coal pickers at an unknown location in Barnsley. *Photograph: E Tasker*

paid their toll. One gang moved into New England, Worsbrough, but the local residents formed a vigilante group and drove them off in the direction of Birdwell. Mr John Frith, a union official, said he did not think members of the Yorkshire Miners Association were involved. With authority breaking down, the Mayor of Barnsley warned that riots and disturbances would be quelled by the police and army. As 100 men from the Suffolk Regiment arrived, traders distributed soup and provisions to the needy but the *Barnsley Chronicle* declared: *'Unfortunately, many who obtained relief were not connected with the stoppage.'* The trouble quickly subsided and the *Chronicle* stated that between 9-16 September, the town was quiet, with miners' lodges meeting and condemning the violence.

The arrival of troops and more police upset trade unionists. At a meeting of Barnsley Trades Council, delegates claimed that 'black-legs' had tantalised strikers who had surrounded their lodgings in Heelis Street, Barnsley. It was said *'their* [rioters] *normal occupation is to prop up street corners and beg and drink at night.'*

The chairman, David Pattison, criticised soldiers who strutted down the streets and policemen who carried cutlasses. W Neal, a typographer, said if the army had not been called in the disturbances at Rockingham and Elsecar would have spread to Barnsley. Another speaker said stone throwing on May Day Green had been provoked by policemen who had been eating at Hudson's Eating House and who had flaunted a piece of meat on the

end of the fork at a window. Rumours were widespread. Troops were sent to Houghton Main Colliery when it was said the manager had been shot but the soldiers later said someone had taken fright at the sight of fox hunters in a wood.

With the approach of winter, coal picking operations were stepped up, one of the favourite sites being Providence Main, a quarry hole belonging to Clarkson's Old Brewery. In their makeshift mines colliers dug deeper and deeper and there were fears someone would be killed if the roof or the sides of the shafts collapsed.

This occurred at the disused Mount Osborne pit in Pontefract Road where Arthur Dodson, aged forty-one, died when the sides of his eight foot deep shaft collapsed around him.

Meanwhile, the miners' long struggle began to pay off. The nation was crying out for coal and the dispute was settled on 17 November, the men returning to work at the old rates. *The Daily Chronicle* declared:

A triumph of labour such as the world has never seen. All along the line they [the miners] *have stood firm through the weary months. Their discipline and loyalty, their sublime endurance, their faith in one another are as unshakable today as they were at first.*

The dispute, involving 300,000 workers in the central coalfields, was the most widespread miners' strike in the nineteenth century. It proved that united action could produce results and paved the way for the successful 1912 minimum wage strike, the first to involve all the coalfields.

Chapter 3

1900-1920

Boom and War

Between 1900 and 1914 Barnsley firmly established its reputation as the coal centre of South Yorkshire. After the 1912 minimum wage strike a coal boom was sustained until the beginning of the First World War in August, 1914. In January, 1914, the *Barnsley Chronicle* declared:

> *The past year has been remarkable, not only for the volume of business but for the high prices. On the other hand working costs and wages have never been higher, the men enjoying a minimum wage. Costs have increased owing to the fact that the miners have not been prepared to toil the whole available working time when they have made a satisfactory wage in a smaller number of days. Yet, with all these extra costs, the colliery owners have enjoyed a prosperous year.*

Although Barnsley could still boast that it was the principal coal town of South Yorkshire, there were the first signs that it would be knocked off the pedestal in the 1930s. Developing the virgin area between Rotherham and Doncaster, where new pits were being laid out, coal owners were predicting in 1914 that these pits would produce a million tons per year. Mr J Hewitt, president of the Barnsley and District Coal Owners Association, speaking at a meeting in February of that year complained that some Doncaster pits were producing coal below the Barnsley price. After suggesting that the new Doncaster pits pay a higher minimum wage to relieve the pressure on Barnsley, where the pits were generally smaller and the seams thinner, he said Barnsley was still the centre of the best quality coal in Yorkshire but warned that the industry was vulnerable to trade cycles.

At that time exports were booming. South Yorkshire pits sent more than seven million tons to Hull between 1913 and 1914, with northern Russia, the biggest

customer, importing one million, an increase of 200,000 on the previous year. Sweden, Denmark and Germany were important importers too. Most of the British coalfields achieved their highest outputs in 1913 when one out of ten workers in this country was employed in the mines. It was the high noon of the industry – although Yorkshire did not reach its production peak until 1924.

In 1914 everything was rosy in the Barnsley coalfield, with coal selling at 12s 6d a ton, compared with 9s 6d in 1912 and 8s 1d in 1911. A large steam trawler business had recently announced the signing of a big contract for South Yorkshire coal. With the coal mines booming the owners had problems attracting enough labour to maintain and increase output and that year the Yorkshire Miners Association heard a complaint that twenty women were employed on the pit banks at Sharlston Colliery, West Yorkshire, because lads would not do the work.

The future of the pits, like the future of the British Empire, looked secure but the war changed all that. In

Shaft sinkers at Elsecar Main Colliery, in the early years of the century. *G. Beedan*

Yorkshire Miners galas in the early years of the century. The banner in the bottom photograph is Wharncliffe Woodmoor. *Loaned by R D Watson, Darton*

This map dates from the early twentieth century.

A deputy below ground, 1912. *Photograph: British Coal, Eastwood Collection*

August war fever spread across Europe and miners, like other workers, enlisted in the forces in large numbers: it was an adventure and many were glad to see the back of their underground galleries. Between August and April, 1915, 13,000 miners from all the coalfields enlisted, resulting in a shortage of coal which pushed up prices. Although production was concentrated on the home markets, exports to France increased as the war progressed but the lucrative markets in Russia and Germany were lost for ever. In the first year of the war national output dropped by thirty-four million tons. Absenteeism was said to be a problem, particularly in Yorkshire and court prosecutions against miners who were absent without a valid reason were weekly occurrences. When it was suggested that drink be prohibited, in an attempt to make workers work harder, a Labour MP said absenteeism was due to a number of causes, illness, daily minor accidents and exhaustion.

As the war progressed almost everything in the nation became subject to Government regulations, from the internment of aliens to street lighting and whistling for cabs! Industrial conscription, though talked of, was never introduced to ease the labour shortages. Wage increases and bonuses averted many disputes, although trouble bubbled under the surface and occasionally broke out in strikes: 170,000 miners were on strike in Yorkshire for a spell in 1914, over the minimum wage, and there was so much disruption in South Wales the coalfield was brought under Government control, a year before the other coalfields.

One problem would not go away – drinking. Drunkenness and absenteeism in industry led the Government into controlling licensing hours through the Central Control Board (Liquor Trade) in 1915. This led to some strange court appearances in Barnsley. Treating a group of friends to a drink became an offence. A group of miners from Wombwell appeared in court in the spring of 1916 after treating each other to drinks at the *George Hotel* and the landlord was fined 10s. At the end of May a Cudworth landlord was fined for allowing 'treating' on his premises.

This photograph was taken on 11 August 1914, when the Parkgate seam was reached at Darton Main Colliery, also known as 'Jaggers'. In the hoppit are the pit owner, Mr Jagger, and the HM Inspector of Mines, Mr Stone. Four brothers of the Sowerby family appear on the picture. A few men from Denby Dale and Skelmanthorpe, were known as 'Yar-sarders' because of their strong accents. *Mr Harris*

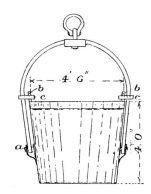

A Hoppit for sinking a shaft. The bow of the hoppit is pivoted on tunnions, ('a' in iillustration). These tunnions are set below the centre of gravity, so that the hoppit can be easily tipped right over by withdrawing the cotter ('b') and lifting the hoop ('c') clear of the pin. The hoppit is attached to the rope by means of a spring hook and swivel.

One of our mystery pictures. It may not have been taken in Barnsley, for there is no record of a local pit opening in 1914, but the scene oozes atmosphere.

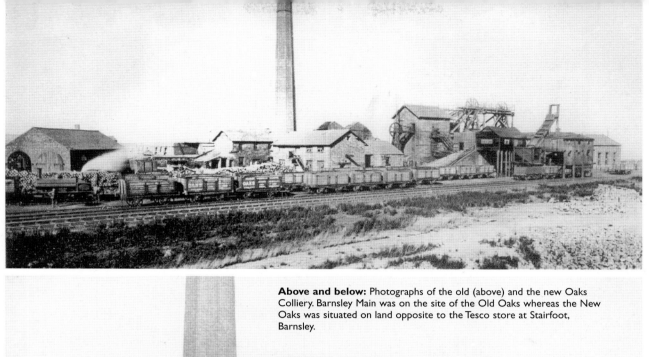

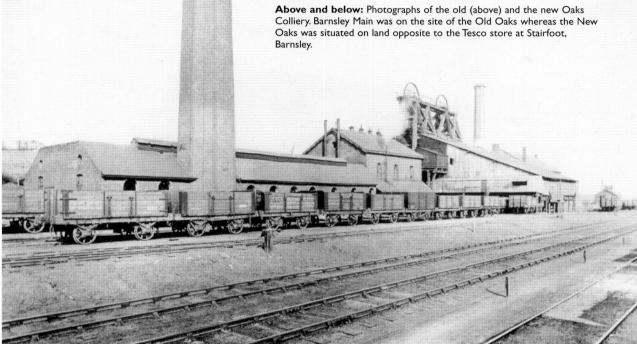

Above and below: Photographs of the old (above) and the new Oaks Colliery. Barnsley Main was on the site of the Old Oaks whereas the New Oaks was situated on land opposite to the Tesco store at Stairfoot, Barnsley.

Darfield Main Colliery in 1910. *Mr G Gill, Wombwell*

Photograph of Dodworth Colliery. In April 1907, a fire caused £50,000 of damage.

In 1912 King George V visited Elsecar Main.

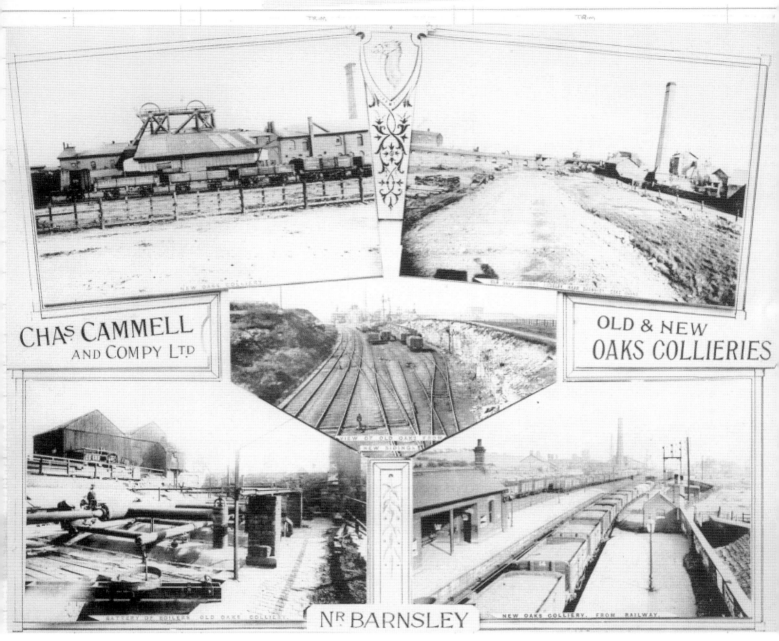

Charles Cammell and Co., Cyclops Works, Sheffield who owned the Old (Hoyle Mill) and New Oaks (Stairfoot) Collieries, produced a photographic record of their premises (above and opposite).

Above: Top left, New Oaks; top right, the Old Oaks; centre, a view of the Old Oaks colliery from the new railway sidings; bottom left, a battery of boilers from the Old Oaks; bottom right, the New Oaks from the railway.

An illustration of the Old Oaks Colliery.

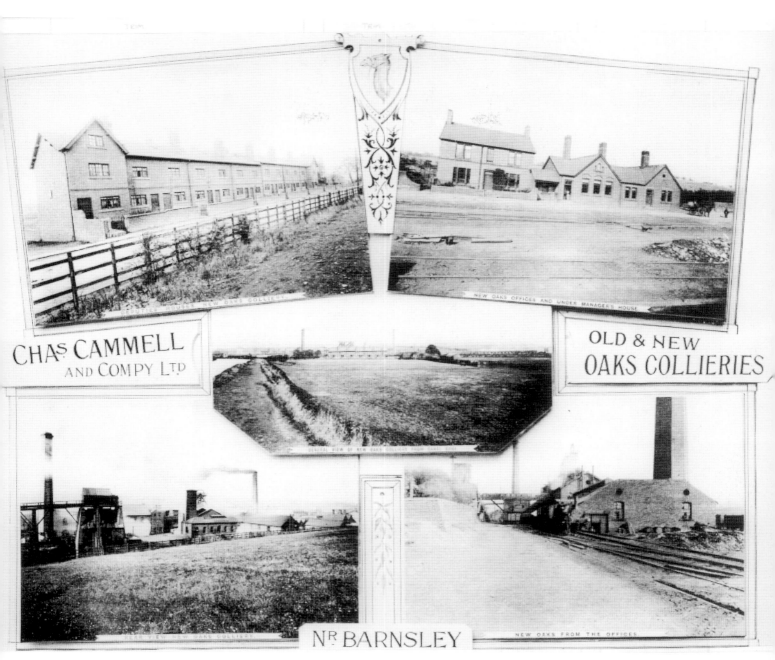

CHAS. CAMMELL AND COMPY LTD

OLD & NEW OAKS COLLIERIES

NR. BARNSLEY

Views of the New Oaks Colliery, Stairfoot. Top left, deputy row; top right, offices and under-manager's house; centre, pit viewed from the canal bank; bottom left, rear view of pit; bottom right, from the offices.

An illustration of the New Oaks Colliery.

More like a scene from a western than the sinking of Elsecar Main Colliery in 1905.
Alan Stevenson, Elsecar

Left: Miners starting to undercut the coal. *Yorkshire Mining Museum/Leeds City Museum*

Below left: Setting a pit prop. *Yorkshire Mining Museum/Leeds City Museum*

Below right: A miner engaged in 'holing'. To give protection to men engaged in holing and prevent coal bursting off from the face in slabs 'cockemegs' are set. The cockermeg consists of a piece of timber two or three feet long, set horizontally and wedged to the floor and roof by the sprags. *Yorkshire Mining Museum/Leeds City Museum*

Below: Hewers at work... 'in a way it is humiliating to see coal-miners working. It raises in you momentary doubts about your own status as an 'intellectual' and a superior person generally. All of us owe the comparative decency of our lives to the poor drudges underground, blackened to the eyes, with their throats full of coal dust, driving their shovels forward with arms and belly muscles of steel.' George Orwell. *Yorkshire Mining Museum/Leeds City Museum*

Below: In 1842 hewers in South Durham worked a six hour day, although coal masters in other coalfields demanded 12 hour shifts. In 1907 coal getters worked 8 hours, 36 minutes a day and other mineworkers 9 hours, 28 minutes. In 1919 a shift was reduced to seven hours plus winding time (36 minutes on average). After the miners' defeat in 1926, the shift was increased to eight hours but shortened to seven and a half hours in 1930. From 1924 to 1938 a six-day working week was regarded as normal. *Yorkshire Mining Museum/Leeds City Museum*

An Edwardian postcard, *The Miner's Dream of Home*.

The Collier, by Sir Frank Brangwyn. *Courtesy of Sheffield Art Galleries*

Knocking out a support ready for dropping and, below right, the result.

In May, 1916, the coal famine led the Government to talk of suspending the *Eight Hours Working Act*, reducing the minimum working age from fourteen to thirteen and employing women on the colliery surfaces. A local coal owner said all the pits were under strength, both underground and on the surface. He said the men who had started work after August, 1915, were making up to some degree for the men who had enlisted but they were still inexperienced and there were few machines for getting the coal out of the ground. By 1917, following the slaughter on the Western Front, the Government switched priorities by announcing to release 500,000 men from the mines for the armed forces. The men to be called up included the following classes: the men who had entered the pits since August, 1915; surface workers and the men who supervised them; and the workers of military age who during the past two or three months had lost on average two or three shifts from an avoidable cause. A coal owner told the *Chronicle*:

> *It means the men must do their duty in the pits or in the forces. It will put the fear of God into the heart of the young, irresponsible shirker, and the sending of a small proportion to the Colours will remedy the evils of absenteeism. The young devils think more of their pleasures than the needs of the gallant men fighting in the trenches.*

There were no objections from the Yorkshire miners

Filling a tub. *Yorkshire Mining Museum/Leeds City Museum*

Pit ponies could sense danger... 'Then the pony stopped abruptly and stood trembling, refusing to advance further in spite of the whip and the oath. Looking past the pony for the cause, the man heard the cracking and rending of timber and falling stone. Going forward he found himself brought to a standstill by a great fall,' wrote Jack Lawson, author of *Under the Wheels*.

Men pushing coal tubs. Yorkshire Mining Museum/Leeds City Museum

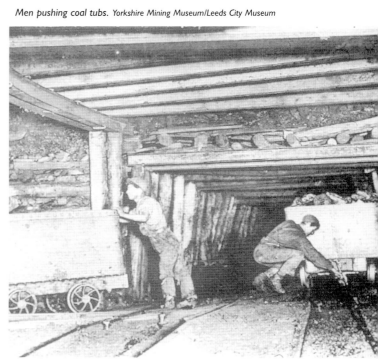

Above: Difficulty in getting skilled men led to the greater use of coal cutting machines in 1909. The HM Inspector of Mines wrote: 'No doubt the use of coal cutting machines and face conveyors working together has a tendency to reduce the dangers of roof falls. *Yorkshire Mining Museum/Leeds City Museum*

The stables.

Above: In an attempt to clamp-
-down on the abuse of pit
ponies, the *Coal Mines Act* of
1911 stipulated that horse-
keepers had to keep a record
of their animals and their daily
condition and movements.
These are two pages from the
Cortonwood Colliery book,
dated 13 and 14 August 1912.
The names of the ponies are in
the left hand column, the
drivers in the next column and
the condition of the animals in
the wide column on the right.
The book was found during
demolition work at
Cortonwood in the 1980s.

A typical miner's family in 1912.

association, the president of which said difficulties would be created in the forces unless the men were released. But he warned that the men would want their jobs back after the war and he believed the end of the war was in sight.

After the war the mines remained under Government control for a time. With trouble brewing in the coalfields the Sankey Commission recommended a pay increase, shorter working hours and the nationalisation of the mines on a permanent basis. But the Government dragged its feet and by 1921 the post war demand for coal was less acute: the mines were returned to the hated coal owners and the stage was set for the 1926 General Strike.

Bath Tubs and Coal

Back in the 1950s my father talked of the old miners he had known in the 1920s . They were born in the 1880s, had received an elementary education and had unusual beliefs: hot water weakened the back and lower limbs and encouraged illness, they said, and they did not like the idea of pithead baths. Their ethos revolved around toughening the body and keeping it in perfect condition to enable them to continue working, since medical treatment cost money. Joe Hall, who started work in 1899 and who later became a national figure, said:

I remember washing at home, with my mother dusting my back. We rarely washed our backs and lower limbs because it was said to weaken them. How my mother kept the beds so clean I will never know.

In Wales they disliked washing their backs because they feared it caused a roof fall. This superstition was not confined to miners: fishermen in Wales did not wash during periods of good catches for fear of washing their luck away. This anti-bathing fear must have taken root in Barnsley in the late nineteenth century because a solicitor reported to a government inspector in the 1830s that Silkstone miners, both male and female, bathed in the same room at the same time with the front door open! Mr Hall, the miners' leader, said it took the union thirty years in the early twentieth century to persuade some branches to accept the idea of pithead baths and one branch spent

five years trying to persuade their members to hold a ballot on the issue. In 1923, when there were one million mineworkers in the country, there were eleven pithead baths. In the North East in the 1920s it was thought that coal dust toughened the back and miners refused to wash it off. During the 1926 lock-out, miners in that area played football with workers in other industries – the miners did not wear shirts and the players and spectators could differentiate between the two teams by looking at their backs, the miners having skin as black as the night. Mr Jack McKenning, the former chief executive of CISWO who lives in Barnsley, grew up in the 1920s and 1930s and his father rarely washed his back.

He came home from work and bathed all over in the zinc bath in front of the fire – except for his back,

said Mr McKenning.

I then rubbed his back with rough cloth and after a while his back had a polished look about it, like ebony. He believed frequent washing weakened the back muscles. I'll always remember coming home from the war on leave and my mother saying: 'Guess what! Your father has started using the pit baths!

The back was important. Arms and legs could be strengthened and hardened but the back had a tendency to let the miners down when they least expected trouble. So when they turned their back on superstitions and started washing their backs, they still took care of them, as in the case of my father who wore a cloth belt to support the small of his back. His was a back that seemed to be perpetually smothered in iodine and lotions of all kinds of colours and strength. The accepted wisdom seemed to be that if it did not sting, it did not work. All those bottles of lotions, often bought off the shelves of the corner shop, were supposed to heal cuts and bruises and cure all kinds of aches and pains which afflicted miners. However, despite all the care and attention, the back still caused problems, some miners developing 'buttons', scabs on each of the vertebrate caused by rubbing their naked backs against the rock roof.

According to George Orwell, the middle classes claimed that miners would not know how to bathe themselves even

Scenes in miners' homes, 1912. *British Coal, Eastwood Collection*

'My cousin who spent his holidays with us, was shocked the first time he saw my father with his face as black as a minstrel's, the white of his eyes contrasting sharply with his face...' (see Mining Memories)

A miner and his bath in the 1920s. Most of the Barnsley pits had pit baths by 1940 but other pits, like Darfield Main, did not have such facilities until 1955. The miners' union had been pressing for pit baths from the early years of this century but there was often resistance from miners who believed that coal dust helped to heal grazes and wounds and that too much washing encouraged sickness and diseases.

if there were more pithead baths. After a visit to miners' homes in Wigan in the 1930s, Orwell said a large number of miners were completely black from the waist down for at least six days a week. *'It is impossible to wash all over in their homes – every drop of water has to be heated up (on the coal fire) and there is no room for a proper bath in the small rooms.'* Orwell estimated he would have to take two baths to remove a day's mine grime and ten minutes to remove the dust from the eye-brows. However, he noted that the myth that washing the legs caused lumbago was dying out. Mine owners were reluctant to provide pithead baths on grounds of costs. Between the wars the owners, convinced that nationalisation was always round the corner, baulked at the idea of investment, not only on the surface but underground.

Coal and dirt were an integral part of a miner's life of

course. The hewers hacked away at the coal at work, had a healthy respect for it because they knew that one slip could end in death or injury and they burned it in prodigious quantities at home where it was seen to be as valuable as money in the bank, better than money in a very hard winter. The wages derived from cutting it at work put clothes on their children's backs, paid the bills and provided them with small luxuries.

It had other uses. It was sucked to relieve indigestion, was thought to be a sign of good luck (soldiers have been known to carry a piece into battle; burglars used it as a charm against arrest), was used by craftsmen to make figurines of miners or miniature coal tubs for display in people's homes, was crushed and put on lettuce to ward off slugs and was given to pigs to empty their bowels in preparation for slaughter.

Young lads getting the coal in, a familiar sight throughout the streets of Barnsley.

Before radio and television became popular, the fireplace was the central attraction in any home and miners' children spent long winter evenings peering into the coal fires. It was easy to see 'pictures' in the blazing coals and dying embers, an amusing and imaginative pastime in the days before soaps and computer games became the predominant occupation of children. The superstitious saw other things in the fire: if the coal burnt unusually bright it was said to be a sign of frost on the ground; a cluster of sparks on the chimney back a sign that news was on its way; a white or black film on the bar denoted a stranger was en route to the home.

Miners loved enormous fires. Thanks to their concessionary coal allowance they were rarely short of coal; whereas other workers would think twice before putting coal on their fires in cold weather, because the fuel was expensive, miners would think nothing of using a bucket full – every twenty minutes if necessary. They derived a sense of pride in the size of the fire. Each home coal delivery was inspected with care, since its quality could vary from month to month and by the late 1960s and early 1970s it was felt by some miners that the coal was deteriorating: the best coal for domestic consumption had been dug and sold in earlier times and the contemporary coal had been produced for a different market, perhaps the power stations. Silkstone seam coal had been

regarded as very good domestic coal. It was known in some quarters as Peacocks owing to the beautiful colours it contained. The colours gave evidence of the coal tar in the coal and formed the base of aniline dyes. In the old days there was coal that produced a sluggish and prolonged fire and coal that was said to be gassy, spluttering and firing bits around the hearth in the early stages of ignition and then settling down to a roar that could be heard round the room with even the smallest lump producing a fierce flame and bubbling coal tar. As the fire went into top gear the coals became a crimson mass of heat that made the occupants push their chairs away from the fireplace or Yorkshire Range in a bid to keep cool. This was the kind of fire a miner loved: it burned swiftly and had a healthy appetite, having to be fed with coal at frequent intervals. It had to be a very hot day before a miner was prepared to peer at an empty grate. It has been suggested that miners needed big fires because they were accustomed to intense heat at work. Writing in

All miners had to start shovelling coal when they arrived home and saw their concessionary coal heaped in the road or in the yard. The coal was stored in the coal shed or cellar.

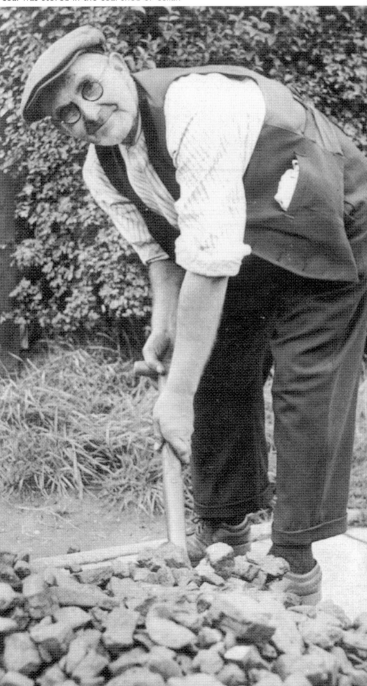

The days of the old tin bath in front of the coal fire are shown in this photograph by former Wombwell photographer the late Joe Short, whose sister, Mrs Rose Hirst, is in the tub and another sister, Mrs Emily Glover, is in the background. *R J Short*

By the early years of the twentieth century, Barnsley was reaching its peak as the coal capital of South Yorkshire, and as a ahopping centre for the surrounding mining villages.

the March, 1993, edition of *The Dalesman,* a woman told the writer, Mr W R Mitchell:

After the warm conditions underground heat was as important as food. He must have a big fire. I remember one day, a few days after we were married, we returned home from a shopping expedition to Pontefract to find the fire was out. It wasn't vital to us but Dick – who had been reared in a miner's home – had never experienced a cold grate in the living room. He actually cried.

There was always something emotional about a coal fire; on a cold and wet evening the sight of flames roaring up the chimney swelled the heart and I have always associated an empty grate with sorrow and loneliness. D H Lawrence wrote of a collier's home:

All the life of the room seemed to be in the white, warm hearth and the steel fender reflecting the heat.'

Writing of his childhood home in Fitzwilliam, near Pontefract, Geoff Boycott, the cricketer, stated in his autobiography:

A place of warmth, movement and caring, a little part of a true community which now seems outmoded and old fashioned.

Large buckets and shovels were indispensable in the home. My uncle's next door neighbour, with the tongue firmly in the cheek, often complained that he was awakened at 7 a.m by my uncle who, having got the fire going, threw a large bucket of coal on the fire, always ensuring that the coal bounced off the fire-back for effect and as a result made so much noise and vibration both houses in the terrace shuddered. My uncle did not realise he was a nuisance, for all miners threw buckets of coal on to the fire with some force, since to do otherwise would have been a sign of a weak man.

Coal dust was rubbed into wounds and grazes to facilitate healing. Old miners said they had enough coal dust inside them, after a working life down a mine, to keep them warm for the rest of their lives. Their backs were pitted with blue scars caused by coal dust embedded in the skin: according to one local woman her father's back was like a road map of England, with all the blue specks, small holes and blue lines. A layer of coal dust was seen as a badge of courage. Joe Hall, after his first shift underground at Darfield Main Colliery, refused to remove the dust for several hours because he was so proud of his blackened features, a confirmation of his adulthood. That kind of ritual was not confined to future miners' leaders. Fresh from his first day down a mine a young miner in the 1920s or 1930s would wash, dress and then walk down the street proud of the dark circles round his eyes, the circles having been created by coal dust engrained in the skin. Some miners would eat a meal before bathing. *'This is not dirt – it's pit muck and it's clean muck',* a miner would tell his wife, who had urged him to get washed. An illogical comment perhaps but it does show that miners had a respect for the stuff. Coal dust intrigued Henry Moore, the sculptor. Commenting on his work as an artist down the pit, he said:

First there was the difficulty of seeing forms emerging out of the deep darkness, then the problem of conveying the claustrophobic effect of countless wooden pit props, two or three feet apart, receding into blackness, and expressing the gritty, grubby smears of black coal dust on the miners' bodies and faces.

When the dust lodged in the lungs, leading to that dreaded disability, pneumoconiosis, it was a different story: dust was something to hate and fear. Old miners out for a walk can still be seen leaning, say, on a wall half way up a steep hill, immobilised by this lung disorder. The affliction has now almost disappeared among younger miners, thanks to all kinds of safety measures implemented underground in the 1970s.

Few workers could have had such a close relationship with the product of their labour. For obscure reasons miners retained large chunks of coal for decades. One of our neighbours, the late Walt Dobson, High Street, Wombwell, kept a lump of coal he had cut at Houghton Main Colliery in 1922 for sixty years; twenty years ago it was used as the focal point at an exhibition on mining at the local parish church. (In May, 1993, the lump was on display at Barnsley Library). Another piece of coal weighing 156 lb, mined at Darfield Main Colliery shortly before the 1926 dispute is now at the Cusworth Hall Museum, near Doncaster. The lump was part of a home coal load delivered to a Wombwell man who, because of its enormous size, refused to break it up. He kept it in the coal cellar for fifty years. When he died at the age of seventy-three his family honoured his wishes that it be kept for sentimental reasons and it was taken to his son's home in Essex, where it remained until 1987. Then the family decided that as it had come from the old Barnsley Bed seam it should be presented to a mining museum – hence its final destination. Miners also became attached to smaller pieces of coal. Recently, I have come across the story of a miner who appeared at the Yorkshire miners' gala in Sheffield in 1909 with a fancifully decorated pick shaft, attached to which was a piece of coal he had won in 1856. At that same gala there were lots of men carrying pick shafts, polished to the last rub, and decorated with flowers.

Coal wielded an almost magical fascination to some men. Many miners hated the sight of coal, having blamed it for turning them into underground slaves; others could not keep away from it. Every village, perhaps every street in the old days, had a character who was strong in the body and who spent his spare time shovelling loads of home coal into miners' cellars for a few shillings. He would clear three or four tons of coal per morning or afternoon without any effort or grumble. Monetary gain was not always the principal motivation for this work, for one man I knew tried to commit suicide during the 1984/85 Miners' Strike (during which no coal was delivered except on compassionate grounds) because he thought no one wanted him. The work had helped the shy and awkward man to forge social contact with his neighbours. My uncle, even in his seventies, would put a couple of tons of coal into neighbours' coal sheds or cellars in a day without a complaint; in his case he appeared to need the physical work to satisfy some inner compunction since he never asked for a penny. Other shovellers would not accept payment but welcomed a couple of buckets of coal, the best bargaining counters in a mining village.

Coal in the shed or cellar was a valuable commodity. One of our neighbours kept coal in the shed for years and I don't think they wanted to burn it. They hoarded it like gold. In the midst of a bitter winter in the early 1950s the children in the yard were fascinated to see that the door had been left open and the shed was empty except for two or three layers of large lumps of coal. It was the first time we had seen that shed almost empty since it had been built. The size of the lumps intrigued our small minds, as the lumps dwarfed the cobbles of coal that had become the norm for home deliveries in the 1940s and 1950s, and we had not seen anything like them before. Within a few days, however, a new delivery of cobbles from the pit had been shovelled into the shed, covering the old coal once again, saving it for another winter. The lumps were in a way the family silver: in the worst scenario they would not be burned in their home but exchanged for money or other goods. Fortunately, for that couple, scarred by their experiences in the 1920s, the bad old dole days did not return.

As the old lady, a born survivor who has street sense, says in the 1941 British film *Love on the Dole*:

I knows nothing about politics but I knows about a load of coal.

Which is not as daft as it sounds. In this major film the young idealist dies penniless in bed but the old lady, the queen of street bartering in the terraced streets of Salford in the 1930s, survives on her 10s (50p) a week pension and her nose for acquiring buckets of her neighbours' surplus coal which she later burns in her home or sells at a profit.

Tragedies

By the twentieth century the titanic disasters involving hundreds of victims belonged to the history books but some accidents continued to capture the headlines. Seven men were killed when they were hurled to the bottom of the pit shaft and six others injured, three of them seriously, in the cage disaster at Barrow Colliery on 15 November 1907. Sixteen men got on the double-deck cage when it was lowered to the Parkgate seam. Then it was lowered to the Thorncliffe seam, where the horsekeeper, the only man to travel from the surface, was set down. When the signal was given to ascend the cage gave a tremendous jerk upwards and began to swing violently, throwing six men from the top deck and one from the lower, and they fell sixty to seventy feet to the bottom of the shaft. The other men were thrown off their feet and all the miners' lamps went out. Realising something was wrong the engineman stopped the cage half way up the 480 yard deep shaft; then it was lowered to the Parkgate seam where the men were rescued.

One of the survivors, George Hargreaves, said:

We were thrown off our feet and some could not speak. The others shouted for the cage to stop, for we thought if

Damaged pit lamps found in the cage.

The Barrow Colliery Disaster

November 1907

The funeral of some of the victims at Worsbrough Church.

The Remembrance Card.

Hoyland Silkstone. *John Goodchild Collection*

we came to the descending cage we would be thrown out. It was a fearful thing and seemed to last three quarters of an hour. We dare not move for we did not know what was coming next, and all we could hear was the groaning in the cage.

After finding six bodies in a heap in the shaft bottom, the under manager at the Silkstone pit, Mr B Miller, a member of the rescue team, said:

They were smashed to pieces. One had the head almost knocked off and another an arm almost wrenched out of the socket. It was a horrible sight; it almost makes me sick to think of it.

The cause of the accident: the flat iron sheet thrown from the mouth of the shaft to the cage to allow the men to pass from one to another had not been lifted away when the cage had started to ascend. The sheet held the cage for a few seconds and then, releasing itself with a jerk, the cage went swinging up the shaft and the men were thrown out. The jury returned a verdict of accidental death and of gross negligence and carelessness on the part of the two men who were supposed to make sure all was clear before the cage moved.

That same year Mr Frank Chandler was awarded the Edward Medal for helping to rescue a man in an accident at an underground boiler-house at Hoyland Silkstone Colliery, Platts Common. Chandler's nineteen year old son died in the accident. A group of men were repairing the boiler-house in the Parkgate seam when a large girder collapsed, bringing down with it a section of the roof: the boiler and piping burst and there was an escape of scalding steam. One man died on the spot and three others were so seriously injured they died in Beckett Hospital, Barnsley, three days later. At the inquest Chandler, a deputy who was in charge of the party, said

they were working on the brick walls on which the girders rested.

There was a big earth bump, my lamp was knocked out and I was scalded by escaping steam. I found a man called Cooke in an exhausted condition; I got him on my back and crept away to a place of safety.

Then Chandler went back to the boiler-house and heard men shouting, including his son Leonard, who said: *'Don't come in here, father, you'll get killed.'* Realising he could not help his son, Chandler crept along in the darkness until he felt the shaft. Tumbling into the cage he was taken to the surface. Later he was told his son had died. After the coroner at the inquest had said Chandler had displayed great courage, he replied: *'I do not think I have done more than any other man would have done.'* The jury returned a

Frank Chander of Jump who received the Edward Medal for bravery.

68

The Wharncliffe Silkstone pit at Tankersley. *Loaned by Mrs G A Greaves*

*The
Wharncliffe
Silkstone Disaster
1914*

The jury in the pit yard.

WHARNCLIFFE SILKSTONE COLLIERY
EXPLOSION TANKERSLEY NR BARNSLEY.

11 KILLED
4 INJURED

The Remembrance Card.

verdict that the four men died accidentally, owing to an earth bump (sudden ground movement), causing the girder to break. They added that the manager was to blame, but not criminally, as the girders were not strong enough to withstand the weight of the roof.

Preparing faces for the resumption of work after the holiday, thirty men were working at Wharncliffe Silkstone Colliery at Tankersley, at Whitsuntide, 1914. Coal cutting machines were being used in the thin Whinmoor seam when there was an explosion and a sheet of flame and accompanying firedamp swept through the workings, killing eleven and injuring four. A hurricane of stone and dust lifted two deputies off their feet, some distance from the explosion, and hurled them fifty yards down a roadway.

A *Barnsley Chronicle* reporter said:

> *The whole affair, indeed, was a matter of a few minutes, and so confined was the area, that men working in other parts of the pit were unaware of the calamity.*

The 2,000-man colliery was usually free of gas and no fire was started after the explosion, thanks to the ventilation and the damp conditions underground. After the alarm was raised the under manager and chief engineer went underground without safety apparatus, halting for a few minutes to turn the cloud of firedamp into the return airway with brattice cloth. Within twenty minutes they had reached the scene of the explosion, about a mile from the shaft. The reporter wrote:

> *It was evident from the conditions of the bodies that the blast had passed them quickly by. In each instance the features were capable of easy identification, the burns, principally of the first degree being on the upper parts of the body and head. In only a few cases was the hair singed or the clothing burnt away.*

Meanwhile, the Wharncliffe Rescue Brigade, on descending the shaft, found no reason to don their safety helmets in the clearing air. The bodies were conveyed to the joiners' workshop on the surface. After identifying the body of his son in law in the workshop, which was used as a mortuary, Mr William Walker, a miner of High Green, said Mr William Fisher, his son in law, had been reading an account of an accident in which a miner had been killed a week earlier and had told his wife: *'Don't be surprised, Nell, if they bring me home like that.'* Mr Fisher also said that he believed the coal cutting machines were dangerous and the jury at the inquest heard that a spark from a machine may have caused the explosion. The Bishop of Sheffield, on visiting the bereaved families, said: *'There were families of three, five and seven children who had lost their fathers in a moment.'* The head of the rescue team had told him that a man whose body was badly burnt told the rescuers to help his workmates. *'That,'* said the Bishop, *'is what I call courage of the first rank and the man deserves the Victoria Cross.'*

What Made Them Tick?

Miners' lives were based on muscle power. *'It is only by having a muscular body that we can earn a living,'* wrote Hemingfield miner Joseph Knowles in his diary. They

This photograph was loaned by Mrs Constance Burton, Stocksbridge, whose father, Mr Francis Levitt, known as Farr, is pictured right. Also pictured is Mrs Burton's uncle, George, and cousin, Majorie, born in the mid-1920s. The father of Marjorie, who is not pictured was Mr William Levitt, president of the Yorkshire area of N.A.C.O.D.S. Mrs Burton's grandfather, Mr Abe Levitt, who lived at Elsecar, collapsed and died at home, through hard work after a shift at the pit. He was in his early 40s.

were men of iron, like hammered statues of iron under a smooth black coating of coal dust, according to one writer who forgot to mention in his spasm of elegant prose the ugly grey streaks on the miners' backs down which flowed the sweat. A vicar of Silkstone, the Reverend J Prince, writing in his book, *History of Silkstone*, published in 1922 and dedicated to miners, said the grimy black of the miners was only skin-deep and they were in the main hardworking men.

It was this unconscious addiction to both hard work and physical prowess – plus their relationship with the nightmarish underground environment and their stoicism – that was the very essence of the coal hewers, the men who cut the coal. As John Wilson, the Durham miners' leader said: *'Forcing me to hew lifted me out of the category of boys at a very early stage.'* The hewers, the elite underground workers, the men who were eulogised by some artists and writers (Auden referred to the *'lurcher – loving miner as black as night'*) had a special quality – strength – and in their eyes that elevated them above other men. Underground they were at home, men who knew every crevice and cranny as well as the temperament of the mine and its seams and who were accustomed to working in deep darkness: *'The darkest night is mere twilight compared to the darkness down a pit,'* wrote Jack Lawson, who started work underground at the age of twelve, became an MP and writer. Outside a coalfield, however, they were more uneasy and did not feel at home in what they saw as an alien world. (Even in the 1980s Arthur Scargill moved the headquarters of the NUM out of London to Sheffield, one of the reasons being that he felt the miners' 'home' should be in one of the coalfields).

Like all industries, mining had its slackers and Mondays were seen as unofficial days off, 'Colliers' Monday' or 'Mabon's Day' (named after a miners' leader) as it was known in South Wales. Being superstitious, miners would not go down a mine under certain conditions; for instance, when a man was killed in the pit the whole pit would stop work that day or on the day of the funeral. But apart from those peculiar customs the average hewer was a conscientious worker, a man who had a sense of pride in his work. Though it was viewed by the outside world as an unskilled job for many years, the hewer needed skills with which to cut the coal in his stall using various pick heads (striking the coal at the right spot would save him time and effort) and he enjoyed exercising his muscles in the daily contest with the wall of coal. The writer George Orwell said hewing took super human effort but the fact that it was often performed in uncomfortable positions, like crouching or on one's side, made the work even more exacting: he said he would not have lasted a week down a mine. Orwell was not a physical man; he admired miners (to demonstrate his rapport with the working classes he slurped his tea out of a saucer in the BBC canteen) but his lack of physical prowess would have been secretly abhorred by miners, who still retained some elements of the old tribal system. They despised anything that was soft or appeared to be soft. That love of muscle-power and work formed two of the acknowledged but unstated rules of a kind of exclusive miners' club from which even their wives and children were often excluded. In their impromptu groups at work and in their spare time the miners indulged in what they regarded as elitist talk about the cleavage of coal, 'wooden' (hard) coal and the 'mini' (minimum wage) and about their pastimes: dogs, pigeons and sport. The groups, large and small, were found in many locations. All towns and villages seemed to have a favourite spot where miners gathered, such as a street corner where they stood deep in conversation, hands deep in pockets, watching the world go by. In Barnsley it was at the bottom of Market Hill, in Wombwell outside the *Prince of Wales* (when there were more than six standing outside the public house, it was seen as a sign that one of the pits was on strike or on short time). Miners also met on allotments, in the tap-room of public houses or back-yards. The discussions, mainly for the edification and enjoyment of the participants, also had the subliminal effect of enhancing the camaraderie among miners.

Down a mine men's safety depended on the men standing next to them, all of which formed a vital bond, and that sense of camaraderie ran through their lives like

Boys started work underground at 13 or 14 years. They were often puny, but once they became hewers they developed muscular bodies.
Yorkshire Mining Museum

71

Above and below: Hewers, the elite workers.

a vein. It also formed part of the texture of the union, for that bond was essential during any strike; most miners realised that one 'black leg,' a renegade, could break a strike. Workmen from other industries, particularly if they had less physical jobs, were often secretly despised and were discouraged from taking part in 'pit talk.' As one ex-miner, Fred Brady, of Thurnscoe, told the *Chronicle* as late as 1993: *'When you get four miners together they talk coal because that's the only thing they know.'*

Coal and work, they were the perennial topics (sometimes it was said more coal was cut in the pub than down the mine). Dick Brown, a miner who worked in South Wales in the 1920s and 1930s said on the television programme, *All Our Working Lives*:

I started work after being indoctrinated by my father and his friends who came to the house. The only topic in the Valleys in those days was work. We accepted that

mining was the only way of life. Quite frankly, on reflection, I was scared stiff by the atmosphere of the pit, the conditions, the stench and the darkness. I cried my eyes out and I told my father I did not want to go back, but I had to go to work to live.

George Thomas, later Viscount Tolypandy, wrote in his autobiography:

We used to listen to stories about life down the pit as lads and felt quite envious. It sounds incredible today but we listened because mining had a manly image.

Mr John Hunt, a pony lad at South Kirkby Colliery and later a pit manager, said there were three types of workers: those who got on with their work and did not require supervision; those who would work under supervision and those who had to be cajoled or bullied to work. A man would be expected to clear a length of coal measuring between eight and nine yards by about two yards in two days. The quicker he cut it the more money he received;

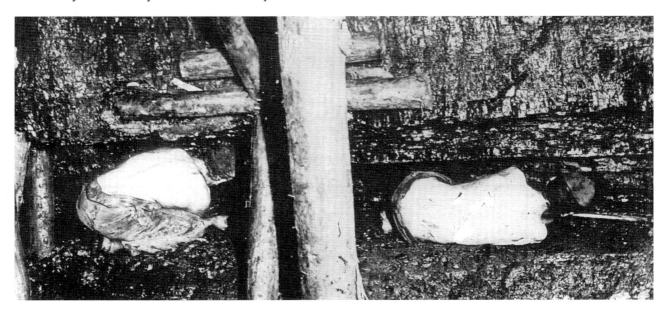

surface workers were paid by the hour. A miner would be expected to buy his tools. Will Paynter, of the South Wales Federation and former general secretary of the NUM, speaking on *All Our Working Lives*, said in his coalfield in the 1920s men had a sharp hatchet (for cutting their own timber for roof supports), several picks with straight blades and a sled to enable the miners to erect wooden supports. Another Welsh miner, Stan Millard, said on the same programme that he had two shovels – *'You always had shovels'* – a box to put the coal in and a sled as well as a number of other tools he had to buy. A Yorkshire miner wrote in 1929:

Taking my tools into my stall I first of all test for gas to make sure my place is safe to work in. I haven't said much about my mate up to now but very likely he has been with me all the way from the pit bottom. There are four men working in my stall, two in the mornings and two in the afternoons. All our earnings are paid for at piece rates and booked to one number, the whole being shared at so much per shift worked each week. When I walk down the gate into my stall, I am facing twenty-four yards length of coal face which constitutes the length my mates and I are responsible for working. There are two kinds of work on the coal face – hard and harder.

Miners have always fascinated people from other backgrounds. Artist Josef Herman, in his autobiography *Related Twilights* recalled seeing a group of miners and the image it produced:

This image of miners on the bridge against the glowing sky mystified me for years with its mixture of sadness and grandeur, and it became the source of my work for years to come.

Eton-educated and former colonial police officer George Orwell said he felt inferior in the presence of miners. The Vicar of Silkstone, Reverend Prince, born into the middle class, was also intrigued, and writing in *The Daily Mail* in 1919, said he had studied the life of the miner.

It is hard work and only a skilled man can get the coal out. Often he works in water, often in great heat – much depends on the place he gets in the pit. I have known miners who after working all week have not had a living wage left for themselves after paying the hurriers [the men who pushed the tubs]. I have tried to understand the miner. It is not difficult: he is a good hearted, industrious fellow, with no wide vision, fond of his beer, his racing, his home; easily influenced, but willing to hear both sides of the question; generally contented.

Mr Prince, who seemed to think miners were akin to children and therefore needed parental guidance to help them avoid the pitfalls of life, was involved in an acrimonious debate in the letters column of the newspaper. In 1919 the pits were still under the control of the Government and there were widespread strikes and, of course, miners were blamed in the newspapers for the trouble. While defending the miners, the Vicar blamed the unions for some of the problems, claiming secretaries and officials had a tendency to mislead the men. Then the vicar criticised the Government, the coal owners (soon to take over the pits again) and the middlemen for profiteering in the past. *'When a man deals in coal he soon stinks of brass,'* wrote the vicar.

I have seen it again and again over the past ten years – fortunes literally piled up out of nothing. If miners see employers, the middlemen and others riding in a £2,000 Rolls Royce, and stinking of brass, can we wonder why they [miners] want a share of the plunder?

A hewer at work in a thin seam in the 1980s. *British Coal*

Hoyland Band, 1926. It was not all brawn and beer. Many miners were gifted musicians. *F W Williamson, Wombwell*

Elsecar Pit Band.

The vicar appears to have had a sincere regard for miners, though treating them like grown-up children, but like many members of the middle class at that time he found difficulty in coming to terms with the concept of trade union officials and found Communists incomprehensible. He was quick to point out there were no Communists in Silkstone during the 1921 Miners' Strike, even though his last quote about the Rolls Royce could have come straight off the lips of what was then known as a Bolshie.

The writer D H Lawrence, born in the 1880s, the son of a Nottinghamshire miner, who often wrote about his father's generation, shared the view that to some extent they were innocents with dirty faces, believing miners were quite content with their lot until agitators and sentimentalists stirred them up in the late Victorian period. He believed miners in the twentieth century steeped themselves in work to run away from the home:

> *Colliers were deeply alive, instinctively. But they had no daytime ambition and no daytime intellect. They avoided, really, the rational aspect of life. They worked together in a kind of intimate community.*

What Lawrence called 'physical awareness' was at its strongest down the mine; when they came up the shaft they 'had to change their flow,' almost as if the world underground was more relevant to them than that on the surface. *'It was hard facts, in the shape of the wife, the money and the nagging home necessities that they fled away from, out of the house into the pit.'* The writer may have been right up to a point but Lawrence had a tendency to see things that were not there, the product of an overwound or exalted imagination. The miner may have run away from the home, like husbands in all walks of life, but not necessarily to the pit. Anyone who has read of the conditions underground before nationalisation would realise that few men could have worked there for prolonged periods and enjoyed it. The miner romanticised his skills and the pleasure he elicited from work but the three feet high dust-filled seams (the dust was thick enough to throw back the light from a miner's lamp) were something different: no rational person would have run away from home to face the subterranean horrors and the dangers of the coal face where a lump of coal big enough to kill a man could shoot out of the roof with the speed of bullet and where he worked in fear of the crack of a wooden prop and the ominous dribble of bits of rock or dirt from the roof, often a sign that something terrifying was on its way. Some men feared they were tied to the pit, its slaves, and that horrified them. They saw the walk to the pit as one long queue from which they opted out in an evening only to catch up with again the following morning. To these men pits were seen as transit camps where men worked until something better turned up. Only the unfortunate or the men who enjoyed pit work stayed the course, they declared.

Invariably of medium build, with strong legs, broad shoulders and firm backs, the old fashioned miners had qualities which not only made them eminently suitable for working underground but which made other workers feel uneasy in their company: their physical aura in a room was palpable, almost intimidating to anyone less physical.

A Derbyshire miner: the pick was the most common tool used down a mine. The blades were sharpened in the blacksmith's department and the hickory shafts shaped by the miner at home using a sharp knife or bits of broken glass. *Frank Burgin*

Again they caused extreme reactions in people.

Miners had a built-in sonar system, and they could pick up the slightest noise or movement underground. My father was sat in Askew's barber's shop, Wombwell, one day when he sensed a mild earth tremor which went undetected by everyone else in that room. The following day a story in the *Daily Express* confirmed there had been a tremor, the epicentre of which was some miles away. He also had a remarkable talent for anticipating sudden changes in atmospheric pressure, particularly in the early hours of the morning when he was on his way to work: when the weather changed dramatically and swiftly with a noise like the crack of a rifle shot, he would turn to his mate and say: *'Told you so!'* When George Thomas, later Viscount Tolypandy, was helping his brother in a makeshift mine during the 1926 dispute, George was suddenly pushed out of the way by his brother and an enormous stone fell out of the roof of the tunnel and landed on the spot where George had been standing. *'How did you know that was going to happen?'* asked George. *'I heard it,'* came the reply. George, who told the story in his autobiography, *Mr Speaker* said he had heard nothing. His older brother, a seasoned miner, had acute hearing which was essential down a mine where you had to wield a pick or shovel while at the same time listen for the crack of a wooden prop (pre-war miners did not like metal props because they gave no warning) as well as the normal creaks and groans in a mine. It was a long time before miners accepted the idea of wearing helmets despite the obvious advantages, because helmets restricted their hearing. Sound was useful in other ways. Most miners could test the coal or roof by sound; they tapped the coal with the pick and shaft to see whether it would take a lot of persuading to move and the roof to see whether it was about to collapse. Having to work in such a precarious environment enabled them to acquire a sixth sense: they could 'feel the weight on the back' before a roof fall, or so they claimed. It is paradoxical that men renowned for their brawn had a sensitive side to them.

But the overriding influence at work and home was the physical side. As well as being indispensable to their survival on the coal face, the miners' physique had other advantages unconnected with work: it opened doors to other worlds. Interest in the mass spectator sports mushroomed towards the end of the nineteenth century and one could write a book, as they say, on the numbers of ex-miners who played league football. It was said that if you needed a centre-forward or 'keeper you just whistled down a mine shaft. Cricket was another sport which attracted miners. Harold Larwood, born in Nottinghamshire in 1904, is regarded as the best fast bowler produced by this country. Having built-up his physique on the coal face no one was better suited to the exacting craft of demon bowling – he had a perfect run up and balance and his wide shoulders and powerful legs enabled him to produce spells of fast bowling which terrified batsmen on the Australian tour in 1932/33. Had Larwood been an office worker one doubts whether he would have had such formidable power in his legs and shoulders, essential qualities in an intimidating bowler. It was not just his physical side; his mental make up had been fashioned down a pit as well and he did not give an inch on the field or give a monkey's uncle about casualties, all of which underlined the cliche that miners worked and played hard.

Miners' strength and skills were useful in time of war. During the First World War when stalemate had paralysed the forces on the western front miners were used to try to force a breakthrough. Tunnelling under 'No Man's Land' miners placed huge land mines under the enemy lines; on detonation by the sappers they created enormous craters. The idea was a success at first but the Germans developed counter measures including sensitive listening devices which picked up the sounds of the men tunnelling, and the allies had to wait until the arrival of the American forces, the tank and the exhaustion of the enemy before the final breakthrough came.

No miner could retain his strength for ever and it was time that broke them. That occurs to all men but the decline is accentuated in men who have had a perfect physique in their youth and who end up on the streets as crippled old men. As young men they worked so hard they developed muscles where none had been before and they developed enormous appetites:

Man is a stomach, wrote Jack Lawson. When fingers, hands, wrists, arms, shoulders, back, body-trunk, thighs, leg balls, feet and toes have been crying aloud, there is only one thing that matters, the stomach.

At work they had a meagre diet, a Dudley or bottle of water plus slices of dried or buttered bread and, on special occasions, dripping, contradicting the assumption you cannot work on an empty stomach; at home they had stew meat, vegetables and Yorkshire puddings in prodigious quantities: it all fuelled the great physical machine. And they had big thirsts, although their favourite tipple at work was water which was needed to replenish the sweat. Chewing tobacco also helped to quench a thirst and keep the mouth moist: when he visited a mine in the 1930s George Orwell was horrified when he put his hand in a brown, soggy lump of chewing tobacco which had been discarded on the face. By middle age some miners were physically spent, particularly if they had worked in their teens with their fathers who, of course, would not have been as nimble as in their younger days. Son had to 'carry' father on the face, virtually doing two men's work and the work became too much. Miners who did contract work in their youth were susceptible to premature ageing as well. As late as 1970 Sidney Schofield, the Yorkshire miners' general secretary, suggested that miners who had worked in the industry for forty-five years should be given the opportunity to retire. He wrote in his annual report:

There is sufficient evidence to prove beyond a shadow of a doubt that many of our members who went into contract work while they were very young – in their teens or early twenties – are really struggling to work beyond sixty.

By 1993 problems regarding miners aged over sixty had almost disappeared. Men in their twenties and thirties were taking redundancy and a working miner aged over forty was rare .

Chapter 4

1920-1940

Strife and Hope

The pits in this country were in deep trouble in the 1920s. Coal demand, production and profits were falling and inflation outstripped wages, all of which set the scene for the 1926 General Strike and the long miners lock-out. Having relied on exports before the First World War to make their profits tick over, the industry now found that nations were producing their own coal or were importing from America and Germany; on the home front the slump dampened the demand for coal.

More than one million miners were employed in the early 1920s (120,402 in South Yorkshire), each man producing 229 tons per year, compared with 260 in 1913, the peak year in the history of mining. Having failed to use their pre-war profits to modernise the mines owners now demanded that the miners work longer hours for smaller wages. The miners, however, claimed their wages had been eroded by a seventy-nine per cent rise in the cost of living since 1914 (in that year miners received 6s 5½d a shift and in 1922 9s 4d). In their annual report for 1925/26, the Yorkshire Mineworkers Association stated:

Coal has been the mainstay of Great Britain. Before the war it was a prospering, fairly tranquil industry and the backbone of the export trade. Now it is a pauper industry, fed by the state, run at a loss and swept by unrest.

According to the report, the world shrinkage in the consumption of coal was due to the increasing growth of other sources of power, such as oil and hydro-electricity; the failure to organise and develop the coalfields on more efficient lines; and unsatisfactory international political relations and unrest.

There had been industrial unrest since the end of the war: a strike in Yorkshire over wages and shorter hours in 1919; a national strike in 1920 and a lock-out in 1921 following Lloyd George's decision to hand back the mines – 'nationalised' during the war – to the owners. That decision shattered the dreams of miners who had been calling for public ownership since the late 1880s. There had been a glimmer of hope in 1923 when a Bill to nationalise the mines was submitted to parliament, prompting Mr Sam Roebuck, the Yorkshire miners' general secretary, to comment: *'Nationalisation is now just a matter of politics.'* However, the miners had to wait until 1947 before their dream came true.

The General Strike was inevitable. For years there had been a feeling that one day the growing power of the trade unions would result in a large-scale clash with big business, behind which stood the all-powerful state. In the early 1920s government kept quiet and prepared to smash the unions in the event of a General Strike by preparing emergency measures. The short-lived Labour Government of 1924 were aware of the plans but they did not tell their

Darfield Main branch banner and union members on their way to a gala. Pictured in Low Valley between the wars.

Jump Distress Committee which fed 1,000 everyday. Front centre of the picture is Councillor Preston and his wife.

A miners' band organised to raise money for strike funds, 1926, in Mapplewell.

A game of miners' golf, 'nipsy', in the Wombwell and Darfield area.
R J Short. Cusworth Museum

trade union friends, for the government is the government irrespective of political colours and the state is incapable of tolerating threats to its stability and power. The trouble started in 1925 when the Chancellor of the Exchequer, Mr Winston Churchill, put the country back on the Gold Standard, thereby increasing the cost of exports by ten per cent. The pits could not compete with the coal industries in other countries and coal stockpiled at the pitheads. When the owners announced wage cuts and a longer working week, Mr A J Cook, the Miners Federation secretary, retorted: *'Not a penny off the pay, not a minute on the day.'* Following a threat by certain unions to support the miners in the event of a strike – it was acknowledged in trade union circles that the miners were much abused – the Government backed away from a confrontation, set up a Royal Commission to suggest proposals to reorganise the coal industry and provided a subsidy to maintain wages at existing levels. Throwing a few crumbs to the miners the Commission recommended that the mines be nationalised at sometime in the distant future; then they said limited pay cuts were inevitable.

The subsidy ran out on 30 April 1926 and the miners, who refused to accept pay cuts and longer hours, were locked-out by the owners. The TUC ordered a General Strike which lasted from 3-12 May. With the government maintaining essential services – the plans for which had been prepared over the previous few years – the unions got cold feet and the strike collapsed. Although militant trade union leaders had always maintained that a General Strike would be the first step towards the overthrow of government, most leaders were not extremists and they were frightened that the strike would lead to instability and revolution. The Russian revolution in 1917 and the

From the 1880s to the Second World War, three quarters of the workers in Wombwell were employed in the mines. That was a high figure even for a traditional mining village or town. It was inevitable that Wombwell would produce men who rose to high union office.

The most notable were Joe Hall, (right) Yorkshire Financial Secretary from 1925-1938, and President from 1938-1952; Sam Roebuck, (above) General Secretary from 1923-1924 and Fred Collindridge, Vice President from 1946-1954 and General Secretary from 1954-1964.

A Barnsley soup kitchen team pictured during the 1926 lock-out.

Lundhill Chapel in the 1920s. The pit had gone but the houses, the pub and the chapel remained. The Chapel was used as a mortuary in the 1857 disaster. Joe Hall, the miners' leader, was educated in the chapel. *Joe Short*

Miners' wives soccer team, 1926. *Mrs M Johnson, Worsbrough Dale*

Making the best of a hot summer nearly 80 years ago
at the old brickworks at Darfield Main Colliery..
R J Short, Courtesy of Doncaster Council, Cusworth Hall

Swimming in Low Valley, Wombwell, 1926. *R J Short*

Fish being distributed during the 1926 strike. Wombwell or Darfield.
R J Short, Courtesy of Doncaster Council, Cusworth Hall

Barnsley Salvation Army soup kitchen in 1921.

virulent 'Red scares' in America in the early 1920s were still fresh in their minds. Despite the reaction of the other trade unions the miners continued their struggle.

Distress in the coalfields was widespread and union funds soon dried up. On 2 September, on the 125th day of the lock-out, a miners' national conference heard that the last money they had paid out was three shillings per head and they had in hand one shilling eight pence per head.

The miners were never solid. Pits in Nottinghamshire continued working and a breakaway union was set up there by an MP called Spencer (history repeated itself in the 1984/85 Miners' Strike). Miners drifted back elsewhere and the conference in September heard that 400 of the 150,000 Yorkshire miners were working. The miners were locked out for six months and returned to work on the owners' terms.

The lock-out influenced miners' leaders for nearly fifty years. Men like Joe Hall, the Yorkshire president between 1938 and 1952, lived with the nightmare that it might happen again, the defeat having rocked the very foundations of the union. Before the General Strike the miners leaders had been confident of victory, there had been talk of a new world, workers' control of the mines and the end of capitalism. When the union funds started to run out the leaders had to face reality and the humiliation of defeat remained with them for the rest of their lives. That lock-out left its mark on miners' sons who were children in 1926 and who later became miners' leaders. Men like Sidney Schofield, the Yorkshire miners secretary in the early 1970s, came to power fearing that history would repeat itself, that miners would slide into a strike when defeat was inevitable. The impact of that lock-out on

the union and miners can never be overstated. When Arthur Scargill came to power he was aware of the humiliation and privations suffered by miners, having heard the stories from his father, Harold, a Communist, but he was too young to have been scarred by them and when his generation took on the Government in the 1970s he had none of the hang-ups of the earlier leaders. To him, the 1972 and 1974 victories were sweet revenge.

After the 1926 lock-out things went from bad to worse. Some miners who had been militants during the dispute never worked again, for their names found their way on to the owners' black list. Men who had worked found they were 'lepers' in their pit communities and one or two men were still ostracised by people when the 1984 strike started. Demand for coal, and wages, remained low and unemployment rose in the 1920s and 1930s. However, South Yorkshire pits began to produce a greater share of the nation's coal, thirteen per cent in 1929 and 14.7 per cent in 1941. More coal was cut by machine, thirteen per cent in South Yorkshire in 1929, 36 per cent in 1934 and fifty-six per cent in 1938. By 1935 Doncaster had replaced Barnsley as the coal capital of South Yorkshire.

In the 1930s Mr Joseph Jones, president of the Miners Federation, wrote in his book, *The Coal Scuttle*:

The low wages of the miners, their hard uncongenial work and the risk of injury or death, to which they are daily exposed, are all matters which are well-known to their countrymen. There has been a quickening of sympathy for the miners, and there has been a keen desire to come generously to their aid in times of suffering and distress.

Mr Jones, a Mayor of Barnsley, said three main evils

The underground stables at Wharncliffe Silkstone Colliery, Tankersley.

Shaft sinkers at the new Upton Pit in the 1920s.

During the 1926 strike, food stations were set up to provide for the needs of the miners' families. These photographs show children collecting bread from a working men's club in Darfield and in Barnsley.

For some young men without any responsibilities, the General Strike of 1926 and the long miners' lock-out were glorious days: under-graduates had the time of their lives driving trains and buses during the national stoppage, and miners looked back on the lock-out with affection – for many weeks they did not have to toil underground and the long, hot summer was one of the best on record. However, miners with families found it all a miserable experience. Debts, accrued as a result of the dispute, were never paid, and some small traders went out of business. At the beginning of the dispute, a special meeting of the Guardians of the Poor was held in Barnsley and the then Ministry of Health were asked for sanctions to provide an overdraft at the bank. Relief was given on loan to families who suffered distress. For the first two weeks, relief was given in provisions, and then a man and wife received 22s per week and each child 4s. In July, according to the records of the Guardians, two representatives of the miners' association, Mr John Mellor (later West Riding County Council Alderman), of Wombwell, and Mr Thomas Tomlinson of Hoyland, asked the board to consider granting relief on loan to single men, some of whom were suffering from malnutrition. Board officials said, if the request was granted, they could be surcharged by the District Auditor. After several meetings with the miners' representatives, the board decided to take the risk and give single men relief under certain conditions, the principal one of which was that the men must be physically unable to work. In July the amount of relief paid during the dispute was £44,120; by August the figure had risen to £133,326. There were reports of men who had made false statements to get relief and court proceedings were taken against at least two men, Mr Henry Foster and Mr Joseph Leech.

dominated the mining areas: unemployment, low wages and oppressive working conditions, adding:

Most people are aware that we have a great unemployment problem; the sad sight of ex-miners begging in the gutters of the cities must bring the fact home to the most casual observer.

In South Yorkshire the number of miners decreased from 116,874 in 1929 to 95,947 in 1934; 56,000 were out of work in the whole Yorkshire coalfield the following year. The average wage per year was £114. Mr Jones again:

The knowledge that men who have to face the perils of the pit and who provide the country with the basis of her material prosperity, receive an average of about £2 per week must cause pain and anxiety to all who have pride in their country.

The national production figures rose in the early 1930s from 253 tons per man in 1931 to 280 tons in 1934. But during the Depression many pits were on short-time and closed down on two or three days per week and Mr Jones wrote:

The effect of short time working is not disclosed by these figures [the national production figures in the 30s], and this was substantially greater in the post war years than in 1914. If the low wages which have been paid in recent years have not had the effect of reducing the miners' output, it is clear that the output has been maintained at the expense of the miners' families, for unless a sacrifice has been made somewhere, our men could not possibly have maintained the strength and energy which are necessary to carry on the work.

The fifteen years following the war brought hardship to mining communities. Thousands were thrown out of work, while thousands who were on short-time working earned low wages. These wages were insufficient to maintain health and strength; families were broken up because men were forced to look for work elsewhere, particularly in London and in the car plants that were being built in the Midlands and in the South. It was hard to believe that in

Coal-picking during the 1926 lock-out. *Artist: Ralph Dyson, Worsbrough Common*

1920, only a few years earlier, manpower in the industry had peaked at one and a quarter million. By the mid 1930s the industry was slowly recovering and the union began to flex its muscles again. In September, 1935, The Miners' Campaign Special Newspaper declared:

The hour has struck. At last, after years of submission and slave-like conditions the miners have decided to press their claim to the payment of reasonable wages. The wages of miners are a disgrace to a civilised community. Shut out from the sunlight, surrounded by dangers, and working with the greatest possible intensity, they receive wages which are insufficient to keep body and soul together. Mining has become a sweated industry. Thousands of miners receive less than £2 per week. The mine owners say they cannot pay more, but the truth is that the fruits of the miners' toil are dissipated by reckless competition and lack of organisation in the industry...

The owners believe that the miners will not force their claim to an issue; they believe the miners were hopelessly defeated in 1926 and that they will not face another stoppage; that is a very unwise assumption...

A big strike was averted but as the Second World War approached the demand for coal increased.

Mr Jones was right when he said there had been a quickening of sympathy for miners during the 30s. There were still some reactionaries in the middle classes, people who believed miners kept coal in the bath, who believed miners were all drunkards and gluttons, but a new generation of writers and film directors were determined to break with the past and they concentrated their talents on the coalfields. George Orwell, author of *1984* and *Animal Farm*, was educated at Eton: he did not see a smoking factory chimney until he was adult and yet he identified with the working man, particularly coal miners. Gathering material for his book, *The Road to Wigan Pier*, he visited Barnsley, described the hard poverty of families living in Peel Street and Wortley Street and in Mapplewell

Miners coal picking in Tower Street, Barnsley, during the 1926 lock-out.

Darfield Main branch of the miners' union pictured at Darfield in the 1920s or 30s. :*W. Swift*

Dearne Valley Colliery rescue team, 1930s, including the instructor, Mr J E Parkinson. The man on the back row, extreme right, was the pit manager, known affectionately as 'Long John Silver', because of his height and grey hair. *Colin Massingham*

Above right: Barnsley Collieries Rescue Station. Barnsley Main No. 1 team, 1931. (Back row, left to right) C. Byron; J E Parkinson (instructor); J B Stringfellow (leader); F Leary. (Front row, left to right) H Hayes; C V Gillespie.

Gedney's private mine at Hemingfield, pictured in the 1930s. The mine, which produced a few tons of coal per week, was sunk in 1930 and a drift was opened up in 1944, when the owner, Mr William Garforth Gedney, lined it with corrugated sheets from an Anderson air raid shelter. The mine was abandoned in 1958. *G Beedan*

The staff at Mitchell Main Colliery, Wombwell, pictured on their annual outing to Scarborough in the early 1930s. *Mr S Winder*

and toured the underground workings at Grimethorpe Colliery, where he said he felt inferior in the presence of miners. A J Cronin, a popular novelist, highlighted the plight of miners in *The Citadel* and *The Stars Look Down*, both of which became popular films. *The Stars Look Down*, made in 1939 and starring Michael Redgrave and Margaret Lockwood, is acknowledged to be the first truly British film. Film critics who watched British films in the 1930s not only condemned their inferior quality to Hollywood products but their bias towards the middle classes: many seemed to be set in drawing rooms south of Watford. The few films set in the north portrayed a working class which bore little resemblance to reality and were usually farces or musicals starring Gracie Fields or George Formby. *The Stars Look Down* took a serious look at a mining community and made a plea for the nationalisation of the mines, strong stuff for the commercial cinema at that time. Our feature films may have not been out of the top drawer but we led the way in documentaries, one of the first of which was *Coal Face* which took the film camera underground and showed

miners on the coal face. This growing sympathy for miners was in some respects a reaction against their treatment in the 1920s when the nation turned its back on them and allowed the miners to struggle through the lock-out.

It became evident in the 1930s that the measures introduced by the coal owners after 1926, longer working hours and cuts in wages had not changed an industry which was still grossly inefficient. The average man in the 1930s had a social conscience and there was sympathy for the unemployed and the deprived, and for the first time for decades miners had public opinion behind them, they were no longer the national bogeymen, and the mood of the nation was moving towards the establishment of a fairer society, culminating in the introduction of the welfare state and the nationalisation of the mines after the war. Not until 1992 would miners have so much sympathy again. The closure of thirty-one coal mines in October of that year led to massive demonstrations and a groundswell of opinion against the Government.

One of the largest disasters in the history of British coal-mining occurred at Gresford Colliery, Wrexham, North Wales, on 22 September 1934. Despite heroic efforts to save the entombed men, over 260 miners lost their lives. In this photograph members of one of the volunteer rescue teams are leaving the pits after hours of fire-fighting.

YORKSHIRE MINEWORKERS' ASSOCIATION
GENERAL ELECTION, 1935

MANIFESTO

THREE OUTSTANDING BETRAYALS!

The "RINGROSE" FIREDAMP ALARM

TO MINERS AND OTHERS

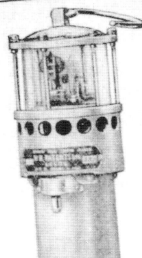

GRESFORD, SOUTH KIRKBY
AND
NORTH GAWBER DISASTERS
MIGHT HAVE BEEN AVOIDED

AMONG THE CRIMES OF THE NATIONAL GOVERNMENT NONE STANDS OUT SO MUCH AS ITS

CALLOUS DISREGARD FOR HUMAN LIVES

Here you see a Photograph of AN AUTOMATIC "GAS DETECTOR," which has been approved on the grounds of RELIABILITY AND ACCURACY, and which would provide an

EFFECTIVE WARNING TO MINERS

Mining disasters haunted the 1930s, a black decade in more ways than one. The worst disaster was at Gresford Colliery in North Wales where 260 lives were lost and where scores of bodies were sealed off in the workings. Yorkshire miners' official Mr Joe Hall vowed that would not happen in Yorkshire but within a few years he had to break his vow, at Bullcroft Colliery. Soon after Gresford came South Kirkby, where eleven men died, and then North Gawber, where Joe said the working conditions were beyond belief. Nineteen men died there and Joe led the rescue team which found the last body: 'He was on a stone with with his face downward. The glass of his pocket watch had melted in the heat.'

MINERS CAMPAIGN SPECIAL

Our Strength is in the Justice of our claim

No. 1

SEPTEMBER

1935

THE MINERS' APPEAL

The Poverty of the Miners

THE hour has struck! At last, after years of patient submission to slave-like conditions of labour, the miners have decided to press their claim to the payment of reasonable rates of wages. The wages of the miners are a disgrace to a civilised community. Shut out from the sunlight, surrounded by dangers, and working with the greatest possible intensity, they receive wages which are insufficient to keep body and soul together. Mining has become a sweated industry. Thousands of mineworkers receive less than £2 a week. Think of it, £2 a week on which to keep a wife and family. *And there is no need for this appalling poverty. That is the awful tragedy of it.*

The mine-owners say they cannot pay more, but the truth is that the fruits of the miners' toil are dissipated by reckless competition and lack of organisation in the coal industry itself. *Because there is no proper organisation of the industry, there is no proper wage for the miner.* That is the simple truth, which has been testified to over and over again. The coal-owners themselves admit it. Read their confessions on page 4 of this issue. They themselves prove conclusively that with better organisation better wages could be paid. AND THE MEANS TO BETTER ORGANISATION IS ALREADY IN THEIR HANDS. THAT IS THE INCONTROVERTIBLE FACT WHICH DISPOSES OF THE ARGUMENT ABOUT THE INABILITY TO PAY.

The Organisation of the Coal Industry

The Coal Mines Act of 1930 gave them the power to organise their industry and pay reasonable wages. Under the Act they can regulate the output, fix prices, and co-ordinate the work of the districts so as to avoid internal competition. Up to the present, instead of doing these things, they have evaded the Act and failed to co-ordinate the prices of the districts. On page 4

may be seen a list of the various devices resorted to by different owners in order to evade the price Schedules of the Act. This list was given to Parliament by the Secretary for Mines himself. Is there any wonder why wages are so low? The resources of the industry are still being squandered i.. reckless and destructive competition between the collieries. But this must stop. The owners must cease to look upon the coal industry as a number of separate pits and districts ceaselessly at war with one another. *They must be compelled to treat the industry as an industry, and to get a price for their coal which will enable decent wages to be paid to the miners. The present position is intolerable ; it must be ended.*

It CAN be ended by giving the industry a new basis. There must be a proper minimum wage paid in every district. The payment of a reasonable minimum wage will relieve the sufferings of the miners and at the same time will compel a re-organisation of the industry. Wages and organisation are but different parts of the same problem. For more than twenty years, the country has placed organisation first. Re-organise the industry, it has said, and good wages will be paid. But so long as the industry is kept going by the serf-like labour of the miners, there will be no reorganisation. Compel the payment of better wages, and reorganisation will assuredly follow. We repeat, that the machinery to better organisation is already in existence, and the driving spur of higher wages will compel the use of that machinery.

A National Settlement Necessary

And just as the Coal Mines Act, 1930, in order to eliminate the competition between the districts, provides for the national control of output and prices, so also is it necessary that the miners' claim shall be dealt with nationally. It is useless for the miners to make approaches to their re-

spective district owners; if they do so they are invariably told that particular districts have to meet competition from other districts, and that an increase of wages is impossible, unless wages in other districts are raised also. The Chairman of the West Yorkshire Coalowners' Association, Dr. Hargreaves, made this statement only last week. The miners, therefore, are making an application for better wages in every district. So far the owners have refused to meet them; for nearly ten years the owners have steadily refused to discuss the wages question nationally, though that is the only logical and sensible way of discussing it; the coal-owners are the only body of representative employers in this country who refuse to treat with their employees on a national basis. Their attitude is stupid and illogical. It is no longer to be borne.

The owners believe that the miners will not force their claim to an issue; they believe that the miners were hopelessly defeated in 1926, and that they will not face another stoppage; that is a very unwise assumption. The miners, it is true, do not want another stoppage; a stoppage of work in the coal industry would be ruinous to everybody; the last one cost the country hundreds of millions of pounds. Surely, in these days, it will not be necessary for the miners to withdraw their labour in order to secure their elementary rights. And yet, if the owners persist in their present attitude, that possibility will become a certainty. The miners want justice, and this time they are determined to secure it. A stoppage of work can be averted only if the force of public opinion is strong enough to compel the owners to adopt a more reasonable attitude to their employees. Therefore, the miners appeal to the public. They appeal to every citizen, irrespective of party and irrespective of creed, to use the utmost influence to ensure a proper consideration of their just claims.

After the exhausting defeat during the 1926 lock out, the miners were
beginning to flex their muscles again by the mid 1930s. A copy of a
Miners' Campaign Special in September 1935. *Peter Taylor Library*

1926 – The Leaders

Dour Herbert Smith, one of three fascinating men who dominated The General Strike and miners' lock out, was no respecter of persons. Prime Ministers, cabinet ministers and coal owners – and even his own miners, whom he saw as being morally and physically superior to the aforementioned – were handled in a distinctive and irreverent manner by 'the man in the cap.'

'Nowt doin', growled Herbert when things were not going his way. Talks between colliery owners and the union halted and everyone went home. *'Ahr 'Erb'* had spoken. He was the dogged, unyielding big boss man of the Yorkshire miners and the Miners Federation of Great Britain during the hungry 1920s. An inverted snob, he sported a flat cap the size of a large dustbin lid and wore an English lever watch the size of small dustbin lid. That was his battle dress: a blatant sartorial warning to his opponents that he relished his working class origins and couldn't be bought. Herbert did not have any finesse, was uncouth, taciturn... but was nobody's fool. Having hauled himself up from the coal face and having met all kinds of men he was a good judge of character. He was also unorthodox, audacious and courageous. And his favourite phrase was *'nowt doin'.'*

Herbert was a big man who attracted tall stories. In 1926 at a meeting in the House of Commons, Lord Birkenhead, who once said that he had never met anyone as stupid as a miners' leader until he met a coal owner, was in evening dress. So was the Prime Minister, Stanley Baldwin, who made an eloquent but long winded speech in which he said the miners had to accept longer hours and cuts in wages. The onlookers gave him a warm round of applause and one or two said: *'Jolly good effort, Mr Baldwin.'* Preparing to make his reply, Herbert paused and appeared to fumble with his dentures, causing sniggers among the Government supporters who thought Herbert symbolised everything that was uncouth among miners, who were still regarded as second class citizens. So Herbert paused again and, with the flourish of a Victorian thespian, removed his dentures, wiped them and put them back in his mouth: *'Nowt doin','* growled Herbert and sat down. A sea of blank faces stared back at the portly figure from the Yorkshire coalfield. First round to Herbert.

'Fine words do not butter parsnips,' was his motto. Born in 1862 he received no formal education (*'Books do not produce coal,'* he said), but he rose through the ranks of the Yorkshire miners, becoming vice president in January, 1904, president in 1906, a post he held until his death in 1938, and president of the federation in 1922, a post he held until 1929. Herbert and his wife, *'Ahr Sally'* came to Barnsley in 1916, and he became a magistrate, alderman and mayor.

Herbert was a national figure during the General Strike and miners' lock out of 1926. When the other trade unions were reluctant to call the strike, Herbert did not hesitate: *'Git onta field,'* he boomed. When they hesitated again he boomed: *'Git onta field,'* for Herbert did not believe in saying the same thing twice using different words – that's why everyone knew what he meant. Herbert had come up the hard way, earning his sharp trade union spurs in the Woodbine-filled and spittoon-filled union rooms where the

Herbert Smith.
'the man in the cap'.

art of diplomacy was for nancies and a filibuster was thought to be akin to filling in a man's face: in other words a blow to the face. As Jack Lawson, the MP and author of Smith's biography said:

You could find Herbert Smiths in every mining village, hands in pockets or stood at the street end. He couldn't hide anything and he did not attempt it.

Apart from A J Cook, the federation secretary, the other major figure in the General Strike was Baldwin, the Prime Minister, and Smith often clashed with him. The late George Wilkinson, a former NUM official at Houghton Main Colliery, who portrayed Smith in the television series, *Days of Hope*, thought Herbert was the one man Baldwin feared. The men were not unlike each other, although their backgrounds were different.

Baldwin was from a wealthy background and well

88

educated: easy going, almost lazy, and one of his election slogans – 'Safety first' – summed up the man. The public saw him as a sound man who did not go in for new fangled ideas; a genial duffer who acted as a buffer against unsavoury ideas that might erupt from the streets or, God forbid, the mine shafts. On the other hand, he had a sincere desire to halt the economic slide in his country and unknown to the public contributed part of his personal fortune towards paying off the national debt. Like many politicians of his generation he looked to the pre-1914 days as the halcyon period and endeavoured to turn the clock back. Smith, born in the 1860s, did not understand the modern world either and had spent most of his life witnessing the expansion of the miners' union (including the 1893 and 1912 victories), not its demise, and a world in which the miners had no political clout was too bewildering for him to contemplate.

Smith wanted to safeguard his members' interests; Baldwin put the nation first, two incompatible ideals. At one point agreement between the Government and the TUC was almost reached in 1926 but unofficial action by printers at *The Daily Mail* provoked the hard-liners in the cabinet and when a representative of the unions went to 10 Downing Street to clarify a point they found the Prime Minister had gone to bed and members of the cabinet had dispersed; the nation tumbled into the General Strike. Earlier protracted talks at 10 Downing Street had their humorous side, however. When Smith strutted into Number 10, the attendant is said to have asked him: *'Can I hang up your cap, Mr Smith?' 'No thanks,'* said Smith. *'I have lost caps like that before.'* This is probably an apocryphal story, for photographs from that period show that he wore a flat cap when dealing with his men – to underline his origins – but a homberg when talking to his so-called superiors; but the story illustrates what the man was like. When the miners' council meeting was held the day after their surrender in 1926 a delegate realised Herbert was deflated and asked: *'Is our chairman suffering from anthrophobia?' 'What's tha' mean?'* came the reply. *'I think it means fear of your fellow man.' 'Fear of my fellow man I'll anthrophobia the lot of you before the day is out.'*

In the lock out Smith was the bulldog; his colleague, Cook, the eloquent dreamer. Whereas Smith was seen as brusque and uncouth – but still a miner – the miners put Cook on a pedestal. One of the most selfless men to hold union office, Cook was the 1920s version of Arthur Scargill, in the sense that he could manipulate an audience of miners as well as fire verbal buckshot at the enemy's rear. It was said he could mesmerise an audience of 80,000 miners. Had you asked Jack Woffenden, the hard-headed delegate at Dodworth Colliery in the 1960s and 1970s to name his favourite miners' leaders he would reply: *'Cook and Joe Hall – they were great men.'* Miners always selected the silver tongued as the pick of the bunch. Cook could spellbound miners with his pulpit-style oratory, a reminder that he had been offered at the age of seventeen a place at a Baptist College. He was born in Somerset but moved to South Wales to work in the mines and that became his power base. Shortly after starting work as a teenager Cook was devastated when a man in the next stall to him was killed in a roof fall. That accident, together with changes taking place in his coalfield, such as falling living standards and the rising power of the newly enlarged coal companies, left a deep mark on him. That underground accident in particular seemed to spur him on to greater things and he always put his members before himself, as if he felt the need to repay some kind of debt; perhaps it was a sense of unjustified guilt arising from that underground accident, perhaps in some small way he felt responsible for it. (It was not unknown for men to change places while working). On his way up the union ladder he adopted radical ideals, including the belief that a General Strike could be the first step towards a new world in which the workers would take over control of government. What he forgot was that most miners were more concerned about a living wage than building a new Jerusalem and the establishment regarded him as an enemy of the state, not as a messiah, and newspaper cartoons of that period depict him as an outlaw trying to hold the Government to ransom. The cartoons reflected the opinion of the general public. Cook appealed to the dreamer in miners, the more pragmatic saw him as a dangerous leader. He exhausted himself during the lock-out, having travelled round the country addressing mass meetings of miners, often going without sleep, all of which had a pernicious impact on his health. Although the miners loved him – even in defeat – there were people on their side who saw him in a different light. The intellectual, Beatrice Webb, of the Fabian Society, described him as *'an inspired idiot'* who was *'drunk with his own words, dominated by his own slogans.'* Miners' leaders said he was capable of inspiring men, like an evangelist, but he was no negotiator. Like Joe Hall, the Wombwell-born Yorkshire miners' leader, he articulated the feelings of inarticulate men, he gave men who had nothing the will to live, to fight for a better future. Unfortunately the General Strike and the lock-out proved too complex and too gargantuan for mere men to handle and the only winners were the cabinet and the establishment, the most powerful institutions in the nation. Cook could not deliver the goods – and I doubt whether anyone else could – and he died a broken man.

One man never forgot Cook. Arthur Scargill is too young to have known Cook but he would have heard stories about the legendary miners' leader from his father, the late Harold Scargill, who lived through the lock-out. On his desk at his Yorkshire miners' offices Arthur had a portrait of Cook to remind him of the bad old days when miners were ground into the dust. Arthur's oratory, his spellbinding speeches much loved by audiences at Yorkshire miners' galas are reminiscent of Cook's. Like Cook, Arthur became the establishment's bogeyman, a man who, they believed, threatened to destabilise society, and the tabloids' editorials of the 1920s were reprinted in a bolder type in the 1980s (when the £ went through the exchange floor during the 1984/85 Miners' Strike the *Sun* had the ridiculous banner headline: *'Blame it on Arthur.'*) But it must not be forgotten that Arthur also modelled himself, unconsciously, on some aspects of Smith's character – for instance, Smith's stubbornness and his refusal to compromise, traits that Cook did not possess, and some people would say traits that prolonged the miners' year long strike in 1984/85.

Pit lads and pony. *British Coal, Eastwood Collection*

Ponies

Pit ponies could expect a working life in the darkness and dust: many did not see daylight until they were pensioned off or until the miners went on strike, and a group of pit ponies in a field could be the first sign to the public that there was an industrial dispute underground. The animals were intelligent, often sensing danger before a miner heard or felt ground movement: they were also perceptive, affectionate and sometimes downright bloody-minded, as militant as any miner with a cussedness all of their own.

A large pit like Grimethorpe would have up to 150 ponies, all employed on hauling pit tubs from the coal face to the shaft. The pony drivers were lads, often new to the pit, who built up close working relationships with the ponies, treating them to their 'snap' and sweets. Ernest Kay (70), Burton Road, Monk Bretton, who spent his early working years at Rockingham Colliery, Hoyland Common, and later at Wharncliffe Silkstone, Tankersley, said on a good day one of his ponies could move forty tons. Joseph Ibbotson, Rotherham Road, Monk Bretton, was employed at Elsecar Main Colliery and recalls his ponies' foibles with affection. Tiger could remove the cork from a water bottle and down the contents in one gulp; even today he wonders how the animal managed it. The pony also liked his snap and would shake the snap tin until the lid came off and the sandwiches fell out. The tin had Tiger's teeth marks on it for years. Wallace had a penchant for clean water and would drink from the trough at the beginning and end of the shift but not from Mr Ibbotson's buckled old bucket at snap time. The bucket was lined with shotfirer's clay and was not the cleanest bucket in the world.

Below left and right: Pit ponies. *Courtesy of British Coal Archives*

I have seen men drink from that bucket but not the pony. Wallace always spent a long time drinking from the trough at the end of the shift and I was always in danger of finishing twenty minutes late.

Tiny, the old pony with bow legs, unhooked the tubs by lashing out with his back legs and then ran off. Another pony had a tail chain twice as long as any other pony's to prevent the driver from being kicked: earlier some men had been carried out of the pit when the pony was in a bad mood. But Toby was the most militant and he had to be banished from the pit because no one would work with him. One man who had worked with horses during the First World War thought he knew how to make the pony move. He put a piece of coal on the pony's bottom and then smashed it with a stick: but the animal did not move.

Many ponies had this stubborn streak. One tub above the allotted number and they would not move until the offending tub was removed. Mr Albert Hayes (78), of Grimethorpe, had one or two tricks up his sleeve. When his pony refused to move he rattled the hook on the last tub to con the pony into believing the tub had been removed, and then the pony moved on. *'I took carrots along for my pony,'* he said.

Some of the ponies could look after themselves and needed little supervision. But a young pony, not broken in, could drag the tubs off the rails. I can remember my mate coming to the house with the words: 'Come on. Albert, let's get down to the pit early and get the best ponies.'

The best ponies were the ones which did not take any coaxing or bullying. At the top of an incline they would halt

Frank Barratt with his pit pony, Dodworth Colliery, 1921.

without instructions and wait for the lad to put the lockers in the wheels to slow down the tubs.

During the 1921 Miners' Strike the ponies at Grimethorpe Colliery were brought to the surface and races organised, the riders being supplied with jockey caps and whips. Ponies, like miners, had their fair share of injuries and fatal accidents and miners resented the recriminations when a pony was killed.

There was always an inquiry; management seemed to think more of the ponies than the men. We were told ponies were expensive to buy and keep.' said a retired miner.

NOTICE.—The reader is asked to imagine that an "old" and "worn-out" Pit Pony is telling the story of its life "underground."

The Life and Adventures of a Pit Pony

"Life stories," of "Famous Men," are published far and wide
And life stories of "Heroes," who for their country died
My life story may interest you, as ever since my birth
My life's been spent, deep down below, in the "bowels" of the earth

For years and years I've worked and done, my duty faithfully
And tried my very best to serve, the Colliery Company
But now my "working" days are "done," I'm "old" and "worn-out" too
So my adventures down the pit, I'll just relate to you

My home's as near "pit bottom" as, it's possible to be
And when my "shift" is ended, that's the place I long to see
But many times when I've reached home, and my "task's" been none too light
They've fetched me out again before, I've hardly had a "bite"

I've had all sorts of "drivers," some were very, very kind
I've also had some brutes," the worst "brutes" you could find
For instance No. 1 I had, he'd treat me like a "Hog"
And if a tub got "off-the-road," he'd kick me with his "clog"

His orders were, my run of tubs, was limited to "four"
But when there was no one about, he'd "hang-on" many more
Sometimes he'd put on "twenty-tubs," which made my legs fair "totter"
And if I could not "pull," them, he'd "bash" me with a "locker"

Driver No. 2 I had, he was a pal to me
He'd often bring a "carrot" or, a "turnip" for my "tea"
A knob of sugar, now and then, when my "shift" was "completed"
And best of all he'd always say, that I was NOT "ILL-TREATED"

He used to drive a mate of mine, old "Tony" was his name
And "Tony" often told me that, he served him just the same
And when my mates at "week-ends," had "extra" work to do
They hoped the lad to fetch them out, was driver No. 2

One day with colliers on the "face," for "water" he was "tapping"
It flooded out the "stalls" while I, was in the passbye "snapping"
He "waded" thro' waist deep to me, "released," and sent me "home"
And then was "carried" back again, by the awful "raging-foam"

Alas, poor driver No. 2, he's in "ETERNITY"
And what is more I feel quite sure, he gave his "life" for me
And when he gets to "Heaven's-Gates," if the good old "Bible's" true
The "King-of-Kings" will say to him, "PASS" Driver No. 2

Driver No. 3 I had, was very hard to please
He'd never try, to see that I, was working at my "ease"
And when thro' "roofing" down a "gate" my "back" was rubbed "red-raw"
He'd merely put some "tub-grease" and, some "coal dust" on the "sore"

Driver No. 4, I had, he was a "football" lad
'Twas, "football" this, and "football" that, aye, he was "football" mad
He'd backed 3 "homes" and 3 "aways," won the "sweepstake" I'll be bound
And nearly got his "coupon" right, to win £1,000

Each "run" on to "main level," he didn't half used to "chin"
And with the other "drivers" he'd, be filling "Coupons" in
He'd then discuss the "Sweepstake" held, at several of the Clubs
And then he'd tell the colliers that, he'd had to wait for tubs

I had a pal named "Jerry" once, who used to "run" a "drift"
He lost his life thro' "carelessness," whil'st working out his "shift"
And when he passed me in a tub, he looked an "awful" wreck
The "door-trapper" had fell asleep, and Jerry broke his neck

I have some "happy" memories, as well as sad ones too
The "happiest" is that "13-weeks," From April "22"
The "Pit-Ponies St. Leger," the "field" beside the "dyke"
I told you all about it in my "Memory-of-the-Strike"

There's one thing that I really think, the "public" ought to know
That's how they treat us ponies, who work deep down below
Our "miners" work, one shift per day, and what I fail to see
Is why we sometimes work 2 shifts, and very often 3

They say that for the "coal" we draw there's "royalties" for the "knobs"
The "royalties" we usually get, are "dicks" and "whips" and "clogs"
No doubt they feel quite flattered as, they at their "Mansions" gaze
But scores of times I've never seen, my "home" for several days

We're only poor "dumb" animals, don't think I've got a cheek
We cannot say when "tired" or "ill", because we cannot speak
But all you drivers down the pit, a word I'll say to you
Be kind and treat your pony as, my driver No. 2.

There's one thing I should like to see, I'll tell you if I may
And that's a "WEEKLY" visit from, the R.S.P.C.A.
A daily "record" of our work, for inspectors, to survey
Also to see we are not worked, above 8 hours per day

Another thing concerning us, that I would recommend
Is that we're brought up in our turns, to "Daylight" each week-end
And now dear reader will you help, to let the country know
There's "still" room for "improvement" in, our "treatment" down below

All the "drivers" in this poem are "fictitious" and do not refer to any living person or persons.   A.M.

91

But they did not have an easy life. Lads enjoyed riding the animals and impersonating cowboys a few hundred feet below ground. The practice was supposed to be banned but that did stop Wild West scenes in the roadways; so management employed a man with a bucket of whitewash to splash the riders as they cantered past in the dark, and the culprits with their tell-tale splashes on their clothes were sent to see the manager.

Many miners had more faith in their ponies than in some of their mates. Mr Ibbotson found himself alone underground one day, the pit deputy having forgotten to remain behind to make sure everyone had finished the shift. When his lamp went out he found himself in darkness as black as a bible. His pony led him back to the shaft, the miner stumbling over the bags of stone dust in the roadways, the nimble-footed pony missing the lot. Mr Thomas Beedan, whose grandson, George, still lives in Wombwell, refused to leave his pony, Jasper, behind when fire engulfed Cortonwood Colliery in 1904. *There is no room for the pony in the cage,'* said the manager. *'Then you had better find room,'* came the reply and Jasper was put in the cage and taken to safety. George Beedan said one of his friends, John Wraith Cusworth, of Hemingfield, was once asked why he took hot tea and cold water down the mine. *'The tea is for the pony and the water is for my lunch,'* he replied.

Charles Wraith was head horse-keeper at the former Mitchell's Main Colliery at Wombwell for more than fifty years and his brother Robert was his assistant (see picture). Charles, who lived at Mitchell's, died in 1968, aged eighty-eight. His son, Charles, who lived at Cudworth, worked as a clerk with his father and uncle in the 1930s when the pit had 103 ponies. Charles, junior, said many of the animals were characters, particularly Donovan who climbed the stairs at the Wraith's home to see his mother when she was ill in bed. The Wraiths walked pit ponies round Wombwell with collection boxes on their backs to raise money for charity, ending their trek at the *Horse Shoe Hotel,* Wombwell, where Donovan would gulp down a bottle of beer for his efforts. Another pony, it was said, could smell his driver 'a mile away', particularly when the man arrived at work with carrots and apples in his pockets. One of the underground stables at the pit was known as 'the cricket end,' not because of the pit's nearby cricket ground in Netherwood Road but because the stables were swarming with insects.

Charles Wraith, head horse-keeper at the former Mitchell's Main Colliery for more that fifty years, is pictured with his brother, Robert, his assistant, and Bill the pony in 1935 during King George V's jubilee celebrations.

When you talk to old miners about the early days, the one common thread of conversation is pit ponies. It's the only time some of them smile because that was their happiest period down the mine. Eventually they would be found other work – on the coal face perhaps – and other lads would take over their ponies. The job of the hewer was onerous, and the conditions in which the work was performed were often appalling: few men have happy memories of that work. But for all the amusing stories

about ponies, and for all the palpable affection between the ponies and the lads, there were cases of brutality which led to the *1911 Mines Act* permitting the owners to appoint inspectors to look after the interests of the animals. By 1914 there were six in the country. John Grayson (80), of Wombwell worked at Mitchell Main Colliery in the early 1920s and he said:

> *Some miners would fake accidents in order to get rid of a lazy pony. Their wages depended on how many tubs they filled and the speed with which they were taken to the shaft. They made sure the accident killed the pony. There was never an inquiry, the ponies were just written*

A lot of hard work must have gone into preparing pit ponies for competition. This photograph shows Dodworth pit pony *Flash* (1st prize winner) with Andrew Kirkup at Woolley Show in 1957.

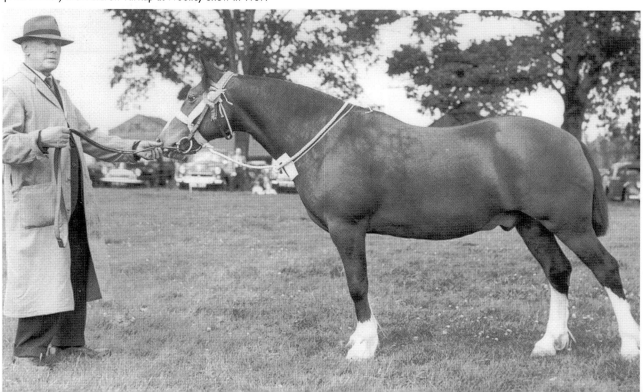

off. Hard working men and hard working ponies – that's what it was like for both man and beast down a pit.

Mr Grayson, a farmer's son, quickly built up a relationship with his pony, Boxer. As a lad he picked the best grasses and carrots and took them to work to treat his pal. Despite such generosity, Boxer, like a good union man, knew his rights and when Grayson tried to persuade him to stay behind to enable the lad to earn some overtime Boxer refused and marched off to the stables. Boxer had his own internal clock and he knew what time his shift ended.

Sometimes ponies had their revenge. Tom, a pony at Monk Bretton Colliery, was said to have killed his driver in 1914. The inquest was told that a fifteen-year old boy was found dead behind a stationary Tom, with blood gushing from a wound in the head. The pony was said to be nasty when whipped but the lad, named Copley, was new to the job and did not know.

In 1913 more than 74,000 horses were at work but by 1947 the figure had dropped to 23,000; in the late 1970s there were still a few ponies, mainly in the North East.

Two Tragedies

Seventy-seven men died in two explosions in the mid-1930s, nineteen at North Gawber Colliery in 1935 and fifty-eight at Wharncliffe Woodmoor 1,2,3 at Carlton in the following year.

At North Gawber a large pocket of methane gas ignited in the 4 South Face on September 12. More than thirty men were working on the afternoon shift when a hot blast swept down the face. As the dust and debris settled, those who could pick themselves up saw that fifteen of their colleagues were dead and that a dozen others were injured, some of them severely. The power was switched off to avert another explosion. After a call was made for volunteers to try a rescue attempt, 4,000 relatives, sweethearts and friends gathered at the pithead, surging forward as each rescue team went underground. The Mayor of Barnsley, Alderman B F Canter, spent many hours at the pithead and said:

They asked for ten rescuers and you should have seen the rush the men made for the cages. Many in their best suits surged forward rolling up their sleeves and casting away cigarettes and matches, eager to go below and face the unknown dangers. They were magnificent.

At the inquest Dr R Millar said all but one of the men were badly burnt and showed signs of carbon monoxide poisoning. A witness said the men had been laughing and joking on the face when there was a sudden gust of wind. The inquest was told of the heroism of Mr Jim Crow, a young overman who was twenty yards from the explosion. Avoiding serious injury he managed to drag two injured miners, Walter Riley and Claude Ackroyd, to safety, although both died later in hospital. He said:

I told Ackroyd to hang onto my clogs as I crawled along. The men were in a bad condition and the air was bad until we got to the middle gate where it became clearer.

The inquiry accepted that a build-up of gas had arisen and that because of poor ventilation the explosive mixture had been allowed to gather until it was too late. The inquiry criticised the mining company for allowing too many shots to be fired. The disaster scarred Mrs D Woodruff, Springfield Road, Hoyland Common, for many years. Her father was Mr Riley, aged fifty-two, of Bridge Street, Darton, who left eight orphans. Mrs Woodruff was fifteen and after the explosion she had to collect £5 every month to keep the younger ones. *'Had it not been for the disaster relief fund, we would have starved because the older ones did not have enough money to help out,'* she said. Her father had been complaining about the presence of gas for months before the explosion.

The explosion at Wharncliffe Woodmoor, caused by an electrical fault, occurred in the Lidgett seam at about 4

The rescue team at Wharncliffe Woodmoor.

A party of rescue workers going to the pithead.

The Salvation Army hand out cups of tea.

Daily Herald

No. 6390   FRIDAY, AUGUST 7, 1936   ONE PENNY

Barnsley Pit Explosion
57 MINERS HURLED TO DEATH IN A FLASH

THE REV. NORMAN KING, vicar of Carlton, Barnsley, prepares, with umbrella, all the patient men of the impressed men.
[Other pictures on Back Page.]

MINE LAMPS GUIDE CORTEGE

From Our Special Correspondent
BARNSLEY, Friday morning.

EARLY to-day a crowd still waited outside the school which has been turned into a mortuary to receive the dead. Miners' lamps were placed along the path leading to it, and the light filtered eerily in the breeze to guide the stretcher-bearers bringing the victims from the ambulances. Many women were weeping when police and doctors, who had made a preliminary...

Daily Herald Free Insurance

THE comprehensive free Insurance provided by the "Daily Herald" for its registered readers includes benefits for all fatal accidents.

Inquiries are being made as soon as any of the victims of the Barnsley disaster are identified as registered readers of the "Daily Herald" cheques will be sent immediately to their dependants.

PAPER BLINDS

ONLY ONE MAN KNOWS HOW IT HAPPENED
Wives See Bodies Brought Up

FROM OUR SPECIAL CORRESPONDENTS
BARNSLEY, Yorks, Thursday.

FIFTY-SEVEN bodies, some of them twisted and battered beyond recognition, are to-night being slowly borne from the Wharncliffe Woodmoor Colliery, shaken this morning by one of the worst mine explosions this county has known.

Along a private road at the back of the pit, ambulances are moving through the darkness to the quaint, disused church school of Carlton, the village in which the colliery stands.

A knot of women, drawn-faced, wide-eyed, are grouped around, silent in the pitiless rain....

So far, 33 bodies have been brought to the surface—many by volunteer stretcher-bearers, who came forward in answer to an appeal by the management.

"There is not the slightest chance," I am told, "of anyone being found alive."

The task of recovering the victims will be resumed at 6 a.m. to-morrow

EFFECTS SEEN A MILE AWAY

THE explosion—some accounts say there were more than one—was so dreadful that its effects were to be seen more than a mile from the spot at which it took place—nearly two miles along an underground railway.

One man alone lived through that frustrating second of death and destruction.

He is an engineman, Alfred Brown, of Smithies, Barnsley; and he is so shockingly injured that he has not yet been able to speak.

Brown was found, bruised and battered, 1,800 yards from where the explosion happened. That shows the merciless frenzy with which death came to his comrades.

WORST SINCE GRESFORD

OF the victims, 19 lived in Barnsley, 14 in Smithies, seven in Carlton and the rest in villages around.

The disaster is the worst since September, 1934, when 265 men were killed in Gresford Colliery.

You can picture the horror of the scene from the account given to me by one of the scores of gallant men who went down to see what could be done.

[Continued on Page 10: "Just a Rescue Man" and Editorial on Page Eight.]

BAREHEADED miners watching rescue workers bring a body from the pithead.

RESCUE WORKERS at the pithead after being relieved by a fresh team.

GERMANY ARMS REBELS
SENDS CARGO OF PLANES
SECRET SHIPLOAD OF BOMBERS SHOCKS BLUM CABINET

FROM OUR OWN CORRESPONDENT
PARIS, Thursday.

NEWS reached French Ministerial circles to-night that a German steamer is now on its way to Spain with a cargo of 28 bombing planes aboard.

The vessel is the 7,775-ton Usaramo, of the German East Africa Line, which left Hamburg on July 31. Pilots and mechanics accompany the planes.

The disclosure created a sensation, and was the subject of immediate editorial discussion between Cabinet Ministers and political personalities of the Left.

CARRYING SHELLS, TOO

A CHALLENGE

SIR D. BANKS IS NEW AIR CHIEF

LAST night 42-year-old Colonel Sir Donald Banks was working late in his office at the General Post Office, as its new Director-General of business chief.

To-day he will take over command of the administrative side of the Ministry as its Permanent Secretary.

[Sir D. Banks' Career, Page Four.]

GIRL TRAPPED UNDER BUS
EIGHT-TON CRANE COULD NOT SAVE LIFE

An eight-ton crane was used by Leeds Fire Brigade last night to lift a bus at Harehills-road, N.E., under which was trapped in thoroughfare girl cyclist, Doreen Crossland, aged 8, of Great Calderwood, N.W.

She was dead when admitted to hospital.

MAINLY FAIR
(See Page Three.)

BROADCAST TO BRITISH SUBJECTS

A urgent broadcast was made at the request of the Foreign Office by the B.B.C. last night to British subjects still in Spain unable to get in touch with relatives outside.

"All are urged to communicate at once with the nearest British consular post, giving their addresses and indicating whether they are able to leave the country, and the message..."

---

3 Britons Die In Alps

From Our Own Correspondent
GENEVA, Thursday.

SWISS Alps claimed two more British victims to-day—making three within the past 24 hours.

Those killed to-day were:— Miss Martha Current, aged 22, of Kingsdown-green, Harpenden, Herts, and Mr. Geoffrey C. Gregson, aged 24, believed to be from Sussex.

Miss Current

Miss Current was killed while climbing with four English friends...

Fifty-seven miners were killed at Wharncliffe Woodmoor in August 1936. *The Daily Herald* referred to 'one of the worst mine explosions this country has known, the worst since September 1934, when 265 men were killed at Gresford Colliery.

The colliery yard and onlookers.

Wharncliffe Woodmoor 1, 2, 3 at Carlton. Viewed from the Royston end.

New Carlton Colliery (later Wharncliffe Woodmoor 4/5).

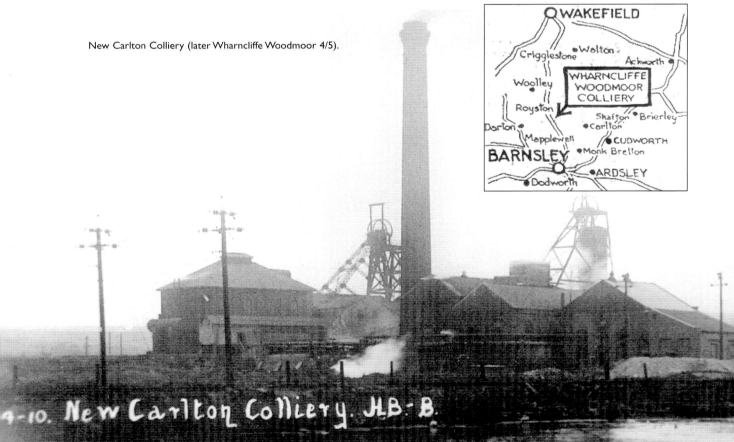

4-10. New Carlton Colliery. JLB-B.

This team had just spent eight hours tackling a fire underground at Wharncliffe Woodmoor 1, 2, 3 Colliery, in the 1920s. The men, all deputies, were, left to right, Instructor Mr Parkinson, Walter Trimby, William Turton, Jack Elrin, Sam Dutton. Mr Trimby, aged 40, died soon afterwards.

a.m. on 6 August 1936. Fifty-seven men were killed outright, and the attendant of the haulage gear, Alfred Brown, was the sole man to be brought out alive but died five days later in hospital. It was said two airway doors had been wedged open with bricks by men taking tubs to and fro, resulting in the ventilation procedures failing to work properly, and firedamp accumulated on the face. The cover of the loader was found to be on the floor and the cover of the electrical starting switch was loose. The presence of combustible material was said to be a contributory factor: 201 tons of limestone had been sent to the pit over the previous seven months, and much of that was said to be combustible. At the inquiry, the Yorkshire Miners Association was represented by the president, Herbert Smith, who said it was his seventy-third experience of a mining disaster, the worst since Gresford two years earlier. Several women, after answering

questions on the witness stand, almost collapsed under the strain and were assisted from the stand by nurses.

All Barnsley and its districts were in mourning. Blinds were drawn, flags on the buildings were flown at half mast and weeping men and women lined the road to Monk Bretton Cemetery on the day thirteen of the victims were buried. Scores of miners, friends of the victims, followed the coffins. At the graveside mothers, wives and sweethearts wept. They were, in almost every case, supported by uniformed nurses.

In 1979 Yorkshire miners' president Arthur Scargill unveiled a plaque in memory of the men who died in the disaster on a site off Laithes Lane. The inscription reads:

On the 6th August, 1936, a firedamp explosion caused by an electrical fault engulfed all face workers at Wharncliffe Woodmoor Colliery. There were no survivors: fifty-seven men died instantly – one survivor died later in hospital. This plaque commemorates the sacrifice underground.

In his speech Mr Scargill said very few families in the surrounding areas were not affected, directly or indirectly,

News Chronicle

ONE PENNY

POSTAGE IN U.K. CANADA, and NEWFOUNDLAND. OTHER PLACES ABROAD 1½d.

2½XT 4ᵈ

FRIDAY, AUGUST 7, 1936

25 STILL MISSING IN WRECKED PIT

Rescuers Find 32 Bodies: One Man Survives

DOCTORS GIVE UP RESCUE HOPE

Gas Sweeps Through Blocked Workings

POLLARD,
BARNSLEY, Thursday

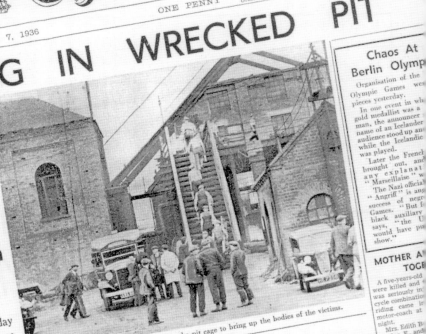

...with stretchers climbing to the pit cage to bring up the bodies of the victims.

Chaos At Berlin Olymp...

Organisation of the Olympic Games we pieces yesterday.

In one event in wh gold medallist was a man, the announcer name of an Icelander audience stood up and while the Icelandic was played.

Later the French brought up any explanat "Marseillaise" w The Nazi official "Angriff" is ang success of negr Games. "But i black auxiliary says, the U would have pu show."

MOTHER A TOGE

A five-years-old were killed and cycle combination riding came in motor-coach a night.

Mrs. Edith B Poplar, E., and victims Bow lett-road, Bow cycle, was tak

'S POWERS AND SPAIN
ENCH ANXIETY
LIES

LAT

Shines Sh so simpl

EASILY OPENED JUST PRESS THIS LEVER

PELA BOOT P

Sold by Co-operative so

DAILY—ONE

You'll be glad you said "MELBOURNE"

No. 30,169 —ESTABLISHED 1718.

The Leeds Mercury.

An All-Yorkshire Journal and a Power in the North for More Than Two Hundred Years.

FRIDAY, AUGUST 7, 1936

32 BODIES TAKEN FROM PIT.

Yorkshire Death-Roll 57.

ONE SURVIVOR OF EXPLOSION.

Hopes of Waiting Women Gone.

A MESSAGE FROM THE KING.

YORKSHIRE WAS STRICKEN YESTERDAY BY A TERRIBLE MINING DISASTER IN WHICH 57 MEN LOST THEIR LIVES.

THEY WERE VICTIMS OF AN EXPLOSION (BRIEFLY REPORTED IN A SPECIAL LATE EDITION OF YESTERDAY'S "MERCURY") AT THE WHARNCLIFFE WOODMOOR COLLIERY, ROYSTON, NEAR BARNSLEY. EARLY THIS MORNING 32 BODIES HAD BEEN BROUGHT TO THE SURFACE. WORKERS IN THE MINE HAD A HARD TASK TO HEW THEIR WAY TO THE VICTIMS.

ONE man alone lived through the explosion. He is Alfred Brown, of Long Row, Smithies, who, though working nearly a mile away from the centre of the explosion, was terribly burned.

Doctors and nurses were fighting for his life in Barnsley Hospital, but though his grave condition slightly improved, he remained unconscious. By his side waited his widowed mother.

The explosion occurred about 3.30 a.m. yesterday, in the Lidgett seam, about one and a half miles from the foot of the main shaft, at a depth of over half a mile.

Moving Scenes at Pithead.

Women Who Waited.

From a "Mercury" Special Correspondent.

BARNSLEY, Thursday Night.
THERE were deeply moving scenes to-night when bodies of the dead in the Wharncliffe Woodmoor Colliery explosion were brought to the surface.

As the bodies were being taken by ambulance to a neighbouring school building, a woman's cry rose above the subdued murmurs. She had identified her husband.

The only thing she saw as the stretcher passed was his boot projecting beyond the blanket, but she said she knew that it was his. Only that morning her husband had wanted his boot eased for him. He could not get it on, he said, and she had cut the boot for him.

By that last service to her husband, she was able to identify him long before official identification took place.

READY FOR CARNIVAL.

One of the trapped men was to have been in Royston Carnival, and one of his three daughters had her gypsy costume ready for the event when the tragic news of the disaster reached their home.

The family was looking forward to a well-earned holiday with relatives in Liverpool. The wife was still hoping late to-night even after rescue parties had warned the crowd to abandon hope.

"It queer how often these thi near holidays" someon

"READY TO RISK THEIR LIVES.—Rescue workers did valiant work in the disaster at Wharncliffe Woodmoor Colliery. Here is a rescue party. (By a "Mercury" photographer.)

RELIEF FUND TO BE OPENED.

Mr. Joseph Jones Coming Home.

From Our Correspondent.
BARNSLEY, Thursday Night.
THE Deputy Mayor of Barnsley, Alderman B. E.
Visited

LIST OF THE VICTIMS.

THE list of 57 men believed to have perished as a result of the Wharncliffe Woodmoor Colliery disaster is printed below.

Alfred Brown, of Long Row, Smithies, is in hospital suffering from injuries.

George Farmery, deputy, 20, Tempest Avenue, Darfield.

Joseph H. Hope, deputy, 30, Mottram Street, Barnsley.

Wm. O. Tompkins, packer, 54, Park Road, Worsbrough Bridge.

Richard B. Grimshaw, Smithies Lane, Barnsley, dataller, 56.

Victor Clarkson, Birkwood.

Frank Cooper, ripper, Sheffield Roa Barnsley.

Richard Wright, ripper, 7, Gray's Roa Carlton.

Arthur Haigh, machine man, 5, Richard S Road, Smithies.

James Green, ripper, 1, Allendale Road, Darton West.

J. W. H. Abbott, ripper, Willow Bank Barnsley.

S. Kirk,

Newspapers dealing with the 1936 explosion.

The Earl of Wharncliffe walking down the colliery yard.

Barnsley MP Mr J Potts talking at the pithead.

by the explosion in 1936.

> It is the price that we have to pay for the coal we need. The town has been built on coal. Many thousands of people owe their lives to the mining industry, and it is right and proper that we should remember this terrifying experience all those years ago.

The memorial, designed in the form of a pithead wheel mounted vertically on a stone plinth, was the idea of the late Councillor Harry Dancer, who felt a memorial should be erected in memory of the men. The oldest man at the

Men pictured at Wharncliffe Woodmoor. *Yorkshire Mining Museum*

ceremony was eighty-five years old Charles Hardcastle, of Carlton, who said: *'If it had happened on another shift, hundreds would have been killed.'*

After nearly sixty years an incident can stir old memories. When there was a public outcry against the closure of thirty-one pits in October, 1992, the *Chronicle* received the following letter from A Marsland, of Darton:

> I have felt the urge to write a story of a simple mining family. My grandfather, Lewis Boyd, worked at Wharncliffe Woodmoor Colliery – he had a son William at the same pit and my father was at North Gawber. One day William went to work his first shift at the mine and never came back – he was killed in the pit cage. Six months later my grandfather went to work at Wharncliffe Woodmoor and was killed in the disaster. My father went with the rescue team to look for his father but couldn't find him. 'Have you seen my husband?' asked a neighbour. 'No, lass.' he said. How could he tell her that he had seen him hanging upside down without his legs. Later they found my grandfather – without a mark on him – trapped behind some air doors. Some years later when I was a child the pit van pulled up outside the gate and the driver got out with a bundle of clothes tied up with a belt – you can imagine what state my mother was in. 'Don't worry, lass, he isn't bad,' said the driver. My father's back was like a map of England with all the holes and scars and he was in pain until his death last November at the age of eighty-one. Michael Heseltine says he feels pain at what he had to do; it's not pain but guilt. Pain is when a mother is told her husband or father is dead, or when a wife is told her husband is in hospital and won't be the same again. Will anyone remember Michael Heseltine with pride?

'...like the messages carried by mysterious means over vast distances among black races, the news had spread from street to street and house to house, and soon groups of men and women from all directions were converging on the pit gates until a great crowd stood there silent...' Jack Lawson, describing a mining tragedy. Mr Lawson was an MP and one of his colleagues in the House of Commons in the 1950s was the Barnsley MP, and ex-miner Lord Mason, who as a child stood in the crowd outside the gates at Wharncliffe Woodmoor, although he cannot be identified on these photographs.

THEY REFUSED TO GIVE UP HOPE

CHILDREN WAITED IN THE RAIN FOR HOURS

FOR HIS MATES

Rescue workers with a pit canary which they took underground to warn them of gas.

There is no mistaking that smile... entertainer George Formby is pictured at Wharncliffe Woodmoor 1, 2, 3 Colliery (Old Carlton) in 1936, shortly after the explosion. Formby (with helmet) is seen with the manager of the Alhambra Cinema, who organised a concert in aid of the disaster fund.
Mrs Needham, Athersley South

Long Carlton Row where many of the Wharncliffe Wodmoor men lived.

Souvenir In Affectionate Remembrance

OF THE

57 MEN WHO LOST THEIR LIVES

At Wharncliffe Woodmoor Pit, Carlton (near Barnsley), 6th Aug. 1936.

W. ALLOTT	J. FLETCHER, 33	R. HULSON	H. HEPWORTH
J. JACKSON, 27	W. BUCKLEY, 44	A. THOMPSON	W. DUERDEN
J. BROWN, 22	A. HAIGH, 26	W. POOLE, 18	A. WHITE
G. THOMPSON	C. E. ISMAY	R. MILLER	R. HODGSON
F. HADFIELD	J. GREEN	BIRD	J. WAUGH
G. FARMERY, 42	J. ROSCOE, 41	F. FOSTER	J. DONNELLY
J. E. HOPE, 34	C. CHAPMAN, 30	W. H. SENIOR	W. ELLIS
R. B. GRIMSHAW	W. SMITH	H. TRAVIS	H. WROE
V. CLARKSON, 33	C. BAILEY	G. WILSON, 33	F. COOPER
S. BROWN, 28	W. A. TOMKINS, 54	G. OWENS, 20	R. WRIGHT
E. DALBY, 34	W. WHITELEY	W. PROCTOR	J. W. H. ABBOTT
H. BIRKHEAD, 29	L. BOYD	H. LEE, 45	S. KIRK
H. HATFIELD, 30	J. D. JONES	C. H. PARKIN	H. WRIGHT, 24
J. T. SMITH, 53	J. BULLINGHAN	H. SCARGILL	H. HALL
W. A. BATEMAN			

(Most of these men have been recovered and identified)

THE KING'S MESSAGE OF SYMPATHY.

"I am greatly distressed to hear of the accident at the Wharncliffe Colliery, and the serious loss of life involved. "Please convey my deep sympathy to the bereaved relatives and my best wishes to the Injured for a quick recovery. I shall be glad to hear how the rescue work progresses."

THE PREMIER'S MESSAGE

"I am deeply grieved at the news of the many lives lost at Wharncliffe Woodmoor Colliery Please convey my sincere sympathies to the families of those who have so tragically lost their lives."

(Sole survivor of disaster ALFRED BROWN, Long Row, Smithes)

Printer; S. Burgess, 8 York Place, Strand. WC.2

A napkin produced to mark the 1936 disaster.

Chapter 5

1940-1970

War and Nationalisation

The industry did a somersault during the Second World War. The owners, ascendant after the crushing defeat of the miners in 1926, lost control of the pits in the war and then became an extinct species after 1947. The union, disunited and disheartened between the wars, became a unified powerful body in 1945 with the formation of the National Union of Mineworkers.

At the beginning of the war, in 1939, the pits were in the hands of a multitude of companies, with the number of directors running into several thousand. The companies owned 2,000 mines, with 700,000 men on the books, 300,000 fewer than in the early 1920s. Output per man improved between the wars but the technical standards could not compete with those in America and Germany. One expert, speaking on the television programme, *All Our Working Lives*, in 1993, said the high productivity levels in Germany before the war were due to superior haulage systems – which moved the coal to the shaft faster and in greater quantity than the British systems – whereas there was little to choose between the calibre of equipment on the coal faces in both countries. He also believed the narrow roadways in UK pits would have been unsuitable for the German-style haulage systems. Others disagreed, believing that the problem was much deeper and wider and that Britain lagged behind other countries in the mechanisation stakes. Another former pit manager, on the same programme, said there had been in the 1930s a widespread belief that nationalisation of the pits was inevitable and there was a reluctance by management to

spend money on an asset which would end up in the hands of the Government in the long term.

As the war approached one chronic problem started to disappear, the dole queue, which had bedevilled the 1920s and 1930s. Within weeks of the outbreak of war there was a chronic shortage of workers in the mines. In the first three weeks 23,000 miners followed the example of their fathers or uncles in the First World War and enlisted. The Government demanded an increase in production from 260 to 270 million tons per year but output fell sharply between 1939 and 1942, and dual control of the pits was introduced: policy was laid down by the Government and the pit manager remained in the employment of the owner. As production fell, absenteeism reared its ugly head, as it had done in the First World War. The public blamed absenteeism for all the ills in the pits. In defence, Mr Joe Hall, president of the Yorkshire miners, said:

A man must be perfectly fit when going down the pit. Ours is an industry where nature has never been kind to us, and never will be. Ours is an industry in regard to which the finest experts and the best mining engineers have never been able to quantify the facts that govern it. Impeded production can take place because of many things: bad roadways and bad ventilation, and our men have to suffer these continued abnormalities and excessive pressures.

In reality the pits were ill equipped to cope with a wartime economy because in the 1930s investment had lagged

Elsecar Main, 1940s.

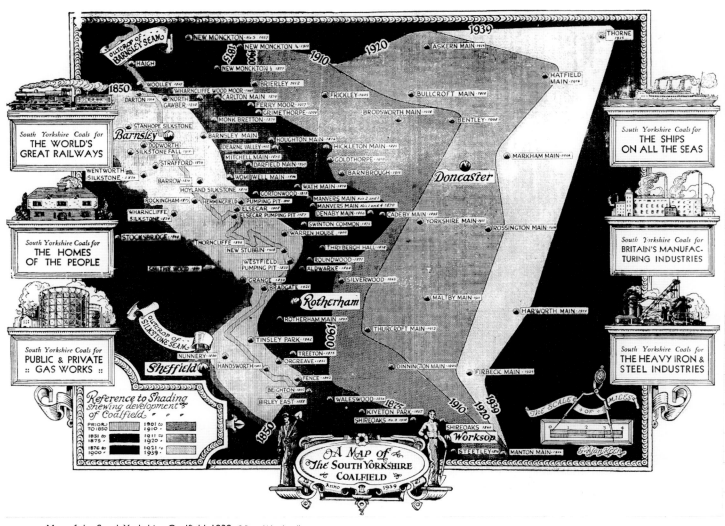

Map of the South Yorkshire Coalfield, 1939. *C Page, Wombwell*

Pit lads at Houghton Main Colliery were asked to gargle with an antiseptic solution during an epidemic of influenza in the 1940s.

SECTION "D."—Continued.

Hemsworth Colliery Prize Band.
Hemsworth

Snydale   Featherstone Subscription Band.
            Ackton Hall   South Kirkby

Frickley   Frickley Colliery Prize Band.
            Brierley   Ferrymoor

            Grimethorpe Colliery Prize Band.
            Grimethorpe

            Royston Silver Prize Band.
            Monckton Main

            Ryhill Prize Band.
Monckton (A)   Monk Bretton

Goldthorpe Goldthorpe Mixed Band.
            Barnbro'

            Upton Band.
            Upton

Y.M.A. Marshals—Mr. A. Jobling, Mr. F. Burns and
Mr. W. Hewson.

Section "E."

Join at Junction of Queen Street and Peel Square.

Hickleton Main Band.
Hickleton Main

Bentworth Prize Band.
Brodsworth Main   Hatfield Main

Bentley Prize Band.
Bentley

Bullcroft Ambulance Silver Band.
Bullcroft

Yorkshire Main Colliery Band.
Edlington   Askern Main

Rossington Miners' Welfare Band.
Rossington   Thorne

Markham Main Ambulance Band.
Armthorpe   Firbeck

Y.M.A. Marshals—Mr. F. Shaw and Mr. G. Jones.

Marshals as set out herein should report at Miners'
Offices, Barnsley, at 10-0 o'clock on the morning of 21st June
for final instructions.

We are, Yours truly,
H. SMITH, President.
ALF. SMITH, Agent.
J. A. HALL, Fin. Sec.
E. HOUGH, Vice-Pres.
J. JONES, General Secretary.

Yorkshire Mine Workers' Association.

Registered under Trades Union Acts, 1871 to 1917.

ANNUAL
Demonstration

TO BE HELD IN THE

LOCKE PARK, BARNSLEY,

ON

MONDAY, JUNE 21st, 1937.

PLACE OF ASSEMBLY

—AND—

ORDER OF PROCESSION.

ROUTE OF PROCESSION.

CHURCHFIELDS,   PEEL SQUARE,
SACKVILLE STREET,   PEEL STREET,
VICTORIA ROAD,   RACECOMMON ROAD,
CHURCH STREET,   KERESFORTH HALL ROAD,
MARKET HILL.   THE PARK.

PLACES OF ASSEMBLY AND ORDER OF PROCESSION.

SECTION "A" WILL ASSEMBLE IN CHURCH FIELDS.
Wharncliffe Silkstone Band will lead the Procession and march
down Sackville Street, Victoria Road, and pause in Church
Street to pick up Sections "B" and "C." Then proceed
down Market Hill, turning on Peel Square, to Peel Street,
Racecommon Road, St. George's Road, into the Park.

The Five Sections Join the Procession in the order
set out below:—

SECTION "A" ... Starts Procession at Church Fields (Rear
Beckett's Hospital).

SECTION "B" ... Joins Procession at Top of Old Mill Lane
(opposite Miners' Offices).

SECTION "C" ... Joins Procession at Corner Huddersfield Road
(Miners' Offices Main Entrance)

SECTION "D" ... Joins Procession at Top of Regent Street
(opposite New Town Hall).

SECTION "E" ... Forms Rear of Procession and joins at the
Corner of Queen Street and Eldon Street, after
the Monk Bretton portion of Section "D" have
turned into Peel Square.

All Sections must take up their positions at the points
assigned to them by 12-30.

Section "A."

Starts Procession at Churchfields (rear Beckett's Hospital).

Wharncliffe Colliery Prize Band.

Wharncliffe Silkstone Nos. 1 and 2   Smithy Wood
Old Thorncliffe   Rockingham   Grange

The Yorkshire Coking and Chemical Works Band.
Glasshoughton   Middleton

Elsecar Band.
Elsecar

Mexbro' Military Band.
Mauvers   Wath Main

Denaby Ambulance Band.
Denaby   Cadeby   Thrybergh Hall

Rawmarsh Band.
Aldwarke   Stubbin

Silverwood Colliery Band.
Silverwood   Rotherham Main
            Treeton

Thurcroft Colliery Band.
Thurcroft

SECTION "A."—Continued.

Workshop Brass Band.
Denaby   Shireoaks & Steetley   Stocksbridge
Dinnington Tinsley Park   Kiveton Park
Nunnery   Manton   Orgreave
Birley   Beighton

Old Silkstone Prize Band.
Wentworth Silkstone   Church Lane   Hazlehead
Old Silkstone

Barrow Colliery Band.
Barrow

National Reserve Band.
Barnsley Main

Y.M.A. Marshals—Mr. R. Athey and Mr. J. T. Pearson.

Section "B."

Join at Old Mill Lane (opposite Miners' Offices).

Monk Bretton Brass Band.
Wharncliffe Woodmoor   Hartshead   Shawcross

Barnsley Boro' Prize Band.
Wharncliffe Woodmoor (A) Howden Clough   Thornhill

Stanley Prize Band.
Newmarket Silkstone   Lofthouse   Park Hills

Flockton Brass Band.
                   Emley   Bowling
Denby Grange   Lepton   Wortley & Farnley
Grange Moor   Kirkinshaw   Waterloo Main
Clayton West   Netherton

Y.M.A. Marshals—Mr. J. Richardson and Mr. C. Thorpe.

Section "C."

Join at Huddersfield Road (near Entrance Miners' Offices).

Darton Prize Band.
            Woodlesford   Rothwell
Woolley

Gawber Britannia Prize Band.
North Gawber   Haigh
Crigglestone   Wakefield Manor

Y.M.A. Marshals—Mr. F. Kirk and Mr. T. Cooper.

Section "D."

Join at Regent Street (opposite New Town Hall).

Wombwell Prize Band.
            Darfield Main   Mitchell's Main
Wombwell Main   Cortonwood
Houghton Main   Dearne Valley

Altofts West Riding Band.
            Sharlston   Walton   Saville Pit   Newland
Altofts   Whitwood

Brotherton Prize Band.
Fryston   East Ardsley

Castleford Subscription Band.
            Pontefract

Mickefield Band.
            Allerton Silkstone
Wheldale   Ledstone Luck
Bowers Nos. 1 and 2   Micklefield

This advert showing the optimism of the NCB appeared in the *Daily Mail* of 1947.

The old Dearne and Dove canal and the Mexborough to Manchester railway line at Aldham, Wombwell. Mitchell Main colliery is in the background. *Photograph: R. Firth, Wombwell*

Wombwell Main Colliery. *Photograph: John Gill*

behind that of our competitors.

In 1943 Mr Ernest Bevin, the Minister of Labour and National Service, worried by the shortage of mineworkers, spent more than £20,000 on advertising nationwide to try to fill the vacancies and some 3,000 responded. Dissatisfied with the response the Government introduced conscription with one out of ten being directed into the mines instead of the armed forces, the famous 'Bevin Boys.' Meanwhile the owners put forward proposals to reorganise the industry; their chief spokesman was the Prime Minister, Mr Winston Churchill, who had called the miners 'the enemy' in the 1920s. Their proposals had come too late, many believed, because there should have been reorganisation in the early 1930s with the emphasis on amalgamated and modern companies with improved marketing, a suggestion resisted by some owners at the time. Counter proposals were submitted by the unions: they had been badgering for nationalisation since the 1880s without any success. The landslide victory by the Labour Party in 1945 clinched the issue with the electorate demanding a fresh start in the nation with new ideas and institutions; this time there would be no return to the bad old days, the nation declared.

The pits were nationalised in January, 1947, and within four weeks the country was hit by a disastrous fuel shortage. The bleak winter, during which more than a million men were out of work because factories had to close, was the moment at which the Conservatives realised Labour was not invincible; at the same time the public turned on the old bogeymen, the miners. It was unfair of the public to blame the miners for failing to cut enough coal. Had there been adequate stocks, the railways would have been incapable of moving supplies around the country. Speaking in the 1970s, Lord Shinwell, the former Minister of Power, said of that winter: *'We had all sorts of problems: shortage of miners, shortage of coal, shortage of railway wagons, and on top of that serious weather – perhaps the worst weather we have had for many years.'* Lord Robens, later chairman of the NCB, said: *'I think the real cause of the 1947 fuel crisis was the abnormal weather coupled with the fact there was an overall shortage of coal.'* Too much or too little coal: the mining industry never got it right at the right time.

In the early 1950s the board stepped up mechanisation and pits were given face-lifts and by the late 50s full mechanisation, using the shearer-loader which put coal on the conveyor belt, was in general use. The unions and the public had been blaming the owners for inadequate investment for years before nationalisation; now was the time for action, declared the Government, and money was poured down the shafts. Whereas there had been a coal famine in 1947, there was a glut of coal a few years later, thanks to higher productivity, and to add to the problems of the pits industries were changing over to cheap oil. More pithead baths were built and mobile x-ray units introduced. Miners, particularly face workers, prospered and by the mid and late 1950s a face-worker could earn £20 per week for a five-day week, putting them at the top of the blue collar wages league, a marked contrast to the earnings in the 1930s. Miners started to buy their homes

A Yorkshire miners' procession outside the *Barnsley Chronicle* in 1966. The group includes Sid Schofield (second left, front row), Ald. Arthur Butler (Mayor), George Brown, Labour Government Minister, and Roy Mason, MP for Barnsley.

Sid Schofield, Yorkshire Miners' general secretary, last of the Yorkshire NUM moderates.

and cars were no longer a middle class status symbol, even if most of their vehicles were second hand. The first cracks were appearing in what had been traditional mining communities, close-knit communities where everyone knew everyone else and where leisure and pastimes were centred on the street or a group of streets, and work meant the pit at the bottom of the hill. High disposable income and the motor car, television and holidays abroad did more over the next three decades to destroy the old patterns and spirit in the villages than all the Conservative Governments have alleged to have done. On the industrial relations front in the 1950s Yorkshire was plagued by petty and unofficial strikes. Often they were caused by friction between deputies, the old enemy who took the flak on the coal face, and miners. For example, deputies were in the invidious position of having to determine special payments to miners; the managers sometimes overruled them and when miners opened their wage packets there was uproar. Public opinion had been turning against miners for some years, for nationalisation had promised too much and delivered too little as far as they were concerned. The public had expected improved productivity and fewer strikes; productivity increased, as did wages, but industrial relations did not change (one old miner said the pits had been nationalised but the bosses were still the same).

Lord Robens resigned from Parliament in 1961 to become chairman of the National Coal Board, a post he held until 1971 when he resigned over the Government's failure to run the industry like a business. During his term of office 400 pits were closed and one job in two, 300,000

Glamour was added to Yorkshire miners' galas in 1947. This line-up was photographed at Rotherham in the mid 1960s.

Pyramid-shaped spoil heaps were familiar sights in Wombwell. Darfield Main 'stack' and the newly opened pit baths in the 1950s. *Colin Moore*

The disused locks at Aldham in the late 1940s. In the background is Mitchell Main. *Colin Moore*

Mitchell Main in the late 40s. The photograph was taken from a spot under Aldham canal bridge.

An area known as Concrete. Flat-topped houses at Cortonwood, Brampton, pictured shortly before demolition, in 1958. The community comprised 106 houses in eight rows, built to accommodate miners when Cortonwood was sunk in the 1870s. A Mines Inspector stated in his annual report at the turn of the twentieth century, that housing for miners was unsatisfactory, criticising houses that looked like barracks and some terraced houses which had good basic amenities but no gardens. By the 1920s, local authorities had embarked on large slum clearance programmes, replacing back-to-back houses with modern municipal dwellings, and the newly established National Coal Board built estates in the late 1940s and early 1950s. In the mid 1970s, highly paid miners were buying their homes. Not that that was unusual. In the coal boom of the early 1870s, miners bought their homes at Worsbrough for £25 each.

A photograph of Mitchell Main in the background, taken in the late 1940s. *Colin Moore*

J McQuillan	J Harper	P. Smith	V Hailsworth	K B Sutcliffe	A Oxley	G E Fowler	A Allsopp
Overman	Overman	U G Electrician	Surface Enginewright	U G Enginewright	Traffic Foreman	Surface Electrician	Pit-Hill Foreman
S Moore	L R Watkin	E Fairhurst	A Watson	E E Crankshaw	R Miller	E Sykes	J A Lowcock
Assist. Cashier	Assist. Surveyor	Storekeeper	Cashier	Under Manager	Assistant Salesman	Chemist	Chief Electrician
W C Jackson	E I Allen	A S Barnes	J L Hay	Maj. P G Roberts MP	E Charlton	S J Lisle	A Sutcliffe	D E Potts
Salesman	Accountant	Co. Secretary	Gen. Manager and Agent	Managing Director	Manager	Surveyor	Engineer	Under Manager

in all, disappeared. It was the age of the axeman. Lord Beeching, chairman of British Rail, cut the railways down to size, Lord Robens wielded the axe on the pits. His reign resulted in a fifty per cent increase in productivity and he also managed to keep a lid on pay rises, although that stoked up trouble for the future when miners realised they were falling behind other workers. According to Lord Robens, two new problems emerged in the 1960s: cheap oil imports and the rise of the militant left in the NUM. He wrote:

One of the ridiculous aspects of the extreme left wing in trade unions has always been their enthusiasm for strikes whereas in the Soviet Union and in the Iron Curtain countries strikes are illegal.

The miners felt threatened in the 1960s. It was the era of full employment and young men left the pits in droves believing it was a moribund industry: high wages could be earned elsewhere without the arduous work and car workers were seen as the elite workers. No longer were miners at the top of the wages league and coalfields like Barnsley were mangled in the pit closure programme. In Yorkshire the militants blamed the right wing leadership for failure to take a hard line against the NCB and the Government and it was clear that the discontent bubbling under the surface would boil over at sometime. The late 1960s saw the emergence of Arthur Scargill, then NUM delegate at Woolley Colliery as a political figure. In 1966 at a special conference called to discuss the Labour Party's fuel policy, Scargill accused the NUM executive of failing to oppose the Labour Government's pit closure programme and argued against the closure of uneconomic pits. He called for an annual output of 200 million tons of coal. All the phrases have a familiar ring about them and nearly thirty years later he was still fighting a Government pit closure programme. At the same time Scargill and a group of miners decided to change NUM policy and in 1967 the Yorkshire left formed the Miners' Forum. The one thing that marked him out from the rest was his youth – he was ten years younger than any other member. His face started appearing on regional television news programmes and his name in the provincial newspapers. He was a born PR man. Whereas the Yorkshire NUM leaders were rather aloof and sometimes inarticulate – the media is incapable of coming to terms with such figures – Arthur was always available for a crisp and rational quote to put some pep or venom into an otherwise staid newspaper story or television programme. It became easier for the Press to contact Arthur, still a pit delegate, than deal with the legitimate leadership who would mumble incoherent comments and release statements

The dawn of a new era... nationalisation. On 1 January 1947 the NCB became the biggest single employer in the country, responsible for nearly 800,000 workers. An independent judicial panel fixed the basic value of the industry for compensation purposes at £164 million. By 1989 the sun was about to set on a contracting empire. Privatisation was the new buzz word.

"UNITED WE STAND"

Charles Bartholomew, Esq.

Samuel Roberts, Esq.

THE

Wombwell Main Co. Ltd.

1853 — 1946

ABOUT the 20th August, 1853, it was decided by Mr. Charles Bartholomew and Mr. Samuel Roberts to sink a shaft to the Barnsley Thick Seam of coal at Wombwell, and start a concern which became known as The Wombwell Main Co. Ltd. · ·

These two families, by personal contact, have directed the affairs of this Colliery during the whole of the 93 years of its existence, up to the nationalisation of the Coal Industry on 1st January, 1947. · · · · · ·

The present Directors hope that the successful results achieved by the team work of the Board of Directors, Officials, Staff and Men together with the atmosphere of mutual affection and respect will not easily be forgotten. · · · · · · · · · · · ·

To this end we present you with this momento and wish you good luck and success for whatever may lie ahead.

Samuel Roberts
Chairman of Directors.

James Bartholomew
Vice-Chairman of Directors.

Peter G Roberts
Managing Director.

C E Bartholomew
Director.

C. W. Bartholomew, Esq.

The Rt. Hon.
Sir Samuel Roberts, Bart. P.C.

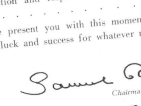

Sir Samuel Roberts, Bart.

Major James Bartholomew, M.B.E.

Major P. G. Roberts, M.P.

C. E. Bartholomew, Esq.

Wombwell Main was regarded as a well managed pit in the nineteenth century. Edward Rymer, a miner born in the 1830s, and who had worked in what he described as 'hell holes' for many years, praised Wombwell Main when he worked there with his son in the 1880s. He said deputies did not have a routine when making inspections and therefore men did not have any warning when a deputy pounced. Coal produced from the mine, known as Wombwell 'hards', had a good reputation in the 1900s – it fuelled French war ships as well as the British navy. Until nationalisation, the Roberts family were associated with the mine for 90 years. To mark the end of the era, employees were presented with these scrolls. This one belonged to the accountant, Mr Allen, whose nephew, Mr R Ogden, of Wombwell, loaned it for publication.

BARNSLEY CHRONICLE
& South Yorkshire News
and incorporating the "Barnsley Independent"

ESTABLISHED 1858
Telephone 3667
VOL. LXXXVIII., 5093
REGISTERED AT THE GENERAL POST OFFICE FOR TRANSMISSION BEYOND THE UNITED KINGDOM.
THREEPENCE
Postage : One Penny
SATURDAY, JUNE 28, 1947

Stern speeches from Westminster leaders at Barnsley

SHINWELL PLEADS WITH MINERS FOR MORE OUTPUT

A candid warning that the future safety of the nation depended upon increased coal output, was given by Fuel Minister Emanuel Shinwell, addressing a massed demonstration of miners in Locke Park last Saturday, following a giant procession through the town in which it is estimated 10,000 took part.

Chief spokesmen in the pep talks to the men of the most prolific coalfield in Britain were the Prime Minister (Mr. Clement Attlee), the Minister of Fuel and Power (Mr. Emanuel Shinwell), Lord Citrine (chairman of the National Electricity Board), and Mr. Arthur L. Horner (general secretary National Union of Mineworkers).

"WHERE'S THE COAL" asks Mr. Shinwell.

"JUST A LITTLE MORE BOYS" purrs Mr. Shinwell in his most persuasive manner.

CAUTIOUS CLEM relies upon his notes.

THE WARNING FINGER shaken by Lord Citrine.

"I WONDER whether all this is sinking in" was the thoughts of Mr. Joe Hall presiding at the Prime Minister's platform.

by courtesy Denton and Co. Ltd.

'Your comrade'

'Common-sense'

Premier speaks

Obligations

ABOVE (left): Banners flutter in the slight breeze last Saturday morning as a contingent marches up Regent-street. RIGHT: Easy going down Market Hill for the Monk Bretton marchers.

"WE WILL CONQUER"

A FEW scattered spectators saw the Prime Minister, Mrs. Attlee, and Mr. Joseph Hall, C.B.E., J.P., step from their car and ascend the Town Hall steps for the civic reception last Saturday morning.

MR. JONES CONDEMNS UNOFFICIAL STRIKES

Unofficial strikes were condemned as reprehensible and indefensible by Ald. Joseph Jones, C.B.E., J.P., LL.D. (adviser on national insurance to the N.C.B. and former president of the Miners' Federation of Great Britain) speaking at a civic luncheon in the Town Hall last Saturday, given in honour of the visit of the Prime Minister, Mr. E. Shinwell and other leading Westminster personalities.

ELYSIAN SETTING: A general view of the Prime Minister's platform at Locke Park where Mr. Attlee is seen warming up in his speech to the assembled miners.

SMILES IN THE MAYOR'S PARLOUR. Group of leading personalities after partaking of refreshments in the Town Hall last Saturday morning. (Left to right): Lord Citrine, the Town Clerk (Mr. A. E. Gillfilian, O.B.E.), Mr. E. Shinwell, the Mayor (Ald. C. Bentley), the Prime Minister, Mr. E. Hall, and Mr. Arthur Horner.

by courtesy Denton and Co. Ltd.

'6-day week may return' warns S. Yorks. leader

Supporting speakers at the platforms in Locke Park all reflected the concern expressed by the Prime Minister and Mr. Shinwell at the fall in coal output, and the main points from their speeches were as follows:

School asked to pay seven guineas for loan of sports field

Lack of playing fields criticised at Barnsley

Concern over the lack of playing fields in Barnsley for young people was expressed at Monday's meeting of the Education Committee, after it was disclosed that a fee of seven guineas had been asked for the use of Shaw-lane cricket ground on the occasion of Longcar Central School sports day.

"And your job in future will be to stamp every piece of coal with N.C.B."

The power of coal – and the NUM – remained unchallenged in 1947. The main speaker at the miners' gala in Barnsley was the Prime Minister, Mr Clement Attlee. The *Chronicle* devoted almost the whole of the front page to the event – even though the news was a week old, underlining the significance of the gala, or perhaps it was just a slow news week. Ten thousand families joined the procession.

Nationalisation of the mines in 1947 produced euphoria among miners. As early as 1884 a miners' leader had advocated nationalisation, and the establishment of the NCB was seen as a dream come true. But other people believed it ws an excuse to employ layer after layer of white collar workers. This view is illustrated in this *Chronicle* cartoon of the time.

Strafford Main, pictured in the 1960s, when it was derelict.
Photographs: A Walker

Shuttle Eye Colliery, near Flockton. Photographed in the 1960s or 70s by Albert Walker.

Pummer Colliery, near North Gawber Colliery. *A Walker, Handsworth*

without a logical beginning and an end. Arthur's face beamed from the television sets, much to the annoyance of the older miners who thought him brash and too left wing. The old men remembered the 1920s and 1930s, the days when working men did what they were told. Arthur wasn't like the old union leaders and did not like being told what to do. He received more space in the newspapers and on television that his union post warranted. My old boss used to say: *'He's only a pit delegate but he is talking as if he is the president of the Yorkshire miners.'*

By the late 1960s and early 1970s a groundswell of agitation was sweeping the coalfields in response to the fear that the miners were tumbling down the industrial wages ladder. With Scargill poised to become the union's Yorkshire compensation agent – the first step towards the Yorkshire leadership – the stage was set for the upheavals of the 1970s.

Barnsley Main

Nine men were killed and twenty-one injured by a sheet of flame which swept through workings 720 feet below ground at Barnsley Main Colliery on Wednesday, 7 May 1947. The explosion, in number three district of the Kent Thick Seam, opened about a year earlier, occurred at about 12.15 p.m. shortly before the day workers were due to finish their shift. The disaster followed the nationalisation of the mines in January and the introduction of the five day week. Soon after the news had spread, wives and other relatives appeared at the scene and after the injured had been taken to hospital, stretchers bearing the dead were carried from the pithead to the first aid room which served as the mortuary.

Believed to have been caused by the sparking of an electric underground cable which in turn ignited dust, the explosion produced a sheet of flame but no fire. Survivors all spoke of a violent rush of air which hurled men six or eight yards and choking fumes. One rescue worker said: *'Down there you could not tell there had been an explosion.'* Another rescue worker said all the bodies had been badly burned and all were killed instantly.

Barnsley Main which closed in the 1960s. *Barnsley Council's Local Studies Department*

One of the dead men is brought to the surface at Barnsley Main. *Mrs M Woodcock, Carlton*

Barnsley Chronicle & South Yorks News Sat May 10 1947.

BARNSLEY CHRONICLE
& South Yorkshire News

ESTABLISHED 1858
Telephone 3667
VOL. LXXXVIII., 5086
and incorporating the "Barnsley Independent"
REGISTERED AT THE GENERAL POST OFFICE FOR TRANSMISSION BEYOND THE UNITED KINGDOM.
THREEPENCE
Postage : One Penny
SATURDAY, MAY 10, 1947

Nine dead, 21 injured — Barnsley Main survivors say—

PIT SWEPT BY SHEET OF FLAME AFTER EXPLOSION

Nine men were killed and 21 injured by a silent flash and a sheet of flame which swept underground workings 720 feet below ground at Barnsley Main Colliery on Wednesday.

The explosion in No. 3 district of the Kent thick seam—a seam which was only opened up about 12 months ago—occurred about 12.15 p.m., shortly before the day workers were due to finish the shift. The disaster on the third working day following the introduction of the Five Day Week was reminiscent of a similar calamity at Barnsley Main in 1942 and cast a gloom over the whole town and district.

They waited . . . .

A GENERAL view of the pit head as crowds gathered to await news of those involved in the disaster.

Soon after news of the disaster had spread wives and other relatives were keeping vigil and there were poignant scenes as, after the injured had been rushed to hospital in a fleet of ambulances, stretchers bearing the dead were carried from the pit-head to the first aid room which served as a temporary mortuary.

So expeditiously did the gallant band of men toil underground that by 4 p.m. the last body had been brought to the surface. All the men known to be down had then been accounted for and the rescue teams were able to be withdrawn.

The accident is believed to have been caused by the sparking of an electric underground cable, one theory being that there was a flash which ignited coal-dust, most of the men suffering burns from the sheet of flame although there was no actual fire.

Survivors all speak of a violent rush of air hurling men six or eight yards and a pall of dust-laden choking fumes.

One rescue worker returning to the surface described the explosion as a mystery. "Down there," he said, "you could not tell there has been any explosion at all. I saw no sign of any fall of roof and there was not a ton of dirt at the coal face where the explosion occurred.

The air is now fresh. The first rescue party wore oxygen breathing apparatus but we have just managed without any apparatus at all. It is four minutes walk from the bottom of the pit shaft to the scene of the explosion. No fire followed the flash but most of the victims are suffering from burns."

Five rescue teams—Barnsley Main, Monk Bretton (two teams), Woolley, and Wharncliffe Woodmoor—were quickly in attendance and they worked unremittingly under the direction of Mr. J. F. Parkinson (supt. Barnsley Mines Rescue Station) who was underground until the last body was recovered.

Dr. A. B. Slack and Dr. McMahon attended to the injured before they entered the ambulances to be taken to Beckett Hospital. Dr. Slack afterwards descending in the cage to see what medical help he could give underground.

Terribly burned

Another rescue worker said the dead men had been terribly burned and it was obvious they were killed instantly.

Following a report to the men employed in all the seams by Mr. Joseph A. Hall (pres. Yorkshire Area National Union of Mineworkers) they, while mourning the loss of their dead comrades, were ready to keep up production by working next morning.

A joint statement issued by Major-General Sir Noel Holmes (chairman, North Eastern Division N.C.B.) and Mr. Hall, after expressing deep sympathy to relatives, said:

"Investigations are proceeding to ascertain the cause of the serious accident. We are pleased to report Mr. Hall has met the workmen and given his report. Full attendance at work on the unaffected faces is expected on the morning and afternoon shifts to-morrow. There is no reason to believe that the affected district will be long delayed in production. Lord Hyndley wishes to be associated with the expression of sympathy of the Board and the N.U.M."

Nine Dead

The list of dead is:—

Harry Storey (31), colliery deputy, married, 117, Colley-crescent, Kendray.

Arthur Edwards (54), miner, married, 47, Rock-street, Barnsley.

Joseph Blaydon (26), miner, single, 63, Neville-avenue, Park House Estate.

William Peake (47), miner, married, 39, Creswell-street, Pogmoor.

Clifford Allen (34), miner, married, 9, Chapel-street, Ardsley.

Harry Crowcroft (26), miner, single, 10, Grange-lane, Cundy Cross.

Harry Irwin Baxter (25), miner, married, 8, Castle-street, Barnsley.

Ernest Earnshaw (53), miner, married, 63, Summer-lane, Barnsley.

John Denton (45), miner, married, 29, Queen's-road, Barnsley.

The injured

Injured and detained in hospital are:—

Leslie Greaves (27), 22, Birk-road, Kendray.

Alec Spence (26), 48, Thornton-road, Kendray.

Ernest Markwell (19), 21, Industry-road, Stairfoot.

Gordon Grocott (15), 34, Doncaster-road, Barnsley.

Everall Lawton (19), 21, Albion-terrace, Barnsley.

Charles Rigby (17), 78, Upper Sheffield-road, Barnsley.

John Chambers (35), 36, Birk-road, Kendray.

Frank Ridge (20), 39, Albion-road, Stairfoot.

Peter Scuffham (16), Obelisk House, Church-st., Barnsley.

Stanley Lea (27), 50, Lambert-road, Kendray.

William Haigh (44), 23, Darley-avenue, Ward Green.

Frank Barron (15), 85, Doncaster-road, Barnsley.

Raymond Allsop (18), 3, Priory-road, Lundwood.

Walter Morgan (35), 15, Crookes-street, Barnsley.

Charles Dodd (34), Park-road, Barnsley.

Kenneth Haigh (16), Barnsley-road, Cudworth.

Charles Spinks (22), 26, Taylor-row, Barnsley.

Horace Jones (20), Sheffield-road, Barnsley.

Stanley Newsome (19), 23, Gerald Place, Kendray.

The injured who were allowed to go home after treatment in hospital are:—

William Bashforth (18), 23, Twibell-street, Barnsley.

Edward Jones (26), 48, Lambert-road, Kendray.

Continued from previous column

Among those who went down to the scene of the explosion with rescue parties, in addition to Mr. Hall, were Mr. W. H. Dixon (manager of the colliery) and under-manager (Mr. J. Atkinson), Coun. T. S. Brown (delegate Barnsley Main branch N.U.M.), Prof. K. N. Adkinson and Mr. J. A. Longden (area general managers), Mr. R. McNeil (area deputy general manager), Mr. E. Hoyle (agent Barrow-Barnsley Main Collieries), Major H. J. Humphreys and Major H. S. Hudspeth (Divisional H.M. Inspectors of Mines), and Mr. John Hunter (production director for the region, N.C.B.).

Mr. Tom Smith (Divisional Director of Labour) and other members of the N.C.B., who were entertaining Joe Baka on his visit to South Yorkshire collieries at a luncheon in Doncaster, hurriedly left and rushed to Barnsley Main on receipt of the news.

For Mr. Joe Hall, who was down the pit in time to help with the rescue of the injured, and gave artificial respiration to one, it was the 36th disaster at which he had joined a rescue party.

The Chief Constable (Mr. G. Parfitt) was among the early arrivals and later the Mayor (Ald. C. Bentley) accompanied by the Town Clerk (Mr. A. E. Gilfillan) was at the pit.

Died instantly

"In the 36 pit disasters I have experienced," said Mr. Joe Hall, "there has never been less trouble in getting men out and getting them away to the first-aid stations established at the pit-bottom and on the top.

"When I got down shortly after 1.30 I found the dust which had hampered rescue in the first place clearing. I was able to lead the rescue teams straight to the centre of the explosion area. The men dead were badly burned and had been killed by blast and asphyxiation. Most of them must have died instantly.

"They were not buried although some had been battered by falling girders and flying metal. We were able to go straight to every one of the bodies and pull them out easily.

"We found my old friend Harry Storey, with whom I had worked on previous rescue jobs and who has done good work as a rescue team leader, knocked out near the coal face.

"We carried him back and on the way I tried artificial respiration. At the pit bottom we all tried but he was dead before we got him to the top.

"We are going down to-morrow (Thursday) to inspect 3's face to see how soon we can get that part back in action on the coal production drive. We want to show the country how soon we can get production going again in spite of this cruel setback. We hope to get the face back at work on Friday."

SCENES AND INCIDENTS at the Barnsley Main Colliery disaster on Wednesday. Top left: Miners and relations look on grimly as a rescue party brings the body of one of the victims to the ambulance room. Right: Worried looks on the faces of relatives of the injured and killed and miners who had been down on the same level as they stand about awaiting news. Below: Fellow workers see one of their injured colleagues despatched to hospital. On the right (in shirt sleeves) is Dr. A. B. Slack who went underground to give medical aid.

GRIM LOOKS on the faces of one of the rescue parties returning from the scene of the explosion.

Ready to help says Member

The Mayor of Barnsley (Ald. C. Bentley) sends the following letter to the "Barnsley Chronicle":—

I should like to convey to the relatives of those gallant men who so unfortunately lost their lives in the disastrous explosion which occurred at the Barnsley Main Colliery on Wednesday last, May 7, the heartfelt sympathy of the Mayoress, myself, the members of the Corporation, and the whole of our townspeople in their tragic loss.

I feel sure the sympathy of the people of South Yorkshire in particular, and the country in general, will go out to the grief-stricken relatives of the men.

Our thoughts turn to those who now lie in hospital severely injured as a result of the disaster, and I express the hope that they may make a rapid and complete recovery.

Mr. Frank Collindridge, M.P., has sent to the Mayor of Barnsley a message expressing sympathy with the bereaved, and he hopes the injured will soon recover.

"I shall be ready to give any assistance required," says Mr. Collindridge.

The Minister of Fuel (Mr. Emanuel Shinwell) informed Barnsley's M.P., Mr. Frank Collindridge, yesterday (Thursday) that if it was considered desirable a public inquiry would be held into the disaster.

He wishes to convey the sincere sympathy of himself and his department with the bereaved, and offers any assistance he can give.

Barnsley Main Colliery employs about [illegible] men and has a production capacity of about [illegible] tons per day.

Continued on back page

Men trapped in pit-shaft faced death for 7 hours

Two men had a terrible ordeal in a pit-shaft late on Saturday night and early Sunday morning. They were Arthur Smith (53), overman, 36, Walton-street, Barnsley, and James H. Lomas (59), deputy, 6, Cawthorne-road, Barugh Green, and for seven hours—from 10.45 p.m. to 5.45 a.m.—they were trapped in mid-air when the cage at the Redbrook pit of Old Silkstone Colliery stopped 150 yards from the surface.

The two officials were ascending on the completion of the afternoon shift and Mr. Smith afterwards described to a Barnsley Chronicle representative how he and his colleague climbed out of the cage into a small hoppit and were hauled to the surface one after the other.

Let Mr. Smith tell the story in his own words.

"We had gone up about 100 yards," he said, "when the chair started spitting fire and there was a whirring noise underneath as if one of the conductors had 'sloughened.' The winder must have realised something was wrong for he brought the cage to a standstill.

"We could not have been very far from the surface for we could hear voices calling to us. It was the upcast shaft, however, and we could not tell what was said until someone started speaking to us at dictation speed.

"Efforts to raise or lower the cage failed to move it. We were afraid they might wrench off the chair if they tried to lift us again so we shouted up to them to leave us where we were.

DRENCHED TO SKIN

"My lamp had burned out by 11 p.m. and we were both drenched to the skin before midnight because of water coming down the shaft. It seemed like an eternity and we dare not use Lomas's lamp except to switch it on and off to see what time it was.

"Shortly before 5 a.m. two shaftmen came down in a hoppit. One of them getting on top of the chair managed to open the cage door and swing himself into the cage. The other manoeuvred the hoppit so that we could climb into it and we were drawn to the surface. I had lost count of time but was told it was then about 5.45 a.m. They did everything they could for us. We were given hot drinks and stimulants and sent home wrapped in blankets.

"The experience has given me a bit of a shock. Several years ago I was buried in the pit and suffered a fractured spine and ribs. The memory of that did not help me."

Mr. A. Bishop (agent Old Silkstone Colliery) stated that an emergency winding gear was erected at top speed to enable the hoppit to be brought into use. Afterwards repairs were quickly effected.

More food is coming

The Regional Ministry of Food headquarters have scheduled over 30 Yorkshire mining districts for extra rations of sugar, fats, and meats for manufactured foodstuffs including pies and confectionery in the shops.

The approved areas include Barnsley, Dodworth, Cudworth, Darton, Worsbro', Silkstone, Darfield, Hoyland, Royston, Penistone, Wombwell, and Wath-on-Dearne.

The centres listed for extra allocations have been decided upon after consultation with the Miners' Union and district food executive offices.

YOUNG MAN TRAPPED AND KILLED IN PIT

A clog, slightly torn at the back, was on view at an inquest in Wombwell on Tuesday when a jury returned a verdict of death by misadventure on George William Jackson (22), haulage hand, Colley-avenue, Kendray, who was killed at Darfield Main Colliery on Friday.

Irvine Dunn, overman, Princess-street, Wombwell, said he got a message that there was a lad fast underneath some tubs in No. 3 level.

He found the lad lying covered up between the roadway and he was unconscious.

He had severe head injuries and was bleeding from the mouth.

Witness noticed that his right clog was missing and his clothes were disarranged as though he had been dragged.

Ronald Lockwood, pit corporal, Blythe-street, Wombwell, said he was working about 150 yards from Jackson about 11 a.m. when he received an assistance signal.

He set off towards the level and when about 50 yards from it Ronald Evans shouted, "Look sharp down here, George is fast between the tubs."

Witness found him lying between the first and second of a run of full tubs. There were 16 on the load. The first tub was off the metals, and the haulage had stopped. From his thigh downwards Jackson was under the second tub.

The clog was lying at the side of the jack-catch between the metals of the full road between 12 and 14 yards from where Jackson was.

MUST HAVE SLIPPED

Witness thought Jackson must have slipped when the tub was moving. There was a mark consistent with the clog being dragged along between the full road metals from the point where the clog was put on as far as the jack-catch.

Dr. G. W. Etches said cause of death was shock following multiple injuries which were consistent with his being dragged.

The doctor thought the wheel might have passed over his pelvis.

The Deputy West Riding Coroner (Mr. S. H. B. Gill) said it was clear that Jackson's feet had caught in some way, and though it might seem a dangerous procedure for catches to be pressed down by the foot it was customary and there was no regulation against it. No one could be blamed.

STRODE BAULKS AS CAGE FELL

Said to have risked breaking his neck by walking across the shaft bottom when the cage was in descent at New Monckton colliery, David Bryce, colliery worker, Poplars-terrace, Royston, was at Barnsley West Riding Magistrates Court on Wednesday, charged with a breach of the Mines Act. He was fined £4.

Prosecuting on behalf of the N.C.B., Mr. A. S. Furniss said when Bryce found himself at the wrong side of the shaft he walked across slippery timber baulks to where the other men were working.

The onsetter had already rung for the cage and it was in descent.

In a statement Bryce said he thought the onsetter had called him to go over.

'Some negligence' — pit death jury

How he was killed in Bank Bottom Colliery by runaway tubs caused by a broken link, was described at an inquest in Barnsley, on Wednesday upon Samuel Dyson (36), miner, Rose Cottage, Silkstone. The inquest was opened on Monday and adjourned when it was stated that evidence would be called that a drag was applied to the tubs.

The jury returned a verdict of "misadventure" and stated there had been a certain amount of negligence.

Dyson died in Beckett Hospital on Friday morning.

The Deputy W.R. District Coroner (Mr. S. H. B. Gill) sat with [illegible] and there were present Messrs. [illegible] Hoyle (H.M. District Inspector of Mines), H. Brown (manager of the colliery), Col. J. O. R. Rideal (representing the colliery owner), F. N. Birkhead and J. Bottom (president and secretary of Old Silkstone branch N.U.M.).

George Stephenson, acting deputy, Lower Cumberworth, said he rang off the tubs after coupling the ropes and looked to see that the tubs were properly coupled before starting them off.

As the tubs passed him he put a drag on the link of the last tub. This should halt runaway tubs by throwing them off the rails or into the roof.

He saw the tubs running back down the drift and rang the bell to stop the haulage.

Mr. Birkhead: Is it consistent with safety to cap off a run of tubs and then attach the drag? Not in the real sense.

He admitted the jack catches were not inserted until after the accident. It was not consistent with safety to use a bent drag.

NO JACK CATCHES

George Ford, overman, Fox and Hounds Inn, Silkstone, said he was in charge of the district. About 2.30 p.m. on the previous Wednesday in the main gate, ten yards from the face he found Dyson lying on his back with his right leg pinned under the left leg and the side of a railing on top of the left leg.

There were four full tubs past him off the rails. Owing to a broken link 17 full tubs had run away. He came to the conclusion the link had broken as 20 tubs were being hauled forward and 17 had run backwards.

In reply to the foreman juror (Mr. A. H. Haywood) witness said there were no jack catches, but there were man-holes all the way.

Ronald Midgeley, miner, Toll Bar, Cawthorne, said he had been working with Dyson. He ran back into the cross-gate about a yard in. The tubs had knocked about four middle lengths from under the girders.

Replying to Mr. Birkhead witness said he neither saw nor heard a drag.

Addressing the jury, the Coroner said it seemed clear Dyson was struck by tubs coming down the incline after breaking away. Stephenson told them definitely he put a drag on the last tub. The drag was afterwards found in a declivity in the roadway. Therefore it seemed certain the drag did not operate.

Dr. L. Friedman, casualty officer, Beckett Hospital, who made a post-mortem, said the cause of death was fat embolism in the artery following a fracture of both legs.

WOMAN GAOLED FOR ASSAULT

Said to have told a pack of lies, Ivy Bowmer (43), Joseph Bowmer (44), and May Baker (19), Wentworth-road, Mapplewell, appeared before the Barnsley Borough Magistrates Court yesterday (Thursday) summoned for using offensive language in a public service vehicle, and for assault and battery.

Ivy Bowmer, who was further charged with being drunk and disorderly was sent to prison for two months and fined £5 and costs.

Joseph Bowmer and May Baker were each fined £10 and costs, and all three were bound over for 12 months in the sum of £10.

Supt. H. E. Legg said the conductress, Lily Siddons (21), Rowland-road, Barnsley, commenced to collect tickets, when Ivy Bowmer, without any provocation, struck her.

P. C. Gregory said that while he was speaking to the conductress, all three defendants came up and the two Bowmers held Miss Siddons while Baker scratched her face.

Ivy Bowmer said she was not drunk and had not struck the conductress. Joseph Bowmer said he had not been drinking, and Baker said the conductress swore at her and kicked her in the leg.

The chairman (Mr. J. Richards) said it was the duty of the bench to stop such acts of hooliganism and browbeating of the public.

Above and opposite page: How the *Barnsley Chronicle* and the *Daily Mail* reported the 1947 disaster at Barnsley Main.

Bear Brand STOCKINGS Lasting Luxury.

Daily Mail

ADVANCE

No. 15,908 ONE PENNY FOR KING AND EMPIRE THURSDAY, MAY 8, 1947

Britain 'gets tough' as dollar reckoning-day nears

U.S. BACKS DALTON PLAN TO SLASH DEBTS

Comment

BABY TALK

THE dear old *Daily Herald* is very upset with us again. We are sorry if we were unkind, for we have a sort of tolerant affection for the sheet.

What makes it bearable is its blundering way of being disingenuous—rather like a clumsy child:—

Awkward, embarrassed, stiff, without the skill
Of moving gracefully or standing still.

The *Herald* complains that our leading article of Tuesday broadened our "æsthetic objections to the building of a power station opposite St. Paul's into a shrieking denunciation of practically everything the Government has done or intends to do."

The writer of that sentence has, characteristically, missed the point. We do not object to the Bankside scheme on æsthetic grounds. What we did was to cite this project as one more example of the higgledy-piggledy planning methods of the Government.

Who defends this particular plan? The *Herald*—yes, but hardly anyone else. Even LORD LATHAM, Socialist leader of the London County Council, is against it, and for the same reason as we are.

No answer

IN a letter to *The Times* he says: "The issue is not only the existence of a power station itself but the dominant influence, contrary to good planning, which it will have on the development of a wide area on the south bank of the Thames."

"Contrary to good planning" are the operative words. They are the words of a leading Socialist directed against a Socialist Government, who claim that they alone are planners.

"Contrary to good planning." That is the criticism we levelled in our leading article against nearly everything the Government have handled. We mentioned housing, transport, coal, exports, and finance.

The *Herald* does not touch on these things in its reply. Not, as we believe, because it is unable to read, but because ("awkward, embarrassed, stiff") it cannot give any convincing answer.

What answer can be given to the homeless thousands who recall the Socialist election statement that housing "can be dealt with in a fortnight."

No planning

WHAT can be said about transport? Only that the Bill to nationalise it was so ill-prepared that the Government themselves had to table 176 amendments on the report stage alone. Is that planning?

Conscription? For months the Government argued that 18 months was the minimum safe period of national service. But they changed their minds in two days under back bench pressure. Is that governing?

SIR STAFFORD CRIPPS says the fuel crisis has cost us £200,000,000 of exports. Why? Because MR. SHINWELL failed to plan for a few million tons of coal stocks last autumn.

This is what we mean when we say that the Government's record has been "contrary to good planning." The *Herald* will say, as it said yesterday, that to mention these matters is politically unscrupulous.

No reports

THIS is part of the endearing baby-talk to which we have referred. But some reproof is necessary, and we may find it in a recent objective analysis of the General Election, published by the Oxford University Press, which says:—

"*The Conservative papers reported their opponents more extensively than the anti-Tory papers. The 'Daily Herald' hardly ever reported an opponent except for an occasional snippet under a derisive heading.*"

This may be because some Socialists really believe that those who disagree with them are fit only for ridicule and contempt.

MR. SHINWELL put it in his own elegant way yesterday when he said that people other than the organised workers "don't matter a tinker's cuss."

In other words—Ministers think, work, and plan not for the nation but for one section. That is why our country is in such dire straits today.

London talks next month

From **JAMES BROUGH**, Daily Mail Special Correspondent
NEW YORK, Wednesday.

THE United States today applauded the decision by Mr. Dalton, Chancellor of the Exchequer, to slash Britain's £3,500,000,000 war debts.

America sees it as the start of another Battle of Britain—to save fast-dwindling dollars and put Britain's finance on a sounder basis.

Assurances have been given to the United States Government that Britain is not asking for any changes in the £937,500,000 Loan agreement.

"That will be repaid in full," a spokesman here said.

"But Britain will refuse in forthcoming negotiations with her creditors to recognise all her wartime borrowing as legitimate debt."

The British Treasury will be tough—it has to be in the growing dollar crisis. If it is proved Britain's debts were incurred in the joint war effort they will be wiped out completely.

Deadline

The American Treasury sees a hard fight ahead for Britain, with July 15 as the deadline for victory.

That is the date when, under the terms of the American loan, Britain has to decide what she is going to do about the "sterling balances" she owes to India, Iraq, Egypt, Australia, Brazil, and other countries.

The total is £3,500,000,000. And there is only £550,000,000 left in Britain's United States Loan bank account.

Ever since the loan was negotiated last summer United States finance experts have been waiting for some such drastic action as Mr. Dalton's announcement last night.

In American financial circles tonight there is a sense of relief that at last Britain has gone into battle to keep herself from bankruptcy.

India and Egypt will be the first to feel the pinch. The Indian Government is firmly opposed to scaling down its £1,250,000,000 sterling balance, but though Britain cannot pay the piper she can call the tune.

No option

Egypt is dead set against cutting her £[illegible] credit, too, but she will have no option, according to British sources here tonight.

The American Government is immensely cheered by the prospect of the Loan being eked out longer than the pessimists have been predicting.

The Treasury Department has been gravely discussing the startling fact that Britain last month drew £112,500,000 from the Loan. That was nearly four times the average monthly withdrawal.

Well over a third of the original credits have now been spent—£387,500,000.

The situation is still acutely dangerous. Spending was originally planned to be spread out over five years, with 50 years to repay.

Navy College to be free

New Dartmouth plan

BOYS of 16 with an educational standard equal to school certificate will be able to enter the Royal Navy through Dartmouth College under a new scheme to begin in September 1948.

Tuition and board will be free of charge.

Announcing this plan in the Commons yesterday Mr. J. Dugdale, Financial Secretary to the Admiralty, said that cadets would be eligible for the executive, engineering and supply branches and spend five terms at Dartmouth before going to sea.

The Admiralty intended to continue the system of recruiting officers from the lower deck, and they hoped it would be possible to select an overall average of 20 to 25 per cent. of officers in these branches from the lower deck.

Ultimately the new system would provide half of the remainder of the officers required.

There was every reason to expect that these officers would be worthy successors to the naval officers of today, he added.

Petition out of Derby?

Hurt in 'Guineas'

PETITION is not likely to run in the Derby at Epsom on June 7.

The injuries the colt sustained when he collided with the tapes and fell at the start of the 2,000 Guineas at Newmarket last week are more serious that was at first thought.

It is feared that he has an internal injury. He has been off his feed since the race.

Sir Alfred Butt, Petition's owner, told Robin Goodfellow yesterday that he was "very pessimistic" about his colt's prospects in the Derby.

Petition, who was rated second only to Tudor Minstrel among the two-year-olds of last season, started second favourite for the 'Guineas,' but finished seventh.

In the betting on the Derby he has gone out to 25 to 1 from 14 to 1.

Robin Goodfellow's Review—BACK Page.

Antiquis note mystery

By Daily Mail Reporter

AN anonymous letter supposed to come from one of the three men involved in the shooting of Mr. de Antiquis in Charlotte-street, London, W., last week was received yesterday by the police.

It is believed that the letter asks: "What will happen to me if I come forward and give information?" and that the writer wishes to turn King's evidence to save himself.

Detectives believe that the anonymous gunman-penman is the driver of the car who, in the flurry of the shooting, panicked, snatched the ignition key, and bolted.

Dalton offer: 5 per cent.

By Daily Mail Political Correspondent

NEGOTIATIONS with financial representatives of India and Egypt regarding outstanding sterling balances will take place separately towards the middle of June in London.

Efforts will be made to obtain a scaling down of the balances in the first instance, followed by arrangements for regulating the speed at which the remaining balances will become convertible.

As regards payment of the balance, if reductions can be agreed, the Government believes that this should take place at the rate of 5 per cent. or 2½ per cent. over a period of years.

PENNY SMOKES

Eire smugglers warned

The price of 20 cigarettes in Eire will be 1s. 8d. from today, an increase of 3d. being announced by Mr. Frank Aiken in his Budget speech in the Dail yesterday.

He issued a serious warning to smugglers, for the price will be only half that ruling across the Ulster border and in Britain.

They wait for news

WITHIN a few minutes of yesterday's explosion, relatives and friends of men working underground had crowded into the pityard at Barnsley Main Colliery to wait for news and to question returning rescue workers. Injured men, of whom 19 were detained in hospital, were still staggering out when the first rescue teams entered the seam where the explosion occurred. Among the first to go down the shaft were National Coal Board officials, including Mr. John Hunter, North-East divisional production manager, and Mr. Tom Smith, labour controller.

Pit not to shut for mourning

Nine die in explosion

From Daily Mail Reporter
BARNSLEY, Wednesday Night.

NINE miners died and 25 were injured in an explosion at Barnsley Main Colliery here today. But the pit will not close for the traditional mourning period. Their workmates have agreed to carry on.

Custom has been waived for Britain's need of coal, and tomorrow 600 miners will be raising their 900-ton daily average.

Soon after the bodies recovered by rescue teams had been brought to the surface, Mr. J. A. Hall, president of the Yorkshire Miners' Association, told the pitmen it was their duty to keep Barnsley Main working.

He said: "The mine is safe to work in, and the whole pit should be working by Friday."

The accident, officially described as an "ignition" at Three's Face in the Kent's Thick Seam of the colliery, swept the men working nearby with flame but did not start a fire.

It sent a blast of air through the workings, hurling men for six or eight yards; plunging the area into darkness and filling the air with clouds of choking dust.

As a pall of coal-dust laden fumes spread across the coal face trapping men behind it, Deputy Bill Haigh, of Darley-avenue, Ward Green, Barnsley, crawled into it in a vain attempt at rescue.

Burned

He was burned and bleeding on face and arms, but gasping and choking, he forced his way nearly 200 yards along the face to reach men who had been killed in the blast.

Then finding he could do no more, he struggled half-fainting along the track to safety.

In hospital last night, covered in bandages through which only his eyes, nose and mouth showed, he told me:—

"*I did what I could to try to save the lads. It was pretty bad going. I couldn't see anything because my face was burned and the dust cloud was pitch black. I groped my way back.*"

When the explosion occurred men on the morning shift were on the point of getting ready to go to the pit bottom.

Suddenly, say survivors, there was a flash, a roar, and a great blast of wind. Lamps were smashed or put out.

There was an immediate call for rescuers, and men ran from all directions to help. Soon five rescue teams—one from Barnsley Main, two from Monk Bretton Colliery, one from Woolley Colliery, and one from Wharncliffe Woodmoor Colliery—were on the spot working under the direction of Mr. J. E. Parkinson, superintendent of the Barnsley Miners' Rescue Team.

They found a scene of devastation at the coal face. Injured men were crawling out but many others lay still and lifeless.

Explanation

Among the first to go down the mine with the rescuers was Dr. H. Slack and his assistant Dr. McMahon. They gave first-aid to the injured who were quickly brought to the surface and taken by ambulance to hospital.

Although no official explanation of the cause of the explosion has yet been given, I was told that there is a theory that it was due to a spark from one of the underground electric cables igniting coaldust.

Nearly all the dead and injured were young men. Some of the boys had been working in the pit for only a few months.

Eighteen-year-old William Bashforth, who had his head bandaged in hospital and was allowed to go to his home in Twibell-street, Barnsley, said:

"I had just come out of the 'gate.' I was lucky. A few minutes more and I might have been back at the coal face when the blast started.

"As it was I was only about 25 yards away. There was suddenly a great noise, a flash and a tornado of wind. It all happened in a split second.

"The next I knew I was blown off my feet and flung for yards.

"Coal tubs had been blown on to men working near me crushing them.

At a late hour last night it was reported that the 19 men in hospital, who are suffering from burns and shock, were very ill and that three of them—Charles Spinks, Gordon Grocott, and Raymond Allsop, aged 18, of Priory-road, Lundwood, Barnsley, were dangerously ill.

MR. J. A. HALL (left) and Mr. John Hunter, production manager of the North-East Divisional Coal Board, went down with the rescue party.

EIGHTEEN-YEAR-OLD William Bashforth, who was blown several yards, pictured with his mother last night.

The dead

Henry Storey, shot firer and deputy in charge, of Colley-crescent, Kendray, Barnsley;

Henry Crocroft, of Grange-lane, Sandycroft, Barnsley;

Joseph Blaydon, of Neville-avenue, Parkhouse Estate, Barnsley;

Arthur Edwards, of Rock-street, Barnsley;

Ernest Earnshaw, of Summer-lane, Barnsley;

John Denton, of Queen's-road, Barnsley;

Henry Baxter, of Castle-street, Barnsley;

Clifford Allen, of Chapel-street, Ardsley, Barnsley; and

William Peaks, of Cresswell-street, Pogmoor, Barnsley.

12,000 GO BACK TO THE PITS

Officials next?

By Daily Mail Reporter

BY midnight yesterday more than 12,000 miners, rendered idle by the strike of 150 Durham engine-winders, had returned to work.

The remaining 15,000 men would be back by the week-end.

The stoppage has cost the country 70,000 tons of coal.

Then came news of another threatened strike by 5,000 members of the British Association of Colliery Officials and Staff—scheduled for May 17.

Meantime, they will not resume Saturday work or overtime until negotiation on matters affecting their pay, perquisites, and rights are opened with the National Coal Board.

And in South Yorkshire the lightning strike by 1,000 men at Monckton 3 and 4 Pits, near Barnsley, continued, adding another 1,000 tons to the production loss.

MAY YET SPREAD

The 12,000 Durham men who resumed on the night shift were lowered to the levels by nine engine-winders who returned to duty.

Up to late last night there were no signs of others following.

Their secretary, Mr. Joseph Walton, is to attend a meeting in Manchester today of the executive committee of the Colliery Winders' Union.

Decisions may be taken extending the strike to South Wales, Scotland, Derbyshire, Lancashire, and North Staffordshire.

Volunteer workers descended the Astley Green Colliery, near Leigh, yesterday afternoon, with the approval of the National Coal Board, for the second time to work right through the night to cut coal for the miners today.

They include managers, firemen, and safety men.

Similar efforts were made at Mosley Common, near Tyldesley, Brackley, Little Hulton, and Parsonage, Leigh.

News of other pits affected includes:—

Shotton (1,750) resuming today.

Bank Hall, Burnley: Ballot showed 73 per cent. of men in favour of returning to work.

Not a tinker's cuss—Shinwell

THE organised workers of this country "are our friends. As for the rest, they don't matter a tinker's cuss," said Mr. Shinwell, Minister of Fuel and Power, at Margate yesterday.

He was addressing [illegible] delegates of the Electrical Trades Union, and declared:—

"If, for example, the Press of the country, who have in recent months been so kind to me and detected in me high qualities which I never believed myself to have possessed, abuse us, laugh at us, revile us, sneer at us, and distort and garble things we say, we expect it.

"Indeed it would be most surprising if it were otherwise, and we would become a little suspicious, not of them but of ourselves."

The loudest cheer was given to this declaration.

"If anyone imagines that the Labour Government is going to stop with the nationalisation schemes they have on hand at present then they are mistaken.

"There was a lot of talk of what kind of a Government will come in after this one, but there is only one possible kind which could come in and that is a Government even more to the Left."

On the problems confronting the Electrical Trades Union when the electric supply industry is nationalised the Minister said that the Government intended to safeguard the rights of every employee.

If certain rights were acceded to in the past they would be accepted as an obligation imposed on the new authority.

"I would wish," he declared, "that every person could be employed in the industry, but it may be that workers will become redundant because of reorganisation.

"In these circumstances there must be a measure of compensation. There is also the question of pensions, and these matters, too, will be safeguarded."

He added: "While we have talked about workers' control and the like, I believe many of these ideas and principles, which have been familiar in the Labour movement for many years, can be achieved in another way.

"We must make provision for the utmost possible consultation between the workers' representatives themselves and those who are appointed to the boards."

The Minister said that many of the delegates present were not in the electrical industry, but in the iron and steel industry. But what he had said about managerial functions would concern them when their turn came.

THE KING

A slight chill

ABOARD H.M.S. VANGUARD, Wednesday.—The King has a slight chill and has been confined to the Royal apartments aboard the Vanguard for two days.

He caught the cold when the ship came out of the tropics into cooler weather.—*Reuter.*

RESULT TODAY

In by-election fight

Housewives who went to vote after queuing for their rations stepped-up polling in the Jarrow by-election yesterday to a peak not anticipated by Conservatives or Socialists.

It was estimated at party headquarters last night that about [illegible] per cent. of the electorate had polled. The result will be declared early this afternoon.

'TESTED' MILK

You can change dealers

From June 1 people will be allowed to change to a supplier of either heat-treated or T.T. milk where the present retailer is unable or unwilling to supply it.

NIGHT WATCH FOR 4 IN LINER

By Daily Mail Reporter
LIVERPOOL, Wednesday Night.

C.I.D. men are keeping watch on the gangways of the 26,000-ton liner Empress of Scotland here tonight in the hope that four young British seamen, alleged to be stowaways, will attempt to get ashore.

The men are said to have escaped from a cell where they had been since they were found two days out from Port Said.

Last night they were safely locked up, but early this morning they had vanished. The hasp and bolt which locked the cell door had been opened.

DISGUISE

The men are: James Martin, aged 23, of Edinburgh; Joseph Hilliard, 23, of Liverpool; Thomas Stewart, 21, of Belfast, and Peter Jackson, 23, address unknown.

Service men leaving the ship have been carefully checked. The seamen, it is thought, may try to disguise themselves in uniform.

The watch will be maintained throughout tonight, as the liner must remain at the landing-stage for the disembarkation of the remainder of her passengers tomorrow morning.

A ship's officer said he did not think it possible that the men could have swum ashore.

Woman and doctor shot

Note on the door

A DOCTOR and a woman were found shot dead in a lonely cottage at Pound Hill, between East Grinstead and Crawley, Sussex, yesterday.

They were Dr. Alan Cecil Gimmell and Mrs. M. F. Smith.

A neighbour found a note pinned to the door of the cottage telling anyone who saw it not to enter, but to inform the police.

Mrs. Smith was lying on a settee in the kitchen. Dr. Gimmell was in a chair, leaning across the table. A pistol was found in the room.

An inquest will be held today.

ROOF RIPPED

26 injured in bus

Twenty-four children, their headmaster, and another teacher were injured yesterday when the double-decker bus taking them to school collided with a low railway bridge in Lancaster-road, Leicester.

The top of the bus was ripped off by the impact. After treatment at hospital all the injured went home.

The headmaster is Mr. C. Clements, of Letchworth-road, Leicester, and the teacher is 19-year-old Miss Cissie Cayless, of Manor-drive, Loughborough.

Defence chief in new storm

Foreign policy is unchanged

By GEOFFREY WAKEFORD, Daily Mail Parliamentary Correspondent

BRITAIN'S foreign policy is unchanged by the Government's time cut in the National Service Bill.

Mr. A. V. Alexander, Minister of Defence, enraged by shouts of "yellow" from the Tories, thumped the dispatch box in the Commons as he said so last night.

Mr. Anthony Eden, Deputy Leader of the Opposition, warned: "This surrender"—the Government's surprise change from 18 to 12 months in the compulsory service clause—"is going to have calamitous consequences."

Someone in the public gallery started to clap. Then Mr. Alexander was up, protesting hotly:—

"There is no surrender on foreign policy. Through the change there will be greater difficulty in meeting the garrison situation overseas.

"On that basis we have taken a risk that between now and 1950"—the Bill takes effect on January 1, 1949—"the situation in regard to our commitments will improve."

He repeated firmly: "We are not throwing any overseas commitments overboard at all. There is cert[ainly] no change in the foreign polic[y of] this country."

But Mr. Eden had been distu[rbed] by Mr. Dick Crossman's "expl[ana]tion" of the reasons which led [the] Government to alter the basis o[f the] Bill.

Mr. Crossman, the only Lab[our] critic of the Government who, [in] the previous debate on the B[ill] before Easter, hinted at a possible change to 12 months, last night went one further.

The Government, he said, had decided that our responsibility for the great Middle East area was "far beyond our strength."

What did Mr. Crossman mean? Mr. Eden seized swiftly on the point, because up to then, after six hours' debate, the Government had disclosed "absolutely no reasons" for the change.

His pressure drew the "no-

BACK PAGE—Col. ONE

BRAZIL BANS COMMUNISTS

Rio de Janeiro, Wednesday.—Brazilian High Court tod[ay] ordered that the Commu[nist] Party should be clo[sed]. Decision was taken by [illegible] votes to two.—Reuter.

FAIR: Weather: Page 4.

Pictured examining their George Cross medals – special awards for bravery in civilian life – outside Buckingham Palace in December 1947 are Syd Blackburn (right) and Harry Crummack with their wives Nora and Annie. They were commended for their bravery after the explosion in May 1947.

Mr Joe Hall, Yorkshire miners' president, said:

In thirty-six pit disasters I have experienced there has never been less trouble in getting men and getting them away to the first aid stations established at the pit bottom and on the surface. We found my old friend, Harry Storey, with whom I had worked on previous rescue jobs and who has done good work as a rescue team leader knocked out near the coal face. We carried him back and on the way I tried artificial respiration. At the pit bottom we all tried but he was dead before we got to the top.

A tragic figure was the father of Harry Crowcroft. Though encased in a plaster cast as a result of an accident in which he had sustained injuries to his spine, he waited for news of his son. It was a distraught father who was led away when he was told his son had been killed. Members of Barnsley Main rescue team worked with the knowledge that one of their members was among the missing men. He was Mr Storey, shotfirer and deputy in charge, whose body was the last to be brought to the surface. Had he listened to his wife's pleas he would not have been at work, for he had been recovering from an earlier accident and had returned home the previous day feeling too sick to eat; he went to bed and was nursed by Mrs Storey, who begged him not to go to work on the fateful day.

There had been tragic events in the life of another victim, Harry Baxter. Suffering from a miners' knee complaint, he had been off work for a month and had restarted work on the Monday, and having found it too strenuous had been found lighter work; Wednesday was the first day in his new job.

The day before the explosion one of the victims had mentioned the presence of gas, the coroner, Mr S H B Gill, was told at the inquest at Barnsley Town Hall. Mrs Storey said her husband said there had been gas in the pit and had arrived home feeling ill the day before the explosion. The jury returned a verdict of death by misadventure and the foreman juror, Mr H Matthews, said the jury did not know whether it was within their province but they thought there had been gross negligence in operating a machine without the cover which was supposed to prevent accidents. The explosion was caused by arcing from an electric cable and the jury felt the electric cable should have been examined at least once a shift by an electrician. And they also felt the ventilation door should have had a foundation. Mr Gill said a previous accident at the colliery had been caused by a trailing cable and when one considered the rough area over which the cable had to be hauled, it did seem important that they should be examined by someone with electrical knowledge. He said: *'While there may have been a case of slight negligence in this case, I could not direct you that anyone has been neglectful in a criminal way.'*

Dr H K Willett, head of the Mines Rescue and Safety Department, North Eastern Division, said he considered it was not an explosion of great violence. He came to the conclusion that the explosion had been caused by an arc from the damaged cable igniting an explosive mixture of firedamp as it was emitted from the waste adjacent to the pan engine. The opening of the ventilation door by a surveying team caused gas to be moved towards the trailing cable.

'Our Joe'

When Joe Hall retired as President of the Yorkshire NUM in 1952, there were no more fights for a man like him. As he closed the door of his office for the last time, he closed a chapter on the history of the miners dating back nearly one hundred years.

To understand Joe, you have to understand his predecessors, for he shared their qualities, their outlook on life and probably their failings. Like his predecessors, he was moulded by a combination of poverty, the Sunday school, the insular mining communities, literature and the boxing ring.

This self-made man followed in the footsteps of John

'That wicked Yorkshireman' – Joe Hall. *Photograph and material, Mr and Mrs A Fowler, Wombwell*

Normansell, the first of the great nineteenth century leaders, who was a product of the Sunday School and the first miner to be elected a member of a town council, in Barnsley; Ben Pickard, the man of iron; A J Cook, the national union official, who was an eloquent speaker, and Herbert Smith, Joe's immediate predecessor as Yorkshire President, who could use his fists.

Their objectives were quite simple – to improve pay and working conditions and, in the later leaders, to nationalise the mines. They started the work – Joe finished it.

Nature – Joe would have said God – had designed him to fight the battles of the 20s and 30s when everything was black and white and when poverty and the pawnshop haunted every street in mining towns. As well as having the knack of raising men's ideals, he was also a fighter.

Joe was a man of his times. Whereas Arthur Scargill would have been as much at home in the 20s and 30s as in the 70s and 80s, Joe would have been out of place today when leaders have to fight different, perhaps harder battles, when miners are not starving and when pits with reserves have to close.

Lundhill, which had a long row of terraced houses, a pit, a pub and a church was his home. Despite its size, it had hit the national headlines before he was born there in 1887. His maternal grandfather had been one of the sinkers of Lundhill Colliery. It was a cursed pit. Several men were killed during the sinking in the 1850s and nearly two hundred men and boys died there in an explosion in 1857. His mother, then a small girl, was walking from Hemingfield to Lundhill when she saw the flames leaping up the shaft.

He was one of eleven children. In the two bedroom house, the boys slept at one end of the double bed, the girls at the other.

At the age of twelve he started work at Darfield Main

Colliery, working in galleries no more than four feet high, carrying oil lamps so feeble as to be almost useless, in choking dust and intense heat. *'There were some months in winter when we saw no sunlight from Sunday to Saturday,'* he said.

At twenty he became a qualified collier in the days when it was still regarded as an unskilled job, and when miners were regarded as 'underground savages.' He said: *'We were untouchables. A miner's daughter had little chance but to marry other than a miner. The miner had no choice but his own kind.'*

But he admitted some of it could have been the miners' own fault:

I remember washing myself at home, with my mother not washing but dusting my back. We seldom washed our lower limbs – we believed it weakened them. How my mother kept the beds so clean when our legs were so seldom washed I could never understand.

At about this time he became a lay preacher in the Wesleyan Reform Church, conducting his first services at the Lundhill chapel, which had been used as a mortuary in the 1857 disaster. Later he conducted services in the Mexborough and Rotherham Circuit. The role of the Sunday school in the development of trade unionism has always been underrated. Union leaders copied the gestures and vocabulary of the old time preachers but focused their attention on coal masters instead of the devil.

So this was Joe's early life, a man influenced by poverty, the dangers of working underground and religion. The rebel had been born. By 1917 he was union branch secretary at Cortonwood Colliery, and a year later he took over the post of checkweighman. He was soon unemployed, however, after he appeared at the Rotherham courts, charged with interfering with the management of the pit. He lost his case and his job.

But Joe was soon back at Cortonwood and he was elected safety inspector and then, when the union's Yorkshire financial secretary retired, the miners chose Joe as his successor.

Within a year came the General Strike and the miners' lock out. There was only enough money in the bank to pay strike pay for four weeks, yet Joe was convinced victory was within their grasp. With a Yorkshire membership of 160,000 behind the permanent officials, and the support of the other unions, the result was inevitable, he believed. When the General Strike collapsed, however, doubts as to the validity of the lock-out grew in his mind, although he never made them public. Not for the first time he found himself opposing the views of his members.

In the 1930s he became Yorkshire President. At public inquiries into disasters he became a despised man: *'Here's to that wicked Yorkshireman, Joe Hall,'* one coal owner toasted him after an inquiry. *'May I never see his face again.'* Yet he also found himself fighting his own membership. The 1926 lock-out had left its mark on him and he was always frightened of things getting out of control again. In one extraordinary case, his old branch, Cortonwood, took him to court after he had agreed to new pay rates with the management without consulting the men at the pit. The Cortonwood miners lost their case.

Demolition work at Wombwell Main in 1969. *R Firth*

Probably his greatest enemy was the Barnsley Bed seam, which produced first-class coal but which clawed back hundreds of lives. In the 30s electricity and coal-cutting machines which kicked up inflammable coal dust were creating new hazards.

In 1942 he nearly lost his life after an explosion at Bullcroft Colliery. He led one of the rescue teams down the pit but then was called back to the safety base, leaving the other members to continue their work. Then he was asked to lead another team down another roadway.

At the face they found it completely blocked. After an hour they heard another explosion, a second disaster. The blast had travelled down the other roadway, trapping the first rescue team: if it had not been for that earlier message, Joe would have been killed.

The district had to be sealed off, to prevent the whole pit blowing up, and Joe had to break a vow. After the Gresford disaster, in the 1930s, when scores of bodies were sealed up, he had vowed no Yorkshire miner would have a permanent tomb hundreds of feet below ground.

After the nationalisation of the mines, he soon found himself at odds with his own members, this time at Grimethorpe. It was known as the stint strike. In one seam the collier's stint was increased from twenty-one feet to twenty-three feet: too much, said the miners, and they went on strike. Soon thousands of miners were walking out in sympathy, making front page news day after day.

Miners are probably the most difficult of workers to lead and control. Once they have made up their minds, the roof caves in, regardless of the leadership. Sir William Lawther, then President of the national union, called the miners 'anarchists,' an insult to any hard working miner. Gallows were painted on walls at Grimethorpe, with the words 'Burn Will Lawther.'

The strike involved most of the South Yorkshire coalfield. It finally fizzled out but not before the miners and public realised that nationalisation had not solved all the problems of the industry. Perhaps just the bosses had changed.

By 1952, when Joe retired, mining had changed beyond recognition from the days of his first strike in 1900, involving the infamous 'troublesome pit lads'. One of his last battles involved opposition to opencast mining, a controversial subject but insignificant in comparison with his earlier battles. It was like a heavyweight champion swatting a fly.

Joe had worked beyond his times and he went into retirement in Wood Walk, Wombwell, spending his spare time serving on the former Wombwell Urban District Council.

It is difficult to assess his achievements. He faced only one major dispute, the lock-out, which was probably too big for any man to handle. He never became national President. He saw vast improvements in pay and conditions, the introduction of paid holidays and pensions; but these may have come with or without Joe Hall.

But, more than anything else, he gave miners dignity. They loved his speeches, eloquent and articulate, and they felt good. He dished out to the establishment what the establishment usually dished out to the inarticulate miner.

He was prepared to take on his own, swim in the opposite direction to his colleagues, often the sign of a great man, and he did not lead miners into any disastrous strikes, for he was convinced that you should not take on the opposition unless you were convinced of victory.

He was often among the first men to go underground after a disaster: a courageous man who earned the respect of the miner.

Workmen salvaging the rails at Wombwell Main. *R Firth*

Chapter 6

1970s and 1980s

Victory and Decline

The miners swept through the country like a tidal wave in the 1970s and even 10 Downing Street was awash in 1974. Those national strike victories, coupled with a revitalised coal industry and rising income which gave the highly paid face workers the opportunity to buy into what had been hitherto the middle-class property market, instilled in the miners a robust confidence and at times a reckless independence in the 1970s and early 80s: their chests, said NUM president, Joe Gormley, were a mile wide. That the miners were so ebullient gave the nation the impression they were invincible, with the result that influential elements in the Conservative Party, convinced that the National Coal Board was a mere extension of the powerful union, decided to do something about Arthur Scargill, the class warrior, and what they regarded as a cock-eyed industry which continued to produce more and more coal – even when there was no demand.

Published in *The Economist* magazine in 1978, a Conservative Party document – the Ridley Plan – outlined radical proposals to combat big strikes. Almost unnoticed at the time of publication the plans played a crucial role in the 1984/85 Miners' Strike, one of the most divisive and bitter in the history of trade unions. In essence the plan mobilised the power of the state and public opinion against the union. At the same time the party looked at ways of dismantling the industry, reversing the tide of nationalisation.

But the long road to the '84 strike – and the subsequent collapse of the industry – began back in 1965 when the Yorkshire miners' council, shocked by the then closure programme, passed a resolution claiming that the Government's planning under their White Paper could not justify closing pits on uneconomic grounds alone.

This Council Meeting, speaking for Yorkshire, is of the opinion that, whilst there may be little we can do to oppose closures on the grounds of exhaustion, can and does strenuously oppose closures for solely uneconomic grounds.

That was the first crack in the miners' hitherto rock solid support for the Labour Party, then in power. The resolution also signified that the Yorkshire miners, after years of single pit strikes, were beginning to harden their policies and widen their horizons. The 1960s was a period of great change and anxiety, not least for the mining industry. Mechanization had brought great leaps in productivity but the pits in Scotland, Durham and parts of Yorkshire were getting older and were closing at a faster rate than in the past. As early as November, 1961, Mr Roy Mason, MP for Barnsley, said the NCB had the wrong image.

The old Yorkshire coalfield divided into different NCB areas with their own offices. From the 1960s the areas began to shrink. By the 1980s there was one Barnsley area with offices based at Grimethorpe.

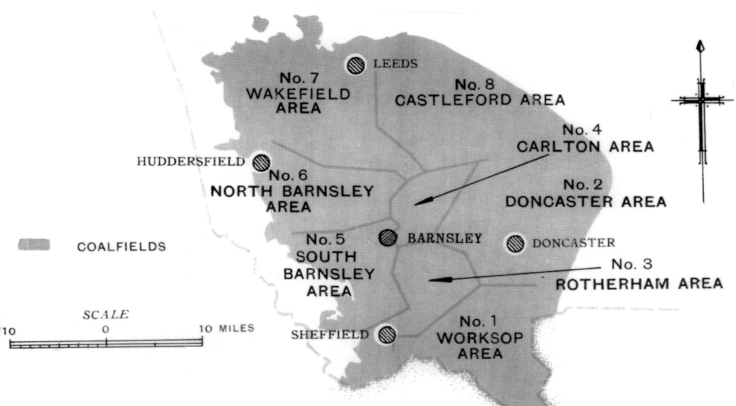

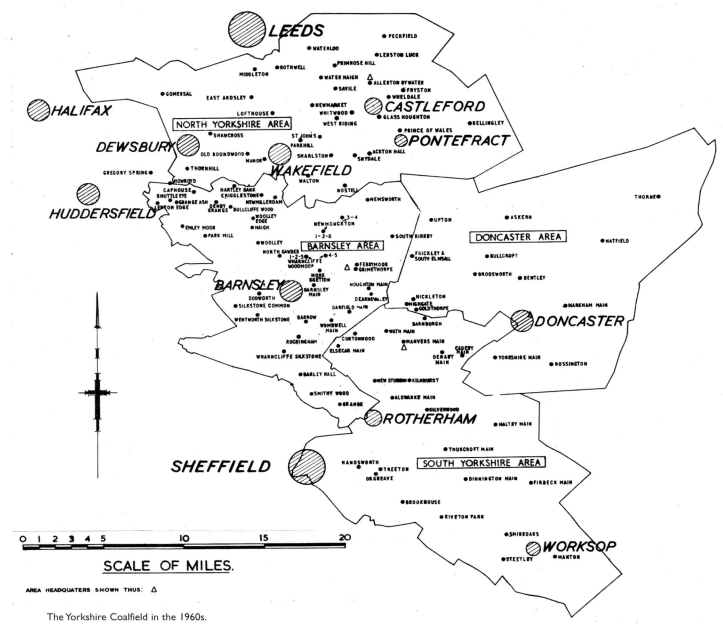

The Yorkshire Coalfield in the 1960s.

It is time the Minister (of Power) *tried to create a fresh image in the minds of the miners instead of the existing one – that of an octopus extending its tentacles throughout the coalfields and squeezing them to death.*

The Plan for Coal envisaged the closure of 200 pits over the next five years, although the Tory Minister of Power, Mr R Wood, said pits would close but output and the number of mineworkers would rise by 1965. On top of closures there was fierce competition from 'modern' fuels such as cheap oil and nuclear power. When 70,000 Yorkshire miners came out on strike over surface men's hours in 1969, Jack Leigh, the Yorkshire vice president, put it all in a nutshell: *'Everybody in the coalfield knows that coal is fighting for its existence and the Yorkshire miners have reached the end of the road.'* Councillor Bill O'Brien, secretary of the North Yorkshire Panel of the NUM, commenting on coal board threats to close Park Mill Colliery during the strike, said: *'We have lived so long as mice that the coal board will still close pits, strike or not.'* The unofficial strike, which involved other coalfields, was a watershed. Left wing miners had almost forgotten what

it was like to organise a widespread strike. Involving 130,000 miners and 140 pits, the strike, like the 1893 and 1912 disputes, demonstrated what mass action could do. It was also significant because it started in Yorkshire with the so-called 'flying pickets,' the precursors of the famous pickets in the 1970s.

Miners, who had been at the top of the wages league after the war and who were still highly paid in 1958, were twelfth in 1970. Their deteriorating position in the league led to another strike. The majority in the strike ballot on pay was not large enough to warrant an official strike under union rules and the subsequent unofficial strike was patchy and disorganised. Lord Robens, chairman of the NCB, claimed irresponsible militants were breaking all the rules and agreements because they did not like the final offer. At Doncaster he was met by 'a yarling mob' of miners, Robens later believing that the mob was the new and unacceptable face of the union and that a new breed had been spawned, union bully boys. The strike demonstrated that the old relationship between the NCB and NUM was crumbling, that a change in the union rules

120

Arthur Scargill, President of the Yorkshire NUM, addressing a miners' gala in the 1970s.

on strike ballots was on the cards and that a new generation of young militants was flexing its muscles. In that year a number of rising union officials, including Arthur Scargill and Ron Rigby of Barnsley produced a pamphlet. *'Miners: Our Demands in 1970'* in which they warned that the nation could not depend on cheap oil from the Middle East in the 70s and that coal was crucial to the future energy needs of the nation. Demanding change in the coal industry through action, they wrote:

As miners we were becoming disillusioned by the contraction of the industry. We started to seek individual solutions. Many of us left the industry. Absentee rates were high. We lost faith in our national leadership. Conciliation, negotiation, compromise brought no real gains. The unofficial strike last October (on surface men's hours) changed all that. The strike forced the NCB to grant its biggest wage increase ever. It rejuvenated the miners. It raised morale.

Men like Scargill, then pit branch officials, started their rise to power at a time when the miners who had started work in the early 1920s and who were in general moderates, solid Labour Party supporters and anti-Communist, were retiring and the number of working men who had working experience of the hungry decades was diminishing. The new miners had not known poverty, victimisation at work and the 1926 lock-out and had, therefore, no hang ups about taking on a Government – perhaps even a Labour Government.

Having achieved some success on the strike front the NUM activists were set for the big strikes which rattled the Government and the nation in the 1970s. At the NUM conference in 1971 the delegates approved a resolution which, the union said, would give them a decent living. At the same time the conference changed the rules to make strikes easier, a sign that the rising tide of militancy was having an impact. Mr Scargill said later:

After the 1969 and 1970 disputes it was clear that things would not be the same again. The pressures on the right wing were so intense that they realised that if they did not do something about the rules of the union,

It was boom time for coal again in the mid 1970s and the *Chronicle* carried adverts each week for miners. The high wages offered halted the drift of workers away from the industry – for a few years at least.

the left and the rank and file would sweep them aside. So they changed the rules of the union to allow strike action to be called with a fifty-five per cent majority instead of the two thirds majority. This was the most decisive rule change in the history of the union. In 1971 we were able to mobilise in every coalfield; we wanted a vote for action and we got it. We had a fifty-seven per cent vote nationally.

After the board had rejected a pay claim, a special

By the 1970s and early 1980s mines which had been big producers of coal were facing closure through exhaustion. Rockingham Colliery at Hoyland Common, which had featured in the 1893 miners' lock out, closed and men were transferred to other collieries with 'brighter' futures. The photographs on this page show Rockingham in its prime at the beginning of the twentieth century and also on a date approaching its closure. On the opposite page is Elsecar Main Colliery, the lifeblood of the village, which also closed during the same period. Many men from that pit were transferred to Cortonwood and by 1984 they were facing redundancy again.

delegates' conference implemented a ballot on strike action and started an overtime ban. Starting in January, 1972, the strike had immediate success with the now famous flying pickets playing a crucial role, descending on pits, power stations and coal and coke depots. On Friday, 7 January the *Daily Express* declared:

> *A colliery shutdown will mean the death-warrant for more of the nation's uneconomic pits. The major victims of the strike will be the miners themselves.*

The response was the proverbial burp from the bottom of the pit shaft. At that time newspapers and the public had not been programmed to accept that miners were capable of crippling the nation, just as in early 1984 the miners had not been programmed to accept the concept of defeat. The important events in 1972 were the body blows to industry: power black outs, the lay offs and the famous Battle of Saltley coking depot in Birmingham where pickets with massive support from other trade unions closed the gates, a turning point in the strike. The events demonstrated that miners were capable of bringing the nation to its knees. To the Conservative Party the closure of the gates was due to ineffective Policing and the pickets' role in the battle was seen as a victory for bully boys. Such views shaped the policies of the future Conservative Government via the Ridley plan. Meanwhile, the Court of Inquiry headed by Lord Wilberforce said the miners had an exceptional case and recommended a twenty-seven per cent wage rise.

Arthur Scargill, who took a leading role in the Saltley incident, was becoming a national figure, vilified by the right and loved by the young militants. Flowing with the left wing tide in the coalfield he was elected the union's Yorkshire compensation agent and then president, filling the vacuum left by the retirement of the elderly moderate leadership. He represented a new type of leader: brash, assertive and articulate with a taste for big cars and executive style suits. He had a reputation as a man who refused to compromise, prompting one NCB official to declare: *'Scargill did not negotiate – he just wore you down.'* At their 1973 conference the national union prepared a wage claim of £35 a week for surface workers, £40 for underground workers and £45 for face workers. When the board rejected the claim in February, 1974, the miners voted eighty-one per cent in favour of strike action. Prime Minister Mr Edward Heath called a general election to try to obtain a vote of confidence from the electorate but the Labour Party won the election, after which they gave in to the miners.

With the dramatic rise in the price of Middle East oil – miners had been warning for years that Arabs would not want to live in tents all their lives – the new Labour Government decided that coal was the fuel of the future. Twenty years of decline in the industry were reversed and newspapers declared that King Coal was back on the throne. The Barnsley coalfield, badly hit by the closure

programme in the 1960s, received a massive injection of £400 million aimed at concentrating production on three centres, Woolley, Grimethorpe and South Kirkby.

The 'fly in the ointment' came in 1978 with the publication of the Ridley Report, which recommended that a Conservative Government build up maximum coal stocks at power stations; make plans for importing more coal; encourage the recruitment of non-union lorry drivers by haulage contractors to enable the NCB to move coal; and introduce coal/oil firing facilities at all power stations as quickly as possible. Mr Nicholas Ridley believed the greatest deterrent to any strike would be *'to cut off the money supply to the strikers and make the union finance them.'* On top of that he recommended the formation of a large mobile police force to uphold the laws against illegal picketing.

By the time the Thatcher Government was elected in May, 1979, politicians on the right were worried about both the NUM and the NCB, which they saw as an extension of the union. To anyone born within spitting distance of a coal mine, that seems to be an extraordinary view. The consensus in the pit communities had always been that the board, while an improvement on the old coal owners, were not angels and sometimes acted like a benevolent dictatorship. When the Government were

Earl Fitzwilliam Collieries Co. sunk two shafts between 1905 and 1908 at Elsecar to work the Parkgate seam. From 1924 the No.1 shaft was deepened to 534 yards to enable the Silkstone seam to be worked. The Thorncliffe seam, 20 yards below Parkgate, was reached by drifting from Parkgate and started producing coal in 1938. The Haigh Moor seam, 200 yards below Parkgate, was opened in 1945. More than one million tons of coal was 'got' from Elsecar Main in 1967. The pit closed in the 1980s. *Albert Walker*

Plastic meal tokens used for pit meals at Elsecar Main.
Kindly loaned by Frank Burgin, Hoyland

Seam closed for at least 9 months following tragedy

The National Coal Board wrote off equipment worth £750,000 this week when they sealed off the Newhill seam where five men were killed in a violent explosion last Thursday night.

The decision was taken by Mr. John Kiers, the board's Barnsley area coalfield director, after consultations with union leaders.

Teams of men worked over the weekend to put permanent 17ft. thick seals on the Newhill seam and part of the adjacent Melton Field seam because of a big build up of carbon monoxide.

Tubes have been left in the seals to monitor conditions in the sealed off faces but it isn't expected that any attempt to reopen the Newhill seam will be made for at least nine months.

Five men die in underground blast at Houghton Main

AS THE SUN SET on Thursday night, crowds of grim faced miners gathered in the yard of Houghton Main Colliery, just a short distance from the village of Little Houghton.

They had just heard that two of their workmates had died in a terrific underground explosion — 1,000 feet from the surface — that another man had serious burns, and three others were missing in the heat and dust.

The pit, which employs 1,350 men, had been cleared, and Grimethorpe Colliery, which is linked to Houghton, evacuated.

"This was a safety precaution," explained Mr. John Kiers, Area Director of the Coal Board, at a hurriedly called press conference in the pit offices.

He said: "The explosion appears to have been caused by gas. The rescue team found a big fall of roof on the main road and one of the dead men was found there."

Coaches arrived with men for the night shift, but except for two teams of hand-picked volunteers they were all sent home.

Mines rescue teams from Doncaster and Wakefield were quickly on the scene and set up their mobile units in the pit yard. Six ambulances waited near the colliery headgear.

On the warmest night of the year, families in the village chatted on the doorsteps while off-shift miners drank their pints in the open air at the working men's club, where there were relays of news from the pithead.

Pockets of men and women gathered at the entrance awaiting news of relatives. Some wives who arrived at the colliery offices were taken to a private room and given cups of tea.

As further rescue workers left the canteen after a briefing, their pit lamps revealed the first result of the tragedy, as an ambulance workers carried the injured man from the first-aid room to the awaiting ambulance.

It was nearing midnight, the crowd was silent, and the ambulance dashed away with a police car escort.

Then in the early hours, the name of the first dead man was revealed by a harassed-looking N.C.B. spokesman. He was named as Mr. Richard Bannister, a 31 years old development worker, of Coronation Avenue, Grimethorpe.

The spokesman also told reporters that Mr. Ken Upperdine, a 38 years old fitter, of George Street, Low Valley, Wombwell, was in Barnsley Beckett Hospital with facial burns and a fractured femur.

As rescue workers toiled through the night, surfacing only when their oxygen cylinders were exhausted, the extent of the tragedy became more apparent.

REMINDER

Quote by Mr. Benn: "This tragedy may remind people, as it has reminded me, that there is still a very high price to be paid in human life for the coal we get in this country."

YORKSHIRE NUM PRESIDENT Mr. Arthur Scargill with Energy Secretary Mr. Tony Benn at Houghton Main.

Energy Minister and NCB chief visit the pit

MR. TONY BENN, Secretary of State for Energy, was an early visitor to the pit on Friday morning and Sir Derek Ezra, chairman of the N.C.B., arrived about mid-morning.

Yorkshire N.U.M. president, Mr. Arthur Scargill and Mr. Owen Briscoe, secretary, and other union officials told Mr. Benn that they would like a public inquiry into the disaster.

SIR DEREK EZRA

The Energy Minister later paid tribute to the work of the rescue teams and expressed deep sympathy with the deceased's relatives.

Sir Derek and Mr. Scargill also praised the work done by the rescue workers.

Sir Derek said "I feel extremely distressed that this has happened. Fortunately we haven't been having many of these accidents lately, but it doesn't make them any less tragic when they do occur.

"Every time I hear of a fatality in the industry, it gives me increased determination to reach the year when we shall not have a single fatal accident.

"I believe it is possible because there are many pits that go for years without a fatality, and if they can do it then it can be done throughout the industry."

GRIM-FACED rescue workers wheel a victim from the shaft to the waiting ambulance.

Above and opposite page: The 1970s were a safey conscious era. The old days of big explosions and almost weekly roof falls had gone for ever. But the coal industry could still produce a few surprises. This is how the Barnsley Chronicle reported the tragedy at Houghton Main Colliery in 1975.

The phone call that saved a life

Fitter Ken Upperdine (38), made an underground 'phone call at Houghton Main Colliery last Thursday — and that saved his life.

He was on the phone when the explosion ripped through the Newhill seam, killing five of his colleagues.

Ken's father, Mr. Mark Upperdine, Palma Rise, Darfield, a former Darfield councillor, made the call some distance from the explosion. It blew him off his feet.

"If he had been working, he would have been killed".

Ken, George Street, Low Valley, had returned to work underground on Monday, after sustaining serious injuries in accidents at the pit.

He was off work for four months after he fractured a bone in his head and had a finger amputated in separate accidents.

His father, who worked at Houghton when six men died in a blast in the Melton Field seam 45 years ago, said: "Ken returned to work at Houghton a year ago. He had worked

THE 5 DEAD

The five men killed in the disaster were:
Mr. Richard Bannister (36), Coronation Avenue, Grimethorpe.
Mr. Irvin Lakin (55), Wath Road, Wombwell.
Mr. Arnold Williamson (59), Norfolk Road, Great Houghton.
Mr. Raymond Copperwheat (42), Narville Crescent, Darfield.
Mr. Leonard Baker, Charles Street, Little Houghton.

A sixth man, Mr. Ken Upperdine, George Street, Low Valley, is in Beckett Hospital, Barnsley, with serious burns and multiple injuries.

Five other men were treated for shock or minor injuries at the colliery. They were: Mr. Fred Woodcock, Mr. Roy Buckley, Mr. W. Arnold, Mr. D. Woodward and Mr. J. Pearson.

as a bus-driver for a time. His wife did not want him to go back, but he is a plucky sort of man."

Ken's son, Christopher, celebrated his 15th birthday on Friday. He has two other children, Tony, who is 14 this month, and Sheryll, who is 16 next month.

Development worker, Mr. Richard Maskell Bannister, said goodbye to his wife, Patricia, and three daughters at 4.30 p.m. on Thursday, and left for the colliery. They never saw him again.

Three hours later he was one of five men killed by the explosion, while working on a split-shift.

Mr. Bannister of Coronation Avenue, Grimethorpe, was born in Ardsley and attended schools in the Barnsley area. He married his wife at St. Joseph's R.C. Church, Kendray, and they moved to Grimethorpe about 11 years ago.

Since leaving school at the age of 15, Mr. Bannister had been employed at Houghton Main Colliery.

His mother-in-law, Mrs. Catherine Bradley of Raymond Avenue, Grimethorpe, said: "Although he lived at Grimethorpe, he maintained he would never leave Houghton Colliery.

RICHARD BANNISTER

"He enjoyed working a split-shift and thought it was the best one", she added.

KEN UPPERDINE

"He was a very conscientious worker, and you could tell he was worried, because he brought his work problems home".

DOUBLE FUNERAL

Mr. Williamson (59), worked at Houghton for 35 years. He leaves a widow and two daughters, Pamela and Sandra.

The two other men who died, Mr. Leonard Baker, 8 Charles Street, Little Houghton, and Mr. Roy Copperwheat (42), of Norville Crescent, Darfield were interred at Darfield yesterday (Thursday), after a double funeral service in the parish church.

Mr. Baker, who had worked at the colliery since he was 14, leaves a widow, Connie, who works in the pit canteen, a son, Danny (25), who is a clerk at the pit, and a daughter, Pat (22).

Mr. Lakin was interred at Wombwell cemetery on Wednesday, following a funeral service at Zion Wesleyan Reform Church, George Street, Wombwell.

The funeral service for Mr. Williamson was held at St. Helen's Parish Church, Thurnscoe, yesterday (Thursday) and was followed by interment at Thurnscoe cemetery.

Mr. Bannister will be buried at Ardsley cemetery today (Friday) after a service at St. Luke's Church, Grimethorpe, conducted by Father Eric Cheetham.

amount of work for the church. His main work concerned young people".

Another victim, Mr. Arnold Williamson, 2 Norfolk Road, Great Houghton, did not like working in the new seam.

His son-in-law, Mr. Graham Howell, a Brierley haulage contractor, said: "He said it was one of the worst places in which he had worked. Water was always coming into the seam.

BIBLE FOUND

A Bible, which was torn apart by the explosion, was found by a rescue team in the Newhill seam.

It belonged to one of the dead men, 55-years-old Mr. Irvin Lakin, 76 Wath Road, Wombwell, who was secretary of Lundhill Wesleyan Reform Church, whose wife, Dorothy, is a local preacher.

He also leaves two sons, Peter (31), an Environmental Health Inspector, who lives in Barnborough Road, and David (29), who is an Assistant Pastor in Birmingham.

Mr. John Hunt, an official at Lundhill said: "Mr. Lakin did a tremendous

Chronicle staff covering the tragedy: DON BOOKER, CLEM NEWHAM, JOHN THRELKELD and ALAN WHITEHOUSE. Photos by STAN BULMER and DON OAKES.

'RUMOURS AND ACCUSATIONS'

The South Yorkshire district coroner, Dr. Herbert Pilling, spoke about rumours and accusations when he opened an inquest on the five victims of the Houghton disaster at Barnsley on Tuesday.

"There have been quite a lot of theories (about the cause of the explosion) bandied about and a lot of rumours," he said.

"Indeed, there have been one or two accusations made publicly. This is very unfortunate in the circumstances, and I think the sooner we can have some sort of answers the better".

Dr. Pilling adjourned the inquest to July 29.

He said that because of difficulties, of which he had been told, it could be 12 months before investigations into the disaster were completed.

But he thought it was totally unreasonable to expect relatives to wait that long for a death certificate and for answers to

problems hanging over them.

The coroner said he hoped he would have enough evidence to reach a verdict about the cause of death of the five victims, when he resumed the inquest in six weeks' time.

If there were too many questions unanswered he would have to adjourn it again to such a time as answers were available, but he did not want to have to do this.

He added: "An inquest is a public inquiry and anybody who has anything relative to say can say it. You don't have to wait to be invited.

"It is a duty, never mind a right, to come and say it".

Formal evidence of identification was given by the deceased's relatives and by P.C. Sam Chambers, acting coroner's officer. Dr. Pilling issued burial certificates.

'I don't know how I escaped'

One of the men who survived the explosion, Mr. Ian Lee, a deputy at the colliery for 20 years, led two men, Mr. Fred Woodcock and Mr. Roy Buckley, to safety after the explosion.

The three men heard each other shouting but it was so dusty, as well as very hot and very dry, that they couldn't see each other, and they had to grope their way along the roadway.

"When we joined forces I found Fred and Roy were very shocked", said Mr. Lee. "They were almost in a state of panic and I did my best to calm them down a bit.

"Then the air began to clear".

The air continued to get clearer as they made their way to the safety of the pit bottom and Mr. Lee stumbled over his snap bag, which he had lost when the explosion occurred.

When he realised the full extent of the explosion, Mr. Lee said: "I don't know how I escaped injury.

"I wish I hadn't to go down a pit again, but I don't know any other job".

In the 1970s Houghton Main had its setbacks. However, it attracted a lot of investment and this photograph shows that modern mines had come a long way from the days of the glorified holes in the early chapters.

considering a successor to Sir Derek Ezra as chairman, Roy Mason was on their possible list. Describing him as a *'tough Labour moderate who understood Scargill,'* Nigel Lawson in his autobiography said *'Mason would not be disposed to contract out the running of the industry to the NUM or give the unions a veto over national policy.'* Mr Mason, now Lord Mason, has confirmed that Lawson submitted his name as a possible successor to Sir Derek adding: *'I did not get it from the horse's mouth but I gather I was turned down because Mrs Thatcher said: 'He is not one of us.'*" Perhaps that was a sign the Government were already looking for a blue-tinted axe man, rather than another Lord Robens; although he was an able man Robens was still, in the view of the Conservatives, an ex-Labour MP. Former NCB men would disagree with

Lawson on the alleged subordinate role the NCB played in the industry, but there was a grain of truth in his views, since the union seemed to have an extraordinary amount of power and influence in the 1970s and early 1980s. Or an illusion of power.

On the NUM side some leaders were convinced that a confrontation was inevitable from May, 1979. In his annual report for 1980, Mr Owen Briscoe, Yorkshire miners' general secretary, wrote: *'I, along with many others, am of the opinion that it is the intention of the Tory Government to decimate the coal industry,'* pointing out that Mrs Thatcher had agreed at a summit meeting on energy in Venice to expand the coal industry yet a few weeks later had ordered two nuclear stations. *'If that is not the height of hypocrisy, and a pointer to pit closures, then the moon is made of green cheese,'* he wrote. But that was it: no more words on pit closures. The rest of the report dealt with

Arthur Scargill (left) and Lord Mason (third from right), pictured in 1979 at the unveiling of a memorial to the mem who died in the Wharncliffe Woodmoor pit disaster. *John Marshall*

bathing and changing time payments (that was probably the most significant argument between the board and the union's Yorkshire area that year), the exploitation of black labour in South Africa and the danger of nuclear confrontation between the major powers, an indication that pit closures had not become a burning issue at that time, although Scargill, still Yorkshire president, was making threatening noises on projected pit closures. The situation changed rapidly. In 1981 Yorkshire miners gave their leaders permission to call a strike in the event of pit closures and the resolution was put in a filing cabinet to await the confrontation. Then Mr Ian MacGregor, aged seventy, and chairman of the Amax Corporation in the USA which had substantial coal mining interests, was appointed chairman of the NCB in 1983: a tough Scots American businessman chosen to reorganise the industry on business lines and to take on the NUM, particularly Scargill. By 1983 the industry was in turmoil. Management were taking a tougher line and miners, afraid their jobs were in jeopardy, became belligerent.

In his annual report presented in March, 1983, Jack Taylor, the Yorkshire miners' President, said:

I believe that very shortly this union will be put to the test in determining the future size and shape of the coal industry. Also at stake is the self-respect and credibility of the union. The future is in our hands.

The penultimate sentence is illuminating. Although the impending strike was chiefly over pit closures, there was also another element, the reputation the all-powerful miners had among their fellow trade unionists: the miners' leaders felt it was their responsibility to ram-raid the Government on behalf of others. When leaders like Taylor talked of 'credibility' and 'self respect' – and Scargill talked of bringing down the Government – the Conservatives took note and muttered about the enemy within. In his report, Mr Taylor also pointed out that the NCB had grown in confidence following the recent union leaders' defeat in the national ballot on wages and pit closures (in favour of industrial action: thirty-nine per cent nationwide, fifty-six per cent in Yorkshire): *'Their attitude at all levels of management has become less understanding and more intransigent. We now find ourselves confronted with a take it or leave it attitude.'* A strike that year at Dodworth Colliery was a sign of things to come in what had become a fractious industry. A relatively minor incident – a miner was sacked for allegedly striking a deputy – exploded like a powder keg. Dodworth sent pickets to all the Barnsley pits and, with miners refusing to cross picket lines, the Barnsley coalfield was at a standstill for a time; at the NCB's Barnsley area headquarters at Grimethorpe there were rumblings that union militants were stirring up trouble, trying to turn the Dodworth dispute into a major coalfield confrontation between employer and employees. However, Dodworth was more likely to have been a spontaneous outburst of pent up anger, a strike right from the gut of the rank and file with no one pulling strings. After all, deputies were more hated than pit managers and the miners demanded the reinstatement of their mate, described by the men as a gentle giant. Bloody-minded and stubborn the Dodworth miners – who had a

The expression in the faces reveal all. Arthur Scargill, Sir Derek Ezra, former chairman of the National Coal Board and Tony Benn, the Energy Minister, at Houghton Main Colliery, the day after the tragedy in which five men died, in 1975. *British Coal*

reputation for militancy – even clashed with their union branch delegate and area union leaders who recommended a return to work pending negotiations on the sacking; the leaders, including Jack Taylor, got it in the neck when they were heckled and booed at a belligerent mass meeting at Dodworth towards the end of the dispute. The reporters who attended that meeting said they could detect an explosive mixture in the air that day, an atmosphere they would feel again on the violent picket lines during the course of the year long strike. The Dodworth strike demonstrated that the old order in the industry, since the mid 1970s a cosy relationship between the lower ranks of the union and the NCB – some pit personnel officers and manpower officers at area level were former moderate NUM branch officials – was breaking down and chaos was spreading. It also revealed there was a prodigious amount of raw energy and anger just waiting to be released. Miners at Dodworth were not only ready to picket other pits – and Doncaster collieries, it was rumoured – they were prepared to confront and insult their own leaders. To the outsider it appeared as if no one was in charge of the rattling coal trains marked NUM and NCB.

In the run-up to the year long strike, during the NUM ban on overtime, similar pit strikes broke out all over the South Yorkshire coalfield, many of which were over petty issues. In contrast to the Dodworth strike it now seemed as if someone in the NCB or NUM was continually pushing a button marked 'strike.' Industrial relations having hit a new low, the union's Barnsley Miners' Panel were about to discuss the strikes when the NCB dropped a bombshell by announcing the closure of Cortonwood and Bullcliffe Wood in March, 1984, an illogical decision if the board wanted better industrial relations, since the

The coal face. This photograph and the others dealing with South Kirkby Colliery on subsequent pages show a modern mine that had received substantial investment. This is reflected in the quality of the equipment. In the 1980s the pit also had a capable management team. *British Coal.*

Barnsley seam, South Kirkby, showing the face entry. *British Coal*

closure of a pit with substantial reserves – Cortonwood – was bound to antagonise the union. It is already part of Labour mythology that the miners were set up for a strike, that Cortonwood, a moderate pit in the centre of the union's Yorkshire heartland, was selected for closure in order to bump-start the overtime ban into a strike. However, according to the then NCB Director for South Yorkshire, George Hayes, he had been asked to reduce capacity and Cortonwood was the obvious choice, the board having failed to sell Cortonwood coal which was piling up at the pithead. By closing Cortonwood at that time he could more or less guarantee miners jobs at other pits. Now it has been suggested in Paul Routledge's book, *Scargill* that the plan to strike in March may have been prepared months in advance by the NUM, not the NCB, and the journalist refers to a conversation between Jimmy Cowan, deputy chairman of NCB, and Mick McGahey, the NUM vice president, in which McGahey is alleged to have spilled the beans, saying the strike would start in March in Yorkshire. Later McGahey said he had been talking in general terms. Had March been fixed in advance as the date of the strike – and had Cortonwood not closed – what would the NUM have used as fuse paper? A pit had to close before a strike could be called. Much has been written about so-called conspiracy theories, mainly from the left wing who claim the state in cohorts with the NCB and Fleet Street engineered the strike and then ganged-up with the judiciary to nobble the miners. But perhaps there was no conspiracy on either side – just a cock-up!

On the day the closure was announced it took sometime

South Kirkby management team: left to right back row: W Bywater, B Simpson, D Thompson, A Hirst, J Henderson, J Sumnall, B Beverley.

before television grasped what was happening. The closure item was the third or fourth item on the evening regional television news programme that Friday night, a blatant error, for someone in the news room had not realised the significance of the event or perhaps the item had arrived too late for it to be given the appropriate treatment. For the subsequent year the strike was never off the television screens.

The significance of the closure was not lost on the miners. The 1981 resolution was removed from the filing cabinet and the strike began three days after the closure announcement by the National Coal Board, 55,000 Yorkshire miners stopping work. What followed was a year dominated by violence, hard poverty and searching questions on a series of issues, including the state of the coal industry, liberty, the power of the state, violence on both sides of the picket lines and the right of men to work during a strike. To digest the ramifications and present a balanced view of the strike is difficult even twenty years on, so the strike has been condensed into this timetable: On 8 March, the NUM executive gave official backing to the Yorkshire and Scottish strikes. By 13 March, 100,000 out of 180,000 were on strike in more than 90 of the country's 174 pits. Meanwhile the board announced a four million ton cut-back plan. On 16 March, the Nottinghamshire miners voted not to strike and on 12 April, Scargill ruled out a strike ballot. Towards the end of March the Central Electricity Generating Board claimed that power station coal stocks were at a record level for the time of the year. In mid-April former NUM delegate at Houghton Main, Terry Patchett, MP for Barnsley East, claimed Police had been bugging miners' phones. Hoax information sent out by miners on the phone resulted in

Police turning up at a meeting place, he said.

It became a violent strike with miners picketing pits in Nottinghamshire, rioting at Maltby Police Station in June and clashing with police at Orgreave the same month (ninety-three were arrested, seventy-nine injured). Peace talks collapsed in July. On 6 July, in the *Barnsley Chronicle,* the NCB strongly refuted claims that thousands of Barnsley pit jobs were at risk and that local pits were in serious decline. A spokesman for the board said: *'Our plans are to maintain a stable work force of between 12,500 and 13,000 mineworkers for many years to come.'* And on 1 August Nigel Lawson said the cost of the strike was a worthwhile investment for the country and it was essential that the Government spent whatever was necessary to defeat Scargill. In September there were on-off talks and on the 20th Derbyshire miners won 'a right to work' injunction. There were more violent clashes at Maltby on 24 September, when police appeared in boiler suits, and the Scottish courts declared the strike in their areas official and lawful. By October, at the Conservative Party conference, John Gummer and Leon Brittan were warning of a fight to the end against the miners. On 12 November Yorkshire saw the worst violence when petrol bombs were discovered. More men were going back to work and the NCB claimed there were 1,900 'new faces' on that day. At the Lord Mayor's banquet in London, Mrs Thatcher linked pickets with IRA bombers. On 17 December, MacGregor dashed the TUC peace talks and John Paul Getty donated £120,000 to relieve the distress of the miners. The 25 February was a critical date, when 3,800 abandoned the strike, a high figure, and the Welsh strike cracked for the first time. At a special delegates conference at Congress House in London ninety-eight voted for a return to work on 3 March; ninety-one were against. The strike was over.

The strike in 1972 had made Scargill's reputation, the

Servicing the shearer Barnsley seam, South Kirkby. *J B Norton*

Advancing powered supports, Newhill seam, South Kirkby. *J B Norton*

strike of 1984/85 broke his power and the back of his beloved union. Twenty years after it started, the strike is still debated, the causes and effects still mulled over. The former aide to Arthur Scargill, Roger Windsor, now a discredited figure in the ranks of the NUM, wrote later:

Let's face it, the NUM were never more than a bunch of amateurs trying to take on the might of the state. We lacked the cohesion, discipline and organisation to run any meaningful campaign, and were led by our Napoleon on to our battlefield at Waterloo.

In the book, *The Coal Strike, Christian Reflections of the Miners' Struggle*, published in 1986, Brian Jenner wrote:

Few of the Yorkshire miners seriously doubted that the Tories deliberately chose conflict with the NUM. Two years previously it had been avoided, but now the loyalty of police and judiciary was assured after massive pay rises. The appointment of MacGregor to run the NCB was seen as a declaration of war and indeed the confrontational style in which he handled the dispute, and which has hardly abated since its end, brought dismay to many senior coal board officials.

Dave Feickert, head of research at the NUM from 1983 to 1993, writing in *The Guardian* in October, 1993, stated:

If the strike was to be won as an industrial dispute, which it could have been, a deal would have had to be struck with the power unions early on. Indeed in May, 1984, Eric Hammond, the EEPTU electricians' leader, privately offered to ballot his power station members if the NUM would drop its political aims and ballot its own members. But Arthur found that politically unacceptable.

However, I believe that the strike failed because the NUM were still living in the 1970s, believing that old style picketing would win the day with some help from General

Arthur Scargill's last Yorkshire NUM Council meeting, in 1982, before becomiing President of the NUM. He is shaking hands with his successor as President of the union's Yorkshire area, Jack Taylor, with branch delegates looking on. Mick Carter (Cortonwood) is pictured far right on the front row. Mr Carter became a national figure during the 1984/85 miners' strike, which was sparked off by the threat to close his pit.

1983, when a miners' demonstration in Barnsley reflected the power of the union. By 1987 the union was a shadow of its former self. *Don Oates*

Winter. But the Government, beginning with the Ridley Report, had prepared for a confrontation, just as the Baldwin Government had done in the 1920s in the run-up to the 1926 General Strike. In 1925 Baldwin had backed off on the grounds that other trade unions would support the miners. Between 1925 and 1926 they built up stocks of coal, imported coal and prepared a plan to keep essential supplies running in the event of a General Strike. When the miners were locked out, the TUC ordered a General Strike which soon fizzled out and the miners had to struggle on alone. The miners had made the mistake of depending too much on the goodwill of other trade unions. History repeated itself when the Conservative Government backed down over closures in 1981. David Howell, Mrs Thatcher's Energy Minister, appearing on television in the latter stages of the 1984/85 strike, admitted that 1981 had not been the right time to take on miners. Coal stocks were relatively low and there was always a danger other trade unions would support the miners. By 1984, however, the trade unions were in retreat, the nation was sitting on mountains of coal and public opinion was against Scargill, who had become a figure of fun and the man-you-love-to-hate in the media.

Not everyone would agree that the Government and the NCB were the villains, since Arthur Scargill's election as President of the NUM was seen by the Government as a confrontational move, a throwback to the bad old days of the 1970s when the unions were said to have too much power; and he was elected with a staggering majority in 1982 – before MacGregor's appointment. In his autobiography, The View from No. 11, Lord Lawson said a strike was inevitable as soon as Scargill was elected,

Yorkshire miners' demonstration in Barnsley, 1983.

describing the NUM president as *'a self-confessed, class-war revolutionary,'* a man *'who spouted the most amazing nonsense'* when they met soon after Scargill's election and whose decision to start the strike in spring was *'astonishingly inept.'* Scargill not only disturbed the Government he frightened some of his own members. There was a great deal of pre-strike opposition to him in some of the coalfields, particularly in Nottinghamshire, and I knew of some clandestine meetings involving pit winders from all over the country in Nottinghamshire long before the strike, meetings which had been called because of what they saw as Scargill's volatile and dangerous style of leadership. He was seen as a wrecker, a man who would destroy the union as well as the industry. The aim of the meetings: to test the water for a breakaway union of winders. Winders, who were in charge of the pit cages, always felt they were superior to miners and until about forty years ago had their own union. The strike intervened and I heard no more about the meetings but within a few

months the breakaway union, the Union of Democratic Miners, emerged in Nottinghamshire. Lord Lawson, in his autobiography, said the anti-Scargill attitude of the Midland miners helped them to win the strike, pointing out that a decision to persuade Michael Heseltine to consider the second application by the NCB to develop the Vale of Belvoir was used as a sweetener to the miners.

There was criticism about Scargill nearer home. As Brian Jenner wrote in *The Coal Strike:*

Contrary to some of the media images, support for the NUM leadership, as personified by Arthur Scargill, was by no means total and by no means uncritical, even in militant South Yorkshire. But if hard things were sometimes said against their own leaders, it was for Margaret Thatcher and Ian MacGregor that the real anger was reserved.' Since the strike the pit closure programme has validated Scargill's predictions, according to his supporters; but when people say that he deserves credit because he had been right in his repeated predictions on projected closures, one of my friends, a former NUM branch official, replies: 'That only proves

Dodworth Colliery, scene of a pit strike in 1983.

that he was given confidential reports and that he can read.

In the opinion of many people Scargill is seen as the man who destroyed his union and the industry. But the strike would have occurred with or without Scargill. The Government were determined to make the industry pay its way – at any cost – and that meant pit closures on a large scale with large cuts in manpower. The miners would have had to stand and fight at some time; the history and the spirit of the union demanded it and perhaps that, in the end, was their most poignant weakness. That was as much the fault of the union, its philosophy and its structure as Scargill. It has been said that things would have been different under wily Joe Gormley, Scargill's predecessor, but Gormley was successful in the post 1975 period because he had a close working relationship with Sir Derek Ezra, the chairman of the NCB, and Ezra had gone by 1984, succeeded by men who would not compromise. Like Scargill, Gormley would have found himself in the same box canyon facing the new hard men in the NCB with the same shadowy Government figures lurking in the background. It is all hypothetical but what could Gormley have done but strike? Execute a strategic withdrawal from the canyon with the voices of young Cortonwood miners ringing in his ears: *'You sold us down the river!'* No miners' leader, moderate or militant, would have been prepared to do that. Scargill has also been criticised for prolonging the strike and putting his members through a winter of hardship. I am not sure whether Scargill could have pulled the plug on the strike – even if he had wanted to do so. As

the Dodworth strike demonstrated in 1983, the union leaders are not always in control of events. In 1984 there was a hard-core of militants who were bitter-enders and whose slogan 'We told Arthur no surrender' could be seen around the coalfield. Had Scargill surrendered, they would have crucified him, ripping apart the union. After Christmas, 1984, most of the pickets and activists realised it was all over but they wanted to soldier on until March to notch up the first anniversary.

To some extent I feel sorry for some pit managers and middle management in British Coal because they may have been conned. Whereas miners have always treated coal owners, the National Coal Board and the Government with justifiable scepticism, the white collar workers went along with the dismantling of the industry convinced that it would not go too deep but they, too, have found themselves without jobs. The Government assault on the industry was also an attack on the whole ethos of the NCB and its past. They were intent on breaking up the NCB as well as the union.

Nearly fifty years after nationalisation, the coal wheel turned full circle. The Government, convinced that nationalisation was out of date, privatised the mines, resurrecting what most people believed had been become an extinct species, coal owners. On 25 June 1993, an ad appeared in *The Daily Telegraph* requesting tenders to buy Grimethorpe and Houghton, the last pits in the old Barnsley coalfield. Back in 1983 it was a different picture with the NCB predicting in *The Barnsley Chronicle* that all the Barnsley pits would make a £25 million profit in 1984/85, which turned out to be the year of the strike. Was that true? Or was it part of a propaganda war to win the minds of the miners in the pre-strike period? As late as

1981 the NCB had described the coalfield re-construction as 'one of the most extensive rejuvenation exercises in industrial history.' Barnsley's eighteen pits and 15,000 miners would move into the twenty-first century on 'a secure and profitable footing.' An article in *Barnsley, An Industrial Heritage,* published by Barnsley Chamber of Commerce added:

> *...by 1984 when we (NCB) start to reap the full benefits of our major schemes, Barnsley will be one of the most productive and profitable areas in the country.*

When the strike ended in 1985 the cut-backs started almost immediately, Barnsley pits losing 3,000 jobs within four months in the biggest shake-out of labour for more than twenty years, and a further 2,000 in 1986, dashing any hopes that the coalfield would make a profit, dashing hopes that the coalfield would survive into the twenty-first century. As well as pits, the area offices at Grimethorpe, which employed 500 workers, were closed and staff offered redundancy or transferred to new North Yorkshire headquarters at Allerton Bywater. Woolley Colliery, once one of the largest in Barnsley with more 2,000 on the books, closed in 1987, two years after North Gawber had been merged with Scargill's former pit. Then followed the closures of Redbrook, Riddings/Ferrymoor, Darfield Main, Royston, South Kirkby, Barnsley Main, the Denby Grange group of pits and finally Grimethorpe and Houghton Main.

The Barnsley coalfield had been one of the largest in the country and before the First World War the pits had exported to Russia, Germany and France: the high quality steam coal fuelled French warships as well as crack steam expresses in this country. In ten years, between 1983 and 1993 the pits were wiped out and more than £400 million investment (at 1980s values) went down the tube.

Strike Memories

Jackie Keating, a miner's wife, of Dearne Road, Brampton, discovered that the miners' strike of 1984/85 had a profound impact on her. In one respect, the strike challenged accepted beliefs – her attitude towards the police underwent a transformation, their actions causing

nightmares. Mining communities, harassed, impoverished and isolated, became societies within a society, governed by their own rules and regulations. In another respect the strike opened up a new world. She

Cortonwood at the beginning of the strike.

wrote *'Our Pit, Our Town'* a moving, honest appraisal of life in the strike. This is an extract:

> *Triona arrived at my home one evening near to Christmas, with Jenny. I was extremely surprised because I hadn't had any contact with Triona since May, and Jenny I hadn't seen much of since my departure from the Action Group. I was quite surprised that Triona had even remembered me let alone gone to the trouble of finding my home. She was very interested in how my own family were coping, and how my parents were. I had spoken of them at length during our last meeting. Fortunately for her, and unfortunately for me, she had caught me at a very upsetting and vulnerable time. Monday of that week had seen some terrible scenes, rioting and violence from both police and miners alike. I had been asked to give first aid to a middle-aged man who had a gaping gash in his leg, showing the bone. Don came and took over and tried to stem the bleeding, while I ran to a friend of ours to use her first aid box. Her first aid box was pretty comprehensive and she always kept the box fully equipped. Ours, unfortunately, being quite small had dwindled and because of lack of money we hadn't been able to replenish items used out of it. After helping the man to hobble to Jenny's house, Don went up to where the rioting was going on at the top of Dearne Road, to try to find his friends and to have the man taken off to hospital. It was no good trying to get an ambulance for*

The start of the big strike: March, 1984. Yorkshire miners' President Jack Taylor (right) and General Secretary, Owen Briscoe, announce that the miners' council have decided to call a strike over the closure of Cortonwood. *John Marshall*

Police, mounted and on foot, line up for a night of confrontation with pickets in Knollbeck Lane, Brampton, near Cortonwood Colliery. The trouble started after a miner went back to work before the end of the strike.
Tony Simpson

Mounted police in the gardens of pensioners' bungalows at Cortonwood.
Tony Simpson

Cortonwood in late 1984, a bowling green roller was pushed down Knollbeck Lane towards the police lines. The roller came to rest on the canal bridge. The slogan, 'We told Arthur no surrender', was removed just before Her Majesty the Queen visited Brampton and Wombwell after the strike. *Tony Simpson*

him as it wouldn't have got through the mayhem. As I walked down the road all hell broke out. Men chased by riot police charged down the road and through gardens. There was screaming and yelling going on all around me. One young lad was caught by a couple of officers who were hitting him with batons. The last time I saw him nine or ten police officers were round him, scuffling. I became aware that more policemen were charging towards me. I began to run; I could hear heavy boots getting nearer and nearer.

On reaching my gate I saw Nikki's frightened face at the window. I was so terrified by this time, expecting at any moment to be hit at the back of my head, that I was fumbling with the door key for what seemed an eternity. First the key wouldn't go in the lock, then my fingers couldn't turn it. I almost fell through the door, slammed it shut and locked it. I was shaking so much by this time I felt as if my legs had turned to water. Both children came running, Darren from upstairs and Nikki from the living room. 'Where's dad?' they asked. Not knowing, I said 'He'll be coming home soon.' The minutes passed and we all heard the yells and sounds of splintering wood, then all went quiet. How much longer passed I don't know, but the shouting and loud noises could still be heard. Sirens sounded in the distance. Then the high pitched sirens of the police vehicle came closer. We all ran to the window to see the doors of the houses opening. Men of all ages and sizes were running into the houses. Remembering that youth I had seen, I ran and opened my door too. About seventeen men ran into my house. Before any police officers came in sight I locked the door again, and ran to make sure the back door was locked. Back in the living room one of the men had the children sitting together on a chair talking to them. Most of the other men were either sitting round the walls or lying on the carpet. 'Come away from the window, love,' one said. 'If the police see you with pickets in your house they will wreck the place.'

About ten minutes later one of the men looked out of

Night convoy. Police vehicles escort working miners into Cortonwood Colliery. *Tony Simpson*

the window and asked if there was a back way out. They left a few minutes later, but the man who had taken care of the children on first entering the house, asked where my husband was.

After I answered quietly that I didn't know, and that he was out there somewhere, he said: 'Lock this door. Don't open it for anyone, only your husband and keep the kids away from the window.' With that he left, but he did wait to make sure I had locked up. They all went over the back fence. Back to the trouble or back home I don't know. One thing I did know was that the few minutes those miners were in my home I felt safer, and without being told I knew they would have looked after me and the children. I can't say the same for the police. Believe me, that takes quite a bit of getting used to.

We all ran to the door when we heard Don's knock (he always knocks in a certain way). I still checked at the window first before unlocking the door. Both children threw their arms around him, hugging him tight; he looked at me and asked if I was all right. Untangling himself from the children he gave me a quick hug and began to tell me how he had managed to avoid the

A photograph which sparked off a row. During a night of violence at Cortonwood some petrol bombs were found by police officers. Later it was claimed the policeman pictured with the bombs was, in fact, a soldier in police uniform, a claim denied by South Yorkshire Police Authority.

Cortonwood Colliery was the scene of some of the worst violence in Barnsley during the strike. A police officer points to a hole in a vehicle, probably caused by a ball-bearing fired from a picketline. *Tony Simpson*

Women's Day of Action in Barnsley in May 1984. Women played an important role during the miners' strike. *John Marshall*

Christmas at the Alamo, the pickets' hut at Cortonwood, in 1984. The pickets could still raise a smile despite the depressing news on the strike front.

Violent scenes erupted outside the Yorkshire NUM offices shortly after the start of the miners' strike in March 1984. Yorkshire NUM President, Jack Taylor can be seen talking to a police officer near the Victoria Road entrance to the offices. A large number of miners had gathered at the headquarters after rumours that the union's assets were to be seized, resulting in brief clashes between miners and policeman. *John Marshall*

Miners and their wives in a festive mood at a rally in Barnsley during the year long miners' strike.

police. Some of the men at the back of the crowd were throwing stones so the police charged. Don, having located some of the injured man's friends, was taking them to him when the charge started. Every man ran but Don. Using his army training, he jumped over the wall into the Chapel garden, lying very still until it had all gone quiet. If you run, then you draw attention to yourself. He was walking down the road later when the second charge ensued. This time he took cover in Jenny's house, checking on the injured man who was by this time going into shock. Luckily a couple of his friends had taken refuge in her house as well and, after the second police charge, they quickly fetched the car and took him away to hospital. We didn't hear about the man again but that injury must have left quite a scar.

Then Don's bleeper suddenly started up. (He was a part-time fireman). He ran out of the back door shouting to me to lock up and not let anyone else in the house. The last we saw of him was vaulting over the back fence.

Don ran through the garages at the back of the houses and out onto the street behind ours, Chapel Avenue. Then he came up to the police cordon across the main street in Brampton, where he was suddenly grabbed. 'Where do you think you are going?', bellowed one of the officers. 'I've just got a fire call', Don replied, grabbing hold of his bleeper out of his pocket. Finally, believing him, the officer said 'OK mate, down there' and pointed in the opposite direction.

'I know the way. I've only been going seven years', Don yelled back, by this time leaving the police behind and running into no-man's land (the gap between the police and pickets). The sky was full of stones, housebricks and bottles. Don never knew how he avoided a direct hit; he managed by zig-zagging those twenty yards. He jumped on the fire tender and they then followed the tender which had already left, manned by full time firemen. They were already putting out the fire, started during the rioting, near to the police cordon. The police then

Ryhill soup kitchen during the miners' strike.

Arthur Scargill at a rally in Barnsley, probably towards the end of the strike.

THE MINER
SPECIAL ISSUE
JOURNAL OF THE NATIONAL UNION OF MINEWORKERS

SATURDAY, JULY 14th, 1984

THE CRACKS ARE SHOWING

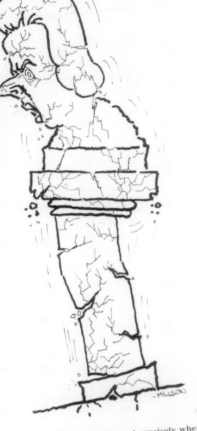

The NUM is heading for the greatest industrial victory in the post-war history of Great Britain.

With Government policies in a state of industrial siege — and financial mayhem growing by the day — both Coal Board and Government are on the rack.

Solidarity action and financial support is being stepped up dramatically by members of the public and the unions. People in all walks of life scent that victory is in the air.

The dramatic fall of the pound, which in turn forces higher interest rates and affects inflation, is ripping Government policies apart.

Billions of pounds have been wiped off share values and the squeals of the businessmen are getting louder by the day.

Retreat in the face of the railmen, Liverpool Council, local government elsewhere, remaining GCHQ union members — and total failure to use anti-trade union laws — is destroying Government credibility at a rate of knots.

STRENGTHENED HAND

A massive addition to the Government's problems is the knowledge that the NUM is now more united than at any time since the start of the strike, with the special two-day annual conference in Sheffield *unanimously* passing a sweeping resolution outlining NUM policy and determination to win a resounding victory.

The NUM goes into the next round of talks with the Board on July 18th with its hand immensely strengthened.

The Board itself is already privately admitting that it has lost disastrously, but wants to avoid mentioning this in public so as to save the Government's face.

But the NUM is fully aware of the dirty tricks department and has made it absolutely plain that the closure list must be *withdrawn* and that there will be NO closures on economic grounds.

The NUM position was clearly spelled out at the Edinburgh talks of a week ago and that position was backed wholeheartedly by the National Executive Committee and the Sheffield Conference.

In key-note speeches at the Conference, the national leadership and delegates were in a mood of cast iron determination to notch up the greatest industrial victory ever recorded.

WORLD ADMIRATION

President Arthur Scargill set the tone in his Presidential Address:

"The magnificent courage and determination of our people will see us through to victory," he pledged.

"Over the past 18 weeks I have witnessed among our rank and file a degree of loyalty, commitment and dedication to principle that has roused admiration around the world.

"I have always felt proud and privileged to be a member of this union but never more proud than at the present time."

The President paid particular tribute to the young miners and their wives who had confounded all predictions.

Together they had inspired "a community solidarity the like of which we have never witnessed in any industry or any union ever before."

It was a theme taken up by General Secretary Peter Heathfield in his annual address. All the predictions that mortgages and HP commitments would ensure that young miners would never fight had been shown to be total hogwash.

"They have shown clearly and precisely where their loyalties lies. They have proudly taken up the struggle of their fathers and grandfathers.

"They had endured brutal police intimidation, appalling media attacks and terrible levels of hardship, but had not flinched.

"They had inspired the whole country."

National Vice-President Mick McGahey said this was the greatest strike he had ever been involved in; with a young President leading young members.

"I would hate to be a scab."

The involvement of the young womenfolk was historic and if they had been involved on such a scale in 1926, "we would never have been defeated."

As for the £ crisis, he said that many workers were forced to suffer crisis every day of their lives — "from the womb to the tomb."

MAGNIFICENT RAILMEN

● ASLEF leader Ray Buckton was given a prolonged standing ovation by conference in deep appreciation of the magnificent support of the railmen.

Glowing tributes were paid to the "marvellous men of ASLEF, the NUR, the NUS and the transport workers who were lifting the whole dispute to a resounding victory."

Their support will never be forgotten and would be repaid a thousand times, NUM President Arthur Scargill pledged.

THE KEY RESOLUTION

The key resolution read:
'This extraordinary Annual Conference, meeting in the 18th week of a strike against pit closures and job losses, reaffirms previous Conference decisions to oppose all pit closures other than on grounds of exhaustion, and any reduction in manpower levels; and reaffirms the decisions of the Special Delegate Conference held on 19th April, 1984.

Conference calls for an expanding and developing industry in line with Plan For Coal. The Government must allocate the same financial assistance to our coal industry as is given to nearly all our competitors. At the same time, Britain must begin to build coal-fired power stations, develop combined heat and power programmes, intensify development of the liquefaction project, the gasification scheme, and fluidised bed combustion.

This will ensure an increasing demand for coal, allowing our industry to fulfill the targets projected in Plan For Coal, and leading towards an annual output of 200 million tonnes as we move into the next century.

Against a background in which the increased use of new technology has combined with a substantial rise in productivity, we demand settlement of the 1983 wages claim. This includes the introduction of the four-day working week, retirement at 55 for all miners on the same terms as those contained in the Redundant Mineworkers' Payment schemes, consolidation of the incentive bonus scheme, implementation of a rate protection scheme (promised in 1981) and all other claims contained in the Union's submission to the Board in 1983.

This Conference places on record its proud acknowledgement of the magnificent achievements of all our members on strike who, together with their families, are providing a lead and an inspiration to the entire British working class.'

An embarrassing headline. The miners were, in fact, heading for defeat. Front page of the union newspaper, *The Miners*.

positioned themselves with shields in front, saying they would give them full cover. Getting on with the business of running a hose reel out, Don found this bit about 'taking care' of him highly amusing. One minute he was an enemy, next a hero! After this incident I teased him terribly about being Wurzel Gummidge and whether he had his good or bad 'head' on.

Almost immediately the atmosphere became charged. A man Don knew called W.... began to yell 'Scab, you're nothing but scabs' and began insulting the fire crew saying to the men that the fire crew were miners and they had scabbed by doing another job. The crowd became very hostile, joining in the chanting of 'Scab, scab'. Don suddenly snapped, ran up to the man and grabbed him by the throat, threatening to rearrange his face if he didn't stop exacerbating the situation. A senior officer dragged him off and made him get back into the cab of the fire tender and cool down. On returning to the fire station, Don and the other retained crew were called in front of the divisional officer. Before the officer could say anything Don owned up to being the one involved. He was carpeted over the incident, but over-all the officer was quite understanding and made no bones about it not happening again.

It wasn't the end of the incident because Don was determined to have it out with this bloke, who suddenly disappeared from the face of the earth and didn't surface again for a couple of weeks. The N.U.M. heard about the trouble and it was brought up at the next union meeting. It was pointed out that the retained firemen had been doing their job for many years and when the bleepers activate they haven't a clue what the job is until they are getting on the tender. Another thing people don't realise is that all 999 calls go through to Sheffield and not to the local fire stations. So the call that day could easily have been to innocent citizens trapped in their homes. Don and the rest of the crew received a round of applause for the work they do and never again did any problems occur involving them. W.... eventually apologised to the fire station and to Don. He was sacked from Houghton Main pit a few weeks later for stealing 'scrap' from Elsecar pit.

Aftermath

I have written at length about the riots in Brampton and what a devastating effect they had on me. I didn't, however, mention that the day the major one happened, Don and I decided that our children would not witness any more chases or violence of any kind. We arranged for my

Cortonwood Colliery, 1984. *Stan Bulmer*

parents to look after them. They (her parents) lived in a mixed community and were quite a distance from any mine, so had not seen the scenes we had. Packing their cases for them and watching them walk up the street with Don made me feel so angry. I wanted to run to the riot vans where the police officers were sitting so arrogantly, and yell at them to go away and leave us all alone. After the

Arthur Scargill.

Below and above: The long road back: miners return to work at Grimethorpe and Havercroft.

Confrontation between miners and police outside the Yorkshire NUM offices, Barnsley, March 1984.

The fitters' shop at Cortonwood.

The pit yard.
Cortonwood Colliery, 1984, D. Colborn

The pit buzzer at Cortonwood.

Maurice Peaker (manager) and Paul Lewis (deputy manager, South Kirkby (Newhill seam), 1985. *J B Norton/British Coal*

children left the atmosphere became more and more tense. Anyone going about their own business would find themselves being watched by the officers sitting around in the vans. People became more and more upset, then a rumour started circulating that the police were to impose a curfew on the village. This just added to the problem and people would gather in small groups discussing the situation. The anger seemed to be reaching gigantic proportions, so much so that the air seemed to be full of hostility.

The police must have realised just how bad the situation was becoming and began visiting the local shops to say they had no intention of imposing anything like that and would people just calm down and go home. This eased the situation, and the atmosphere became calmer, although there was still a sort of rumbling going on just under the surface and it wouldn't have taken much to ignite the whole situation again.

I became terrified of police officers. If any of them passed in a van, or on a bike, I would feel threatened by them, and if ever the Metropolitan Police were known to be in the area, the atmosphere would instantly become hostile. These policemen were notorious for using unnecessary violence against people, and had become known as the 'Gestapo'. Like the original group of that name they enjoyed their work enormously.

During the days of the riots the police began to stop the buses from running through Brampton. They would board the buses at the Yorkshire Traction bus depot and tell everyone who wanted to go into the village to get off and walk. This included the old and young alike.

Sue, my neighbour, came to our house one day, shaking and upset by one such incident. She had been on her way home after doing some shopping, to be home in time to collect her young son from school. She, like the rest, was told to walk. She told them she would be late to meet her son. It didn't make any difference, she still had to get off. She was so worried, not knowing what Andrew would do if he left school to find no mummy. Would he wait? Or would he try to cross the road to make his own way home? Luckily he was late out of school, and was standing looking for her at the gate when she arrived breathless and carrying the shopping bags.

We just couldn't believe that police officers could be so dense – aren't there any fathers in the police force any more? And what would they have done if their wives had been prevented from collecting their children from school on time?

After sleepless nights caused by the rioting, the village became quieter; it was nice to go to bed for some undisturbed sleep. But every time I fell asleep I would have violent nightmares about the police chasing me through gardens. It would always be the same: I would be running and running with nowhere to hide; at the point where I was grabbed by the hair from behind, with lots of other police officers crowding round, I would wake up,

Cortonwood before closure. *D Colborn*

North Gawber Colliery, merged with Woolley in 1985.

Demolition at Cortonwood. *Stan Bulmer*

Darfield Main Colliery, 'closed' in 1985, then reprieved and later merged with Houghton.

Going... going... the chimney is demolished at Elsecar Main Colliery in 1985, later to be followed by the rest of the pit. *Don Oakes*

The old Elsecar branch of the miners' union banner discovered in a box at a Hoyland snooker hall in 1988.

NUM officials at a mass meeting called to dismiss the proposed closure of Woolley and Redbrook Collieries in 1987. From left to right: Eric Richardson (Redbrook), Jack Taylor, Yorkshire Miners' President, Mr Derek Reeves, NUM area agent, Arthur Scargill, NUM President, and Terry Patchett, MP for Barnsley East.

Redbrook Colliery which closed in 1987.

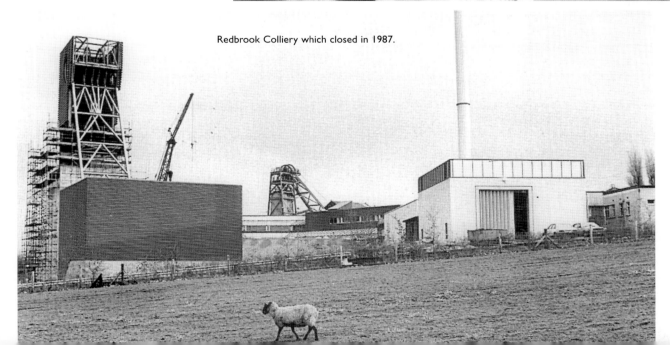

The ghost pit. Woolley Colliery, once one of the biggest pits in Barnsley, employing 2,000 men, closed in 1987. Photographer Don Oakes, a frequent visitor to the colliery in its prime, said there was an eerie atmosphere in the empty pit yard when he visited the pit on the last day.

The shafts at Cortonwood were capped in 1988. Colin Fletcher, a former Barnsley Chronicle photographer, captured the sombre mood hanging over the colliery site that summer. After the pit closure, the surface buildings and headgear were demolished in almost indecent haste, as if everyone wanted to eradicate the bitter memories of the largest industrial dispute since 1926 as quickly as possible. The brass plaque on one of the shaft pillars was soon removed by a souvenir hunter. The pit site is now a booming business and retail park.

Barrow branch of the NUM banner and miners, appearing at the National Miners' Gala in Barnsley in June 1989. Barrow Colliery closed at the end of the miners' strike and the men transferred to the new Barnsley Main Colliery. But the banner survived. *Stan Butler*

Barnsley Main was closed in the 1960s. After the 'Plan for Coal' the then National Coal Board announced it would be reopened. At the end of the year long miners' strike in 1985 Barrow Colliery was closed and the men transferred to the new mine, one of the most modern in the world. In 1989 it was said the colliery was making a profit but the pit closed within two years. Its reserves could not be mined economically. Much of the coal was under residential areas and the cost of repairing subsidence damage made the extraction expensive.

terrified. This went on for a week or more. I was worn out
by working and not daring to go to sleep. I began to dread
the nightmares. They were so real and I just didn't want to
go to sleep in case I was back in the gardens again.

I had read somewhere that to conquer your fears you
had to first face up to whatever it is that frightens you. So
I decided to 'face' up to the police by walking through a
police line. I had to stop those wretched nightmares
somehow. Of course thinking and putting into practice the
thoughts are quite, quite different. Reaching the top of
Dearne Road and looking down to where the 'Alamo' was,
with the double police line and what seemed like
thousands of pickets (probably fewer than a hundred in
reality), I confess I would have liked to turn around and go
back home, back to my own four walls. Don asked me if I
had changed my mind and if I was still determined to go
through with it. I could quite easily walk up to my parents
along the alternative road leading out of Brampton.

He walked with me, up to the last few yards before the
police line. He was staying as part of the picket. I was
expecting at any time to be grabbed, as in the dream. It all
seemed to happen in a haze. The next thing I remember is
walking past the riot vans full of more police officers. They
were there as a back-up, in case of trouble breaking out.

I turned to Don to let him know I was all right. He gave
me the thumbs up sign and waved. I asked him later if I
looked as terrified as I felt, and he said that apart from
being white I looked quite normal.

Looking back, I can laugh about it; time heals. But I was
glad at the time that no-one could see the 'real' me who
was a quaking wreck inside. It did stop the nightmares. I
only had them occasionally after that, if anything
happened to trigger them off again.

Darfield Main colliery.

Houghton Main branch of the NUM, Yorkshire miners'
gala, 1987.

Darfield Main Branch of the NUM at the 100th Yorkshire miners' gala
in 1987

Something to smile about... miners pictured with a young lady after Houghton/Darfield Main produced a million tonnes of coal in 1988. *British Coal*

Above: The village of Grimthorpe. *Don Oakes*

Above right: Grimethorpe Colliery. *Don Oakes*

One of the biggest coal preparation plants in Europe at Grimethorpe, in the 1980s. Note the size of the parked cars. *British Coal*

It was not all gloom and doom in the 1980s. Grimethorpe Colliery created a record when they produced five tonnes per manshift in 1988. *British Coal*

Royston Drift on the point of closure. Men waiting to be deployed on the afternoon shift.

Anton Want

A group of Grimethorpe miners pictured at the pithead, waiting to go underground to deal with a fire caused by methane gas, in September 1989. More than £20 million of coal reserves and equipment were sealed off in the coal face.

Chapter 7

1990s

The Long Goodbye

'*It is an extraordinary Government that can make Arthur Scargill a hero'*, said Patrick Hannan on a news programme, *Tea Junction* on BBC Radio 4 in April, 1993. Probably the most hated man in this country in the 1970s and 1980s Arthur led a march for jobs through some of London's wealthiest areas in October, 1992, and was mobbed by admirers. The same people who had jeered at miners and shaken fists at the television screens during the 1984/85 Miners' Strike were now applauding the miners because the Government had become more unpopular than miners, and that takes some achieving! '*He was the man they loved to hate'*, trumpeted the *Daily Mirror* the following day.

> *But yesterday, thanks to bungling John Major, Arthur Scargill was both a hero to rich and poor. In swanky Park Lane, an admirer handed Arthur a bouquet of white chrysanthemums – and even the Police shared in Arthur's delight.*

The whole nation seemed to be behind Arthur and the miners after the Government had announced the big pit closure programme in October: thirty-one pits and 30,000 job losses. For the first time in more than fifty years miners were receiving widespread public support and Arthur, vilified by the tabloids for decades, chimed with the times. These were indeed extraordinary times. President of the Board of Trade, Mr Michael Heseltine, was castigated for his handling of the closures – small when compared to the scale of the closures in the 1960s, during which one out of every two jobs in the industry vanished, and to the 70,000 job losses announced by British Telecom in the early 1900s – and there was a backbench revolt by Tory MPs led by Winston Churchill, grandson of the man the miners loved to hate: a figure who was despised by two generations of miners. Scargill and a Churchill on the same side? Strange bedfellows indeed; Arthur's late father, a miner who lived through that appalling decade, the 1920s, would have been nonplussed. Tory MP Michael Clark admitted: '*The Government has misread the mood of the country and the mood of the miners. They do not want charity.*'

The groundswell of public indignation against the proposed closures was not just motivated by a sense of injustice or love of miners; there had been a growing cynicism about the new Government since its election in April, 1992, and the closures proved to be a catalyst. (A similar mood, cynical and corrosive, had been detected in America where big government was under attack from public opinion, a mood which led to the election of an outsider, Bill Clinton, as President in November, 1992). It is difficult to get excited when the Government is booted out of the Exchange Rate Mechanism or euphoric when discussing the finer points of the Maastricht treaty, but 'blood on coal' is an emotive and straightforward subject, the massaging of which enables a nation to let off frustration and steam. Later, with rising unemployment and further gaffes by the Government, the sting went out of public protests on pit closures and when the pits closed there was hardly a whisper of protest from the general public. The popularity of the Government continued to slide and by May, 1993, it was said to be the most unpopular since the war, Gallup revealing that the

In August 1992, the statue on the Oaks Disaster Monument at Kendray had to be removed for repairs. The monument had stood since 1913. In October 1992, the closure of the last Barnsley pits was announced.

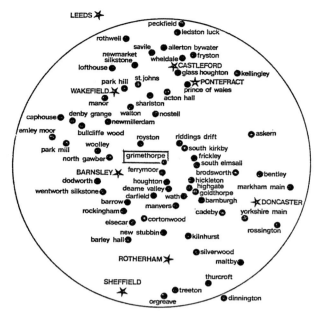

The Yorkshire coalfield in 1978.

reminiscent of the one made by the young miner at Cortonwood Colliery when he *appeared for a few seconds on News at Ten after the announcement to close the pit in 1984: 'Unless we save this pit there is going to be a plague right up the (Dearne) Valley.'* Mr Hancock was upset but not surprised that the 210 men made the two-to-one decision to accept the package.

The Grimethorpe closure marked the end of the thirty year decline in the Barnsley coalfield. In 1961 half the town's working population was engaged in mining and quarrying and the coalfield employed 33,500. But Barnsley Council were already warning that new industry was needed to replace old pits. By the mid 1960s the Government's first big pit closure programme was on the way and the axe fell on the Barnsley coalfield, one of the oldest in the country, and in six years the pits went down like ninepins: Haigh, Wharncliffe Silkstone, Monk Bretton, Wombwell Main, the Wharncliffe Woodmoor Collieries at Carlton, Barnsley Main and the Monckton collieries. There was no public outcry. Lord Mason, a former Labour Minister of Power and former MP for Barnsley, said in one year in the 1960s thirty pits closed nationwide. But at that time there were still plenty of pits where redundant miners could find a job and the nation's unemployment levels were not high. He introduced the over fifty-five scheme which enabled redundant men who did not get a job to receive financial assistance until the age of sixty-five: *'the real beginnings of miners' redundancy payments,'* said the former Barnsley miner. By 1974 the Barnsley coalfield employed nearly 20,000, half the 1960 figure. Saleable output had fallen from eleven million to below seven million tonnes in the same period. An NCB (Barnsley) official said in 1974:

Despite the age of the coalfield (the average age of the pits is over eighty years), the twenty-four seams now being worked contain 268 million tonnes of classified workable reserves, including sixty per cent of the national coking coal reserves.

For a while the coalfield seemed to be in terminal decline but then massive investment at local pits – following an unexpected upsurge in the demand for coal – resulted in the NCB in 1983 still being the most single economic

Government's approval rating had fallen to sixteen per cent. Only the first Wilson administration in 1968 had rivalled Major's lack of public esteem, with a figure of eighteen per cent. Large majorities of voters – more than sixty per cent – thought Major's Government was ineffective, short-sighted and out of touch.

But that was cold comfort in May in the Labour stronghold of Barnsley, where the remnants of the old coalfield, Houghton Main and Grimethorpe, closed. Despite a big campaign and big parades to try to keep the pits open, Houghton shut on the last day in April, Grimethorpe a week later. The men at Grimethorpe agreed to take British Coal's enhanced redundancy package, the same package accepted earlier by the Houghton men. Grimethorpe NUM branch secretary Ken Hancock said: *'There seems to be a cloud of despair hanging over the whole community. There is a smell of fear and uncertainty not only at the pit but in the village,'* a quote

The washery at Woolley. *Don Oaks*

Look after their future...

ACCESS TO WEST PIT SHAFT

A fact sheet produced by the Coalfield Communities group.

Britain is often called an island of coal. Reserves are measured in hundreds of years. If the mines close much of this will be lost for ever.

Britain has limited alternative energy sources. Nuclear power is too expensive (at least 3 times more than coal) and requires substantial government subsidy. Gas reserves are scarce – only 40 years at the present rate of consumption, far less if used to generate electricity.

Most experts say electricity from gas is more expensive than that from coal, even if coal power stations are fitted with equipment needed to burn coal cleanly.

If our coal mines are closed, Britain will become reliant on imported coal and gas for its electricity. A recent government report admits that over 80% of our energy needs will be imported by the year 2000.

Most British pits are now profitable and production costs are still tumbling. Experts (including the power generators) predict that within five years British coal will be as cheap as imported coal – sooner if the exchange rate continues to fall.

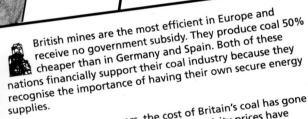

British mines are the most efficient in Europe and receive no government subsidy. They produce coal 50% cheaper than in Germany and Spain. Both of these nations financially support their coal industry because they recognise the importance of having their own secure energy supplies.

In the last five years, the cost of Britain's coal has gone down 28% in real terms, but electricity prices have continued to rise. This indicates there is something seriously wrong with the electricity market. We know that one distortion is the £1.3 billion annual subsidy to nuclear power paid for by you, the consumer, in your electricity bill. But no-one will reveal how much extra consumers will pay to cover the higher costs of electricity from the new gas stations.

Elsewhere in the developed world, countries are moving massively away from nuclear and expensive oil towards coal for electricity production. The USA's use of coal is set to rise 20% in the 1990s.

In a time of deep recession and against a backcloth of flawed economic evidence, the government is to spend at least £2 billion to close pits – much of it on redundancy payments and unemployment benefits.

Last but by no means least is the unnecessary destruction of the livelihoods of 30,000 miners and at least as many again in supporting industries. They don't want aid, they want to keep working.

10 REASONS why the 31 threatened Coal Mines should stay open

Above and right: Houghton Main Colliery. *Don Oakes*

influence on the borough and the biggest single employer, operating the following pits: Dodworth/Redbrook, North Gawber, Woolley, Grimethorpe, Houghton Main, Barrow/Barnsley Main (in the process of reopening), Ferrymoor/Riddings, Darfield Main, Kinsley Drift, Dearne Valley, South Kirkby, Royston Drift and the Denby Grange, Bullcliffe Wood group. The NCB paid two million pounds in wages into the local economy every week and a similar figure in rates to the local council. It was a smaller, rejuvenated coalfield, one of the most modern in the world; it had been created by pumping more than £400 million into the pits and cutting the number of workers. A report by Barnsley Council, Coal Mining and Barnsley, published in 1983, stated:

> *It has been Barnsley's good fortune to have good coal reserves, using the Government's criterion, to justify the investment it has received, while other areas now face the complete collapse of their coal industries. It is ironic that the shedding of over 20 per cent of the NCB's Barnsley area workforce in a decade can be classed as good fortune...*

Between 1977 and 1983 5,750 out of nearly 20,000 Barnsley mining jobs were lost and, according to the report, management planned to shed at least 1,000 more by the end of 1985 *'though no colliery is immediately at risk.'* It was anticipated that by 1986 there would be 16,000 mineworkers in Barnsley. The pre-strike shedding of labour in Barnsley pits was done with the approval of the unions as part of the modernisation programme, but there was an understanding that the remaining jobs would be retained for years. Had there not been the modernisation programme pits would have closed before the strike. The 1984/85 miners strike, triggered off by the closure of Cortonwood and Bullcliffe Wood Collieries, was a watershed in many respects, ushering in a new era in the industry. The NUM argued that the strike was planned and implemented by the NCB and the Government to break the power of the union to pave the way for the

dismantling of the nationalised industry. Within months of the end of the strike British Coal, formerly the National Coal Board, began carving up the Barnsley coalfield.

The first sign of the shape of things to come appeared when British Coal did not open Redbrook and Barnsley Main in a fanfare of publicity at the end of the strike in March, 1985. Dodworth and Barrow had been closed under the modernisation programme and a reduced workforce transferred to Redbrook, which had been rebuilt, and Barnsley Main, a new pit on the site of the old colliery closed in the 1960s. The strike interrupted the transfer of men and the official openings. Before the strike the new pits had assured futures; after the strike coal became a new ball game with new rules and a new referee and linesmen, and British Coal knew both mines would not survive many years in the new harsh climate, so the pits were opened without any fuss.

Other pits where millions of pounds had been invested and where jobs had been originally 'guaranteed' for fifteen or twenty years were closed over the next few years because the pits could not match new productivity yardsticks. After the strike the economic goal posts were moved: pits had to produce more coal at a low cost. On top of that each pit had to repay the high interest on its capital investment, instead of it coming out of a central or regional fund, and in the case of the Barnsley pits there had been huge investment: more money than in any other coalfield apart from Selby. *We are being crippled by high interest charges,'* became a familiar quote from NUM branch officials as the pits closed. What had been seen as the saviour of the old Barnsley coalfield – investment – now became a cross that was too heavy to carry and between 1985 and 1993 pits were closed at a faster than anticipated rate. Meanwhile, questions were asked about the validity of the investment in the first place. Why was so much money invested in on old coalfield where the seams were thin? How could a 'new' coalfield disappear so fast? The NCB argued that the market for Barnsley coking coal, the coalfield's prize asset, had been scaled down over the years. The country's largest reserves of coking coal were under the 120 square mile coalfield but the market collapsed with the contraction of the old steel industry before the coalfield reconstruction programme was complete. It was also pointed out that a 'new' coalfield took many years to plan and bring into full production, and during that period markets and the needs of the national economy – or, perhaps, the energy fads of the two principal political parties – could change beyond recognition.

By October, 1992, only Grimethorpe and Houghton Main remained in the once mighty Barnsley coalfield, both pits having seen big reductions in manpower in the aftermath of the strike. Then they were included in the doomed list of thirty-one pits. Arthur Scargill, describing the October closure programme as vandalism, said:

The only reason for closing these pits is an act of vindictiveness on the part of the Tory Government and on the part of the people who want to destroy the NUM. It is nothing but malice for 1974.

(Scargill is consistent: in the 1960s he used emotive language about pit closures; in 1980 he claimed that the NCB had secret plans for the closure of up to fifty pits over three years, an allegation denied by the board at the time). What followed became known as the People's Revolt, with *The Observer* declaring on 18 October: *John Major is facing a catastrophic Commons defeat over pit closures unless the Government makes substantial concessions.'* Tory MPs believed that public feeling was so strong that the Government might have to promise a review – and a delay – to the pit closure programme.

Below and right: Darfield Main and its demolition.

Arthur Scargill, a hero in 1992.

However, Neil Clarke, BC's chairman, told the Trade and Industry select committee that only a radical transformation of the market for coal would save the pits and at present there was no market for the coal. Miners had been breaking productivity records but the coal was piling up at the pitheads. British Coal officials argued that if the Government had split the power generators into four or five companies, the 'dash for gas' would not have occurred, and the need for such massive colliery closures would have been avoided. By 19 October, after a public outcry, Heseltine was forced into announcing a provisional reprieve for some pits and consultation on others. On 26 March, however, the *Barnsley Chronicle* announced that Grimethorpe and Houghton had not been given a reprieve – but the fight went on – with Ken Hancock saying: *'We have got to fight on or accept that for the rest of our lives we will be on the dole – I am not going to settle for that.'* NUM national vice president Frank Cave said:

Despite the public anger over this issue and despite all the evidence and arguments in favour of maintaining

the UK coal industry, Michael Heseltine has announced the closure of thirty-one pits. The Government knows the market is rigged against coal. They know that electricity from gas and nuclear power is more expensive but they have chosen to do nothing about it.

The Observer said:

The essential problem for the industry is that the Government is neither prepared to protect the market for coal nor devise a coherent long-term energy policy based on the balanced use of Britain's oil, coal, gas, nuclear and other resources... New or planned gas-fired power stations are scheduled to replace up to thirty million tonnes of coal by the late 1990s... Nuclear receives a subsidy of £1.2 billion a year, which if magically transferred to the pits would transform the economics of the mining industry.

In June *The Observer* announced:

It was a swift, silent execution. Nineteen coal mines

Grimethorpe miners at a protest meeting in Octobert 1992.

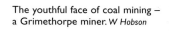
Ian Walker, a Grimethorpe miner and son, Richard, at pit demonstration.

The youthful face of coal mining – a Grimethorpe miner. *W Hobson*

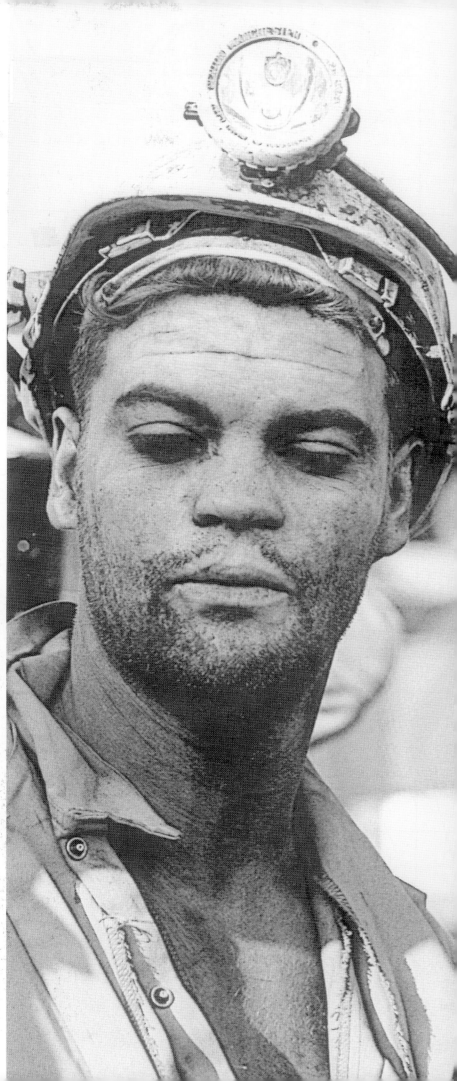

Above and below: Protests at local and national level. The Barnsley Women against Pit Closures are seen in London during the October demonstration.

A demonstration in Barnsley.

have closed in the past six weeks, pushing to 18,000 the number of miners made redundant since October. More casualties are expected by the end of the year. Yet hardly a placard has been waved in protest. Eight months after the nation rose up in anger at Michael Heseltine's plans to shut thirty-one pits, the President of the Board of Trade is well on the way to achieving his original goal almost unchallenged. Only a handful of the reprieved mines are expected to survive. The miners are still protesting and demonstrating, but they are fighting a forgotten war. And they are weakened by deadlines for accepting redundancy.

Seumas Milne, in *The Guardian* wrote:

If ever there was a testament to the cynicism of public life in the 1990s, it must surely be the silent six-week closure of almost half of the British coal industry. Since the end of April, nineteen pits have been shut and their work forces bullied and cajoled off colliery books. More than 17,000 miners have been made redundant since last October... all this has been executed without a murmur from either Government or opposition, media or trade unions. One miner said that if they blew up the pit now they [the media] would not report it. It was all so different last October.

Miners and their wives and children protest at pit closures – pictured in London and en route to the capital by *Barnsley Chronicle* photographers.

Miners, councillors and families demonstrating against pit closures.

In Lord Lawson's words: *'Diversification of energy sources... was code for freedom from NUM blackmail.*

Heseltine was still saying there was no market for coal – and Labour politicians were still claiming that the energy markets had been 'rigged' in favour of gas – when Grimethorpe-Houghton went up for sale as one unit in June as part of the coal privatisation programme.

In 1993 the last local pits closed and since then there has been a transformation in the town. In some respects Barnsley is heading for a new era on the back of Old King Coal. Some of the sites of the pits are sprouting factories and offices instead of headgear and spoil heaps, creating jobs for the future, and that's rather ironical. In the early 1980s, when £400 million of taxpayers' money was pumped into Barnsley pits, British Coal 'guaranteed' there would be jobs at some pits into the millennium, but after

the 1984/85 Miners' Strike, that quixotic idea vanished without trace. Barnsley has never been over endowed with tailor-made conventional sites for new industry, so the council and other agencies – such as English Partnership – have turned to pit sites. By concentrating on developing these sites they can create jobs, clear dereliction and enhance the environment in one move.

Redbrook is a good example. That pit was reopened in 1985 following a £20 million refit; yet five years later the new surface buildings were demolished and the shafts filled in, and the site was converted into a business park. The site of Dodworth pit is also a successful business park, thanks to its close access to the motorway system. The biggest success story, however, has been Cortonwood where the 1984/85 Miners' Strike started. Its location was not promising since it had poor access roads

A torchlight protest at Grimethorpe. *Wes Hobson*

but the construction of the Dearne Towns Link Road changed all that. The site now boasts a supermarket, other retail units and a call centre, all of which are highly successful, another sign that that part of our area is changing faster than anywhere else in South Yorkshire. Large scale development is also under way at the Grimethorpe Colliery site. That pit, for most of its life one of the largest in the Barnsley coalfield, was known as 'the sleeping giant', for it never reached its full potential in its coal digging days. That story is expected to change and a new Grimethorpe, vibrant and expansive, will be created as a result of the redevelopment of the site. Meanwhile, other pit sites have not been successful in terms of industrial development. Darfield Main, for instance, has poor access roads and that area has now been landscaped to blend with the neighbouring reclamation scheme on the site of the former Mitchell Main Colliery, which closed in the first closure programme in the 1950s. Both sites are now part of a country park, luxuriant and picturesque in summer, a sharp contrast to the old Mitchells, a rancid spot with its pit, chemical works and greasy canal. In a way the clock has been turned back to the 1850s when London journalists on a trip to the Barnsley pits described as rich and beautiful the countryside at Wombwell, Worsbrough and at Aldham.

Big changes are underway elsewhere in Barnsley. For years, the council has been worried about the state of the town centre which has failed to attract any large-scale stores since the development of the Alhambra Centre twelve years ago. With the help of Yorkshire Forward, the council is planning to create a new town centre and the existing Metropolitan Centre, built in the 1970s, has been

The pit closure programme displayed in placards.

bought with the intention of demolishing it as the first phase of a proposal to revitalise the area. One idea is to have a beam of light projected 1,000 feet into the sky to act as a kind of beacon: it would be seen as far away as Doncaster. The men behind the project say it would help to draw visitors and shoppers to this area. Another idea is to design a town centre that would resemble a Tuscany hill village, around which shops, houses and parklands would be built.

There is a familiar ring about this idea. D H Lawrence, a miner's son from Nottingham, who was seen as a major

Above: Grimethorpe Colliery.

The southside drift at
Grimethorpe.
British Coal

Farewell to Grimethorpe Colliery ceremony,
14 May 1993. A wreath was laid to commemorate
the men who died at the pit.

Grimethorpe, 1993. *Wes Hobson*

literary figure in the twentieth century, once said that his home city might have looked like one of the lovely hill towns of Italy had it not been for the Victorians who created formless ugly surroundings. Enlarging on that argument in *Pits 2*, I asked one hypothetical question: what would have happened to Barnsley if there had not been any mining? Mining filled the vacuum left by the decline of the linen industry and the new pits averted the collapse of the local economy; but mining also turned the town and the landscape into an eyesore.

Just strip Barnsley of its estates, terraced streets, most of the town centre and the factories and, in your mind, you will be left with what could have been an attractive hill town. I wrote.

However, I did not expect that, fourteen years later, someone would produce an idea for a Tuscany hill village in Barnsley. What a thought! Those old miners who lived and worked in a town built on coal must be revolving in their graves. Other people viewed the touch of Tuscany as a kind of black joke played on the good people of Barnsley, a few that the town needed to be forward thinking and they welcomed the idea.

The (coal) dust won't settle on this argument for years.

How it has changed. These photographs show the site of Cortonwood after demolition of the surface buildings and what has been built there since. The business and retail park is home to Morrisons and a B & Q as well as a call centre and other units. *Wes Hobson.*

Chapter 8

Mining Memories

(Researched and written in the 1980s)

Roy Mason

At the age of twelve, in 1936, Roy Mason was at the pit-head at Wharncliffe Woodmoor 1/2/3 when the bodies were brought out. He remembered vividly the huddled groups of women in shawls and the weeping; Father King, who led thousands in prayer at the pit head; the temporary mortuary in the school hall near the pit; and George Formby appearing at a later fund-raising show at the Alhambra Cinema.

Two years later, on his second shift at the sister pit, Wharncliffe Woodmoor 4/5 he saw a dead man carried out on a stretcher. *'My charge-hand said they always brought out dead men feet first with a cover over the body.'*

The future Labour minister was buried three times at the 4/5 colliery. On one occasion he was talking to two men in charge of a power machine when a shouted warning alerted him to danger.

> *Mr Laverack, who saved my life, shouted 'Look out!'. He had seen a prop buckle. I found myself spread-eagled with a large stone on my back. My lamp had gone out and it was dusty, but I could see lamps bobbing about in the distance and I shouted for help. I was carried out on a stretcher badly bruised.*

Injuries were nothing new to the Mason family. His grandfather lost an eye and his father was crippled for life, dying at the age of sixty. His father was a committed trade unionist and on his first pay day (wage 19s 6d) his father

Lord Mason, former Minister of Power.

told him to go to the union office and pay his contributions. He has been a member of the union for forty-nine years.

Private enterprise was the arch enemy. The coal getters received a small basic wage and the bonus depended on the number of full tubs. Sometimes there was a shortage of empty tubs; delays caused frustration and when an empty tub appeared miners fought each other to claim ownership. The market system, whereby a group of men who did not have regular jobs were directed to fill vacancies elsewhere, gave deputies enormous power and influence. They could pick their mates for the best jobs, leaving the rest to be transferred to lower paid jobs.

The village had its own class system, Long Row being

for the miners, Stone Row for the deputies and the large detached house for the manager.

The 1930s were hungry years with the demand for coal remaining depressed and pits closed for part of the week. Miners worked three days and had three days off, receiving three days pay and three days dole. If the pit opened for a fourth shift it was not uncommon for someone to sabotage a shift by removing a prop to cause a roof fall. Some of the men were then sent home. The miners' three days on, three days off income was higher than four days pay and no dole.

Roy Mason was responsible for maintaining and repairing machinery and on one particular occasion he spent twenty-seven hours working on a vital breakdown job underground. Eventually his family turned up at the pit-head to find out what had happened to him. Every few hours a bottle of water and sandwiches were sent down to him. His snap usually consisted of a bottle of water and four slices of bread and lard, worse than a prisoner's diet. Pork dripping was a luxury and, working in a confined space with a one-way air flow, the rest of the men soon realised what he was eating. The snap was wrapped in paper (many miners could not afford a snap tin) and on reaching the face he would tie a piece of string round the food and suspend it from a girder to try to hoodwink the mice. Mice were all over the workings, having hitched a lift in the sacks of grain sent down for the pit ponies in the underground stables.

At twenty-three he was elected a union branch committee man. He had been studying mechanical engineering on a day release course. On nationalisation in 1947 the NCB introduced a system of six days pay for a five day working week, provided miners worked for the five days. The proposal was introduced because of a shortage of coal and because of absenteeism. Because of the day release course, he missed a shift every week and the family could not afford to lose the money. He asked the union to do something about it, nothing happened and he missed his examinations. So he contacted the MP for Hemsworth, Mr Horace Holmes, who persuaded the Government to amend the Act. To shake-up the union he stood for election and became a committee man. At twenty-five he was elected branch delegate. In 1953 he was elected MP for Barnsley, determined to improve society, an ambition he had nurtured since the death of his mother at an early age.

Ernest Bamford

Retired miner Mr Ernest Bamford is proud of the fact that he spent all his working life in the pit and said: *'I have done more miles on my knees than most marathon runners have done on their feet.'*

Mr Bamford, aged eighty-six, of Waddington Road, Pogmoor, started work in 1914 at Church Lane screens (Dodworth Colliery). When he moved to North Gawber Colliery he was to remain there for thirty-five years and was involved in the 1935 explosion in which nineteen men were killed. One of the men, Albert Ibberson, managed to write a message in chalk as he lay crippled. *'I will never forget the words he wrote,' said Ernest, 'It was a message to his wife, "Farewell Fanny, my love."'*

A Deputy, he was involved in the subsequent inquiry into the disaster. The inquiry concluded the pit had been seriously lacking in ventilation and it was agreed massive alterations to the system were necessary.

'Miners were the salt of the earth. They treated each other like brothers and were always willing to help each other. I knew all the men at the pit by name.' For Ernest the annual concert at Sheffield City Hall stands as a fine example of the community spirit among miners. *'It is fantastic to listen to the colliery bands and choirs.'*

Anonymous

An anonymous miner aged eighty-one, who lives in Doncaster Road, remembers miners fainting from lack of air, and having to drink pints of water because of the heat down the pit. He started work in 1919 on the same day as his brother, who had just returned from the First World War. After working as a face worker for forty-seven years, he retired in 1970, receiving a lump sum of £203 when he left the pit. *'Human beings were never made to go underground; they turned into animals when they went down a pit and became slaves.'*

Albert Haynes

The day sailors arrived at the 'watercress pit' (it earned its nickname because it was so wet) are recalled by Albert Haynes, aged seventy-eight, of High Street, Grimethorpe. The pit (Grimethorpe's sister pit at Ferrymoor) was flooded and the navy were called in because there was a shortage of labour as a result of the First World War.

I remember them arriving in their bell-bottom trousers and the word got round that the navy had arrived. The sailors went round the village handing out tins of bully beef to the children.

The watercress pit was one of the smallest in the coalfield. *'The shaft was 90 yards deep and from the surface you could shout to someone in the pit bottom.'*

He recalls the strikes of 1921, 1926 and 1947 – which started at Grimethorpe – mainly because of the hot weather.

Miners were coal picking behind Deputy Row in 1921 and they were as brown as berries and the heat was so intense it melted the tarmac on the roads. In 1947, after nationalisation, management increased miners' work stint without telling them. More coal was produced but the men did not get any more pay, so they came out on strike and it became known as the stint strike.

Albert worked at Grimethorpe Colliery which produced coal known as Barnsley Bed Hards: *'Our concessionary coal consisted of lumps as big as a television set.'*

Alf Parker

During fifty years spent working down the mines, Alf Parker tackled virtually every job that was going. Now seventy-seven years old, Alf, of Gerald Crescent, Kendray, started work in 1924 at Wombwell Main and then worked at Mitchell Main, Wombwell, and Barnsley Main until it closed in 1967. He spent his last years at Barrow Colliery, retiring in 1974.

I started off at Wombwell Main which was an easy pit. I soon found out what mining was all about when I moved to Barnsley Main in 1925. I did not like the time I spent at Mitchell Main and I lasted a couple of months there. The area I worked in was red hot and the ventilation was awful. It was like working in an oven.

He was a member of the rescue team and was called in when there was an explosion at Barnsley Main. Officials were examining the pit after a fire, but when the stoppings were removed there was an explosion.

One of my friends, Stan Parry, was a deputy at the time. I brought him out of the pit with a face like a tomato after he had been left for dead.

In his fifty year career he did not escape injury and an incident with a pit pony left him with two broken ribs, although his broken nose was caused by a spade which he accidentally jumped on. 'The most enjoyable time I spent down the pit were the last eight years. Until I retired I worked seven days a week driving the paddy at Barrow, and the manager ordered a specially made seat for me. It was the best job I ever had down the pit.'

John Grayson

The 1926 miners' lock-out was a glorious time for young men without responsibilities. Like miners in the 1984/85 Miners' Strike, some of them experienced weeks of uninterrupted sunny weather for the first time in years. At Wombwell, where he lived, the public health inspector reported that the health of miners actually improved during the dispute. They may not have had enough to eat but the fresh air, the warmth and exercise did them a world of good.

'We came out of the pit in May and did not go back until November. It was the best time of my life,' said the eighty-three years old. *'My father had a job on the council and we did not feel the pinch like other families. We spent our time playing sport and walking.'* He remembers a miner with a motor-bike travelling on to the moors to steal sheep and miners waiting at a spot where the trains had to slow down so they could steal food and goods off the wagons.

His favourite miners' leader was Joe Hall, from Lundhill, Wombwell, whom he recalls being carried shoulder high through the streets of Wombwell to Brampton where he made a speech to a large gathering of miners.

A lot of miners worshipped Hall who was capable of making rousing speeches. The mounted Police were at Brampton and at one point it looked as if things would get nasty. A horse and cart carrying a load of bricks came down the street and I expected the miners grabbing the bricks and throwing them at the Police. But nothing happened. At other times the Police were brutes. The authorities must have chosen the biggest Policemen they could find to send to Barnsley. If three miners were walking down the street together, the Police would disperse them. The Police were used to escort 'black-legs' from the pits to their homes. I remember one black-leg who lived at Cortonwood. When he got to the safety of his home, he would turn and challenge the miners to a fight.

Arthur Akeroyd

Arthur Akeroyd started work on the screens at Barnsley Main Colliery in 1925 but within a few months the miners were locked out and he went coal picking at Pogmoor, charging 6d a bag for 'spitting coal' (so called because it contained bits of pot and other objects which spat in the fire) and 1s for riddled fuel; and at Silkstone Fall which worked during the dispute, and at what was known as the Bluebell Seam in Dodworth Road, where he was sometimes chased by Policemen.

'It was a glorious time – the weather was beautiful and I was sixteen,' said Arthur, a retired pit winder who now lives in Shirland Avenue, Athersley. In a way he had been lucky for before the lock out he had worked on the surface, where most of the men were members of the General and Municipal Workers Union; his union paid strike money whereas the miners' union ran out of funds within four weeks.

During the General Strike there was some trouble in the Gas Nook, Barnsley, where a bus was turned over. The TUC said all transport workers had to stop work but this bus was still operating.'

More than fifty years later he portrayed one of the miners' leaders in 1926, W G Richardson, in the BBC television series, *Days of Hope*.

In 1928 most of the surface workers transferred to the Miners' Federation, although they did not receive the same perks as underground workers.

When the underground workers paid their contributions, the union officials gave them a Woodbine but the surface workers received nothing.

Thomas Franks

The muscular world of mining was in the blood of Thomas Franks (seventy-four), who spent forty-nine years in the industry. The former Woolley Colliery miner had the strength – and knack – to lift half ton tubs back on to the underground rails. And he was prepared to work seven days a week, often in terrible conditions and often in danger.

He saw three men killed in separate accidents and after finding one buried he nearly gave up the job. He was buried twice, broke a leg and had numerous injuries; but it never dampened his appetite for hard work and the pits. Working down the pit had its compensations. During one week in 1948 he earned £25, blue-chip earnings when £7 was regarded as a decent wage. But he had to work over the Easter holidays – with double shifts on Easter Tuesday – to hit the jackpot.

The job has got easier over the years; during the period before my retirement I had to carry the tackle (belting, timber and girders) for men working on a heading and I was still working harder than the younger men.

His most embarrassing moment: he was called to the manager's office for alleged absenteeism, a serious offence during the Second World War, during which discipline was as tight as in the army. *'It was all a mistake – I had worked six months without having a day off.'*

George Henry Taylor

George Henry Taylor (seventy-two), Sheffield Road, went down the pit at thirteen and a half working as a pony driver. When he was seventeen he was buried in the pit and went to Beckett Hospital, Barnsley, where he was encased in plaster. It took him two years to recover and as a consequence his wedding had to be postponed. He spent fifty years in the industry, twenty-five of which were at Monk Bretton. He also worked at Barnsley Main, missing the explosions of 1942 and 1947 through illness.

Walter Darlington

Walter Darlington (seventy-seven), Doncaster Road, believes he had a lucky escape. He went down the pit at sixteen, in 1926, for which he was paid £2 7s a week. It came as a shock when after only seven weeks the miners were locked out in the 1926 dispute. Walter considers he was lucky as he quickly found work in a butcher's shop and never returned to the pit.

John Haughton

John Haughton (seventy), Pontefract Road, was working at Rockingham Colliery, Hoyland Common, when the roof caved in and killed two of his pals. John had been working with one of them the previous day and when the news went round Barnsley Main Colliery his brother thought John had been killed.

The two men had been doing some repair work when four girders dropped: 40 tons of metal and earth fell on them. We spent most of the day digging them out. I was off work a week because I was so upset.

John Haughton worked in the Lower Fenton Seam. Some of the seams were so close that debris fell from one to another.

In 1948 I remember finding a racing pink newspaper, dated 1912, which had come from the Top Fenton seam which had been worked in the early years of the century and which had not been worked for years. The odd coal tub came down too. From Rockingham you could make your way into the underground workings of Barrow, Skiers Spring, Platts Common and Pilley Collieries. We kept the airway clear in the old Pilley Colliery and to do this work we had to use the disused shaft. So much water came down the Pilley shaft we were glad to reach the surface.

He worked for forty-two years in the mines, at Rockingham, Barnsley Main and Barrow. *'There was nothing but hard work down a pit – my health has never been better since I left.'*

Edward Slater

Edward Slater remembers his father's body being carried from a horse-drawn ambulance into his house in 1921, after an accident at Barnsley Main Colliery. Consequently seven year old Edward did not look forward to a life in a mine.

When Edward left school there were no jobs outside mining and even the pits were on short time. So Edward and his brothers, John and Thomas, went to work at Barnsley Main, where their father was killed. In Edward's case history nearly repeated itself. On 7 May, 1947, he was working on a new face when there was an explosion, killing nine men and injuring twenty-three. At his home in Samuel Road, Gawber, he said:

I remember cap lamps were coming in and I was fortunate enough to get one. The force of the blast took the helmet straight off my head. I had my back to the blast so I was thrown flat on my face. I pulled my cable to retrieve my helmet and light but it made no difference, everything was a mass of dust. My mate and I scrambled along the tailgate by instinct and we were on our way to the pit bottom when we suddenly went cold: our skin had shrivelled as a result of the flash.

Edward was in the ambulance room when the first of the stretchers arrived.

That was enough for me. I left and went to see my own doctor. I think I was the only man in the explosion not to go to hospital. Barnsley Main claimed my father and nearly claimed me.

Eli Sumnall

Mrs Winifred Gillespie (eighty) of Scarborough, said time could not dim the memories of the old Yorkshire Mineworkers' Association. Her father, the late Eli Sumnall, was secretary of the Wharncliffe Woodmoor 1/2/3 branch of the YMA for more than thirty years. The union and the miners were his life. Always the knock-knock on the door: *'Is your dad in?'* or *'Can you help, Eli?'*

Ill and breathless with pneumoconiosis, maimed, disabled, human beings, denied recognition of liability for their injuries. My father spent demoralising hours arguing for their rights. Many frail old miners kept in the union so as to qualify for the death benefit of £6 to help bury them. So important was the union to him that in 1933 he took us to Tolpuddle in Dorset for the commemoration of the 100th anniversary of the Tolpuddle martyrs, the men who formed the first trade union. What depth of feeling to stand where they once stood. Our names are in the Book of Remembrance.

The nationalisation of the mines in 1947 was his dream, and when the flag was raised at the pithead he quoted one of the Proverbs from the Bible to the effect that *'hope deferred made the heart sick, but when the desire came it turned out to be the Tree of Life'*. And so it seemed for a while but disillusionment set in and in the end he said that they had changed the name but the bosses were the same. *'Today (1987) there is no trace of Wharncliffe Woodmoor but thank God we still have the union.'*

Albert Clarkson

Albert Clarkson has bitter memories of one strike which took place at Cortonwood Colliery during the Second World War. Late in 1941 the Cortonwood Colliery Company successfully applied for Government permission to cut the face workers' wages by one third. The company claimed the reduction was necessary because one of the seams had ceased to be viable. Miners downed tools in protest and held out for five hard weeks over Christmas and the New Year before going back on slightly better terms. They had recouped 2d of the 6d cut. Albert Clarkson, aged seventy-three, of Fearnhouse Crescent, Hoyland Common, a face worker at the colliery said:

We had been paid 1s 6½d a ton for the coal we produced, but the company suddenly turned round and said they could not pay it. They had previously introduced a new system of cutting coal in the Silkstone seam which made it look as if we were unproductive, but the new system was not working properly.

To support his wife and two children Albert used to retrieve old wreaths from a refuse tip in Hoyland, after which he would strip them down, re-decorate them with holly from the wood and then sell them to mourners.

In those days we had what we called Parish Relief. The first time I applied for it was four weeks after the strike had started and I received twenty two shillings. The man who was handing it out said that if I spent it on anything but food I would be sent to prison. After the strike we were taken to Rotherham Magistrates Court by the company for going on strike. We were fined by the magistrates and one of them said if he had enough power he would line us up against a wall and shoot us for being unpatriotic. But that wasn't true – we were as patriotic as everyone else.

Ernest Woodhead

Ernest Woodhead (twenty-one), was a hard and willing worker but, for some reason, he was unwilling to travel from his home in St John's Terrace, Buckley Street, to the colliery on 4 February, 1943. His reluctance was not shared by his mother, Harriet, for words were exchanged and he set off to work. That was the last time Mrs Woodhead saw him alive. Shortly after 3.45 pm that day Ernest was working with William Henry Glover, aged forty-seven, of Churchfield Lane, Kexborough, trying to erect a roof support girder at Woolley Colliery after the firing of six shots when three tons of stone fell on him.

Ernest Woodhead

Ernest suffered a fractured skull and died almost immediately. One of the first to be informed was his father, Frank, who was working in a different part of the pit the same day. The man with Ernest, William Glover, a ripper, died of asphyxia. At the inquest there was a difference of opinion between H M Inspector, a Mr Green, and the deputy in charge that day, Mr Charles Hinchcliffe Jackson, of Bridge Street, Darton. Green believed the additional timber safety props should have been placed in position before the shots were fired but Jackson believed every reasonable safeguard had been taken and the quickest and safest way had been to set the girder as soon as possible after the firing of the shots. The verdict at the inquest: death by misadventure. Some weeks later colliery proprietors Fountain and Burnley paid the family £150 under the *Workmen's Compensation Act.* That sum was the equivalent of Ernest's wages for twenty-five weeks.

Alfred Smith

Sixty-seven-year-old Alfred Smith, of Darton, worked at Woolley Colliery for twenty-six years, beginning in 1933 at the age of fourteen; in 1936 he began work underground. On his first day he had to walk and crawl three and a half miles to get to the coal face.

At the end of my first shift I did not realise everyone had gone and the deputy had to come looking for me. He said he had been looking for me for half an hour.

He still has nightmares over his brushes with death.

On one occasion there were two of us in the cage when the engine man must have been given the wrong signal, believing he was dropping coal. The cage dropped almost one thousand feet at such a speed we hardly had time to be frightened but the bad air meant we could not breathe properly. The shock hit us when we reached the bottom and we had to be hauled out of the cage.

On another occasion when the lockers failed to hold the tubs, and he had not altered the points, he was nearly responsible for the death of twenty men.

The tubs were heading for a cage holding twenty men and I could not stop them. My cries of 'runaway!' warned them and they managed to get out of the cage before the tubs hit it. That could have been an awful accident and it would have been my fault.

The best part of the day when he was a lad was the ride back to the stables.

At the end of the shift, against all the rules, I used to ride back to the stable on my pony and I only banged by head and fell off once. I do remember on one occasion knocking the Under Manager over when I was riding back to the stables and I had a lot of explaining to do. The pit manager fined me five bob.

Alf Smith left Woolley in 1959 with a lung ailment.

Ralph Dyson

Ralph Dyson (fifty-nine), Highstone Road, Worsbrough Common, recalls the humour and comradeship as well as the hard work underground. In 1942 he left school on a Friday and started work at Old Carlton Colliery on the Monday. Later he worked at the other Wharncliffe Woodmoor Colliery, Barnsley Main, Wombwell Main, Grimethorpe, Haigh, Barrow, Woolley and North Gawber as well as two private pits, Brook's at Silkstone and Robinson's at Cawthorne.

When I started conditions were primitive, but they improved after nationalisation. The trouble was they nationalised the pits but they did not nationalise the bosses, and the number of bosses increased after 1947.

Every pit had its hate list of deputies. One deputy, known as 'Black Charlie' at Barnsley Main, was injured in an accident and none of the men helped him: *'He was rotten – rotten to everyone.'*

There were plenty of characters. During the war it was not easy to get transferred to another pit. The manager at Haigh Colliery was a rough diamond who had worked his way up from the coal face. He had no finesse and he was well schooled in the art of ungentle persuasion. Ralph Dyson wanted to leave the pit because of the conditions but the manager outwitted him. One day he went to the manager's office determined to get his transfer. Convinced that he had won, he went to the offices with a note from the manager, expecting to be paid up, only to discover that the note was for a new set of picks. On another occasion the manager made him feel guilty by telling him: *'Things can't be that bad here – you have put some weight on and you have colour in your cheeks.'* Eventually he did leave.

Managers did not get their own way all the time. At another pit the area manager was on his rounds when he spotted two lads asleep. Poking one with his stick, he asked: *'Do you know who I am?'* Rubbing his eyes, the lad turned to his mate and said: *'There's a bloke here who doesn't know who he is.'*

In the old days tragedy was just round the corner. Ralph Dyson's father rarely had a shift off work but one day he met his relatives and they all ended up at the club at Long Row, Carlton. His father missed the shift; his mates who had been drinking with him went underground and they were killed.

Ralph's career came to an end when a large stone and metal bar pinned him to the ground in a kneeling position at North Gawber, the deputy rescuing him by removing the dirt from underneath his knees. In the ambulance room the medical staff asked him to go to hospital but he refused because he was needed at home and struggled to the bus. His back was badly injured and later he had to be treated in hospital and was off work for three years.

John Allen

John Allen said he would do someone a favour – and as a result almost died. While working at Wentworth Silkstone Colliery, near Stainborough, in November 1960, a machine amputated his left leg and almost severed the right. John of Devonshire Drive, was working with his son-in-law on development work when the accident occurred.

It was the end of the shift – ten minutes past one and we decided to go for the paddy train. The afternoon shift was following on and I changed my mind, deciding to do them a favour. I thought I would push the machine back to give them a good start. We put a rope round the machine, tightened it and got out of the way. The machine was switched on, but the rope broke and the seven foot jib swung round and caught me with its sharp teeth. My left leg was taken off at the knee and my right leg was almost cut off.

He managed to struggle over the tension (a belt drum) and crawled thirty yards down the face. By then the rescue team was on its way. They gave him a seven pint blood transfusion. *'I was conscious and I could not feel any pain. As the minutes went by I decided I had a chance if I saw daylight.'*

In the ambulance room on the surface he still couldn't feel any pain and men were going down like ninepins because they could not stand the sight of his mangled body. In the hospital casualty department he finally lost

consciousness – for a week – and was in hospital for six weeks.

After learning to walk again with the aid of artificial limbs he had a number of jobs in mining, retiring in 1975 from Dodworth Colliery. *'It has been a long hard slog – if I didn't have my wife I would have gone under.'*

It was not the first tragedy in his life, for his brother was killed by a runaway tub in 1939, the family receiving a lump sum of £90 in compensation.

I was a seven days a week man at the pit and I have gone in to work on a Sunday evening but if I had my life over again, I wouldn't work like that again.

Derek 'Chocker' Reeves

The 'powder monkey' strike at Darfield Main Colliery started Derek 'Chocker' Reeves on his union career. As a teenager 'Chocker' and the other pit lads wanted one shilling and five pence a can to carry the explosive powder down the pit, a job colliers would not do. The tin carrier was known as 'a powder monkey' and the lads downed tools when managers declined to concede the payment. At the end of the week-long strike a compromise was reached – the men had to carry the cans.

At sixteen (1955) he sought election as a union man and lost by seven votes. He was a likeable militant and the lads caused so much trouble that the manager, with a twinkle in his eye, put them on the 2 pm to 10 pm shift. The pubs in those days closed at 10.30 pm and the manager thought by restricting their drinking time he would turn them into moderates.

Life down the pit was never dull and the lads indulged in jolly japes. Chocker once attached a bucket of water to a hook, above head height. Then he attached a rope to the bucket and hid in an alcove underground. His mates got a whiff of his plan to shower them with water and did not come near; instead an unsuspecting miner turned up. Unable to see the miner in the dark, but hearing his footsteps, Chocker went into action and the miner ended up soaked to the skin with an upturned bucket on his head.

Dashing out of the alcove with a raucous *'I've got you!'* Chocker found himself face to face with what appeared to be an Australian bush ranger, complete with metal helmet. A muffled voice inside the bucket sighed: *'The lad must be mad.'*

On another occasion the pit knock-out cricket team accepted an invitation to play a game at an RAF training college. The upper-class RAF officers thought they had invited the Yorkshire Council side from Mitchell and Darfield. The pit team arrived in an old van enveloped in clouds of choking exhaust fumes and as the motley crew jumped out of the van with their Albert Hirst shopping bags full of gear, one of the officers was heard to say: *'I say, is that a cricket team?'*

The pit team included a sixty-year-old miner who tried to put his pads on back to front, and a couple of jokers who sat down on the boundary smoking, when they were supposed to be fielding. They were out classed to say the least and after the match the teams were enjoying refreshments when one of the jokers, Alan Beck, strutted up and down with a cricket box clasped to his mouth declaring: *'Angels one five, bandits at four o'clock.'*

Chocker was so embarrassed he breathed a sigh of relief when they were on their way home – although he believes the match is still talked about down among the gin and tonics in the RAF mess.

*Derek 'Chocker' Reeves was elected Barnsley area agent of the NUM in the early 1980s, being responsible for more than ten pits and 15,000 men. He retired in 1991 and died in 1993, aged fifty-four. He was a born comedian and much loved by miners. At the funeral service Wombwell Parish Church was full and the mourners included Arthur Scargill, President of the NUM.

Charlie Bennett

A letter from Charlie Bennett, Middlestown Wakefield, in *The Yorkshire Miner* newspaper in August 1987.

I started work at Woolley Colliery in 1928. At that time, men going into the workings would strip off most of their clothing at the pony stables about 200 yards from the shaft bottom, because of the heat. Some men would travel more than half an hour before reaching their workplace.

Your older readers will know all about tramming. For a period, I was a 'market trammer', which meant you were sent to tram for any collier whose trammer had not turned up. At that time wages were paid 'aht o't cap.' A market trammer might have to find five different colliers for his money, and most colliers would try to pay market trammers less than he should. Many fist fights developed in the pit yard on Fridays.

Any man who might have proven troublesome to the management would find himself blacklisted and, because the same owners owned most of the pits in the area, a man blacklisted would not be set on at any of the pits. Victimisation gave the union plenty to do. Pits in those days, under the old contract system, were a jungle. Men were conditioned to behave like beasts, to develop teeth and claws.

One can only hope that Britain's miners of today, as well as the British people, will not allow privatisation to return to the coalfields.

Arthur Brant

Lady luck deserted Arthur Brant when he was killed in the explosion at North Gawber Colliery in 1935.

He had always regarded himself as lucky. He had served in the First World War, had been gassed several times and had been badly injured when a shell exploded near him. Yet he had survived the war.

His widow, from Four Lane Ends, Mapplewell, who identified his body after the pit explosion, said she could hardly recognise the body because his face had been nearly burned away. Earlier a neighbour had told Mrs. Brant she had seen her husband on a stretcher on his way to hospital and it looked as if he had survived the disaster. But it transpired that the man on the stretcher was Mrs. Brant's son, William, a deputy at North Gawber.

A reporter with the *Yorkshire Evening News* wrote:

The warmth of the September sun brought no comfort to the homes where husbands and sons were missing, their burnt and battered bodies lying in the improvised mortuary at the colliery. I toured the homes today and, as I talked to weeping women and their wide-eyed children, I realised the stark horror of the disaster. They told me of fearful visits to the mortuary, where they were called upon to identify their men, and spoke of the terrible burns and other disfigurements.

A survivor told the reporter:

All at once there was a gap in the atmosphere underground. Then it seemed that some giant breath was dragging me forward with tremendous suction.

Just as I was falling there was a terrific flash and I was flung against the coal face. Eventually I was pulled away before the fire reached me.

(Nineteen mineworkers were killed in the explosion).

Eleanor Bayley

Mrs Eleanor Bayley, of Macclesfield, was nineteen years old and a nurse when she witnessed the sight of fifty-seven white shirts and coffins lined up for the victims of the Wharncliffe Woodmoor explosion in 1936.

I was between training courses in nursing and had been asked to help out with relief duties for the District Nurse – that is how I became involved in the rescue operations.

Eleanor, (nee Caswell) was roused from bed at 4 a.m. by her father, a member of the pit rescue team, with the words: *'Cum on lass, there has been an accident at the pit.'* It was 6.30 a.m. when the first man was brought out. He died a few hours later. *'We saw rescue workers going in with canaries and bringing them out dead so we expected the worst.'*

The bodies were brought out, washed and then laid on straw for identification.

We had to get down on our knees and armed with buckets of water we washed the grimy, burned and disfigured bodies – it was a pitiful sight that will never leave my memory.

Eleanor was working alongside the midwife, Mrs. Bateman.

We came across her brother-in-law but didn't realise it was him until we had washed the dirt away. Then came the body of my Sunday school teacher and lads that I had gone to school with. Last messages to wives, mothers and sweethearts, and hidden in their pit clogs, were handed to the authorities.

Charles Page

Charles Page (eighty-three) Stonyford Road, Wombwell, started work at Darfield Main Colliery in 1918 and his first job involved putting metal discs (motties) on nine inch nails.

The discs were collected by miners before they went underground and then the discs were put on the tubs so that office staff could identify the miners who had filled them when the coal arrived on the surface.

When the pit ran out of discs, miners used chalk to put a number on their tubs.

Mr Page remained in the office for a month and then the pit bought its first Ford-T truck to replace the horse and cart used to deliver miners' home coal.

Charles Page

I got the job as a driver's mate.
The driver was Irving Camplejohn, whose family later ran a bus company, and we delivered coal to miners' homes. We also delivered loads to the owners of the pit, the Mitchell family, who lived at Wath and at Upperwood Hall, Darfield. All the coal had to be hand picked for the Mitchell family. I worked on the lorry for nine months and then went underground.

He remembers receiving what was known as the Sankey Money (named after Lord Sankey who awarded the miners a big wage bonus at the end of the First World War).

I was just over 14 and I thought I had received a windfall. The one-off payment was probably a £1, more than my weekly wage.

Newcomers were not supposed to take a pony down the pit, the rules stating that they had to be accompanied by an experienced lad. But Mr Page was tall for his age and management allowed him to take charge of a pony on the first day.

My pony was called Tigser; he was so intelligent he could do the job without help from humans. Management thought a lot about ponies. When there was a big roof fall one day, the manager asked: 'Are the ponies all right?' Ponies cost money but we get men for nothing.

Pensions were small in the 1920s and 1930s and men worked until they dropped. Just before he left Darfield Main, to work at Upton Colliery in 1929, there was still a seventy year old man called Finch working on the coal face.

I remember talking to miners in their late 60s and telling them that one day we would get holidays with pay. The didn't believe a word. But we got three days with pay in 1938 and a week with pay in 1940.
In those days, old miners were always punctual. When we were children, we knew what time it was when we saw the men, many with walking sticks, making their way from Low Valley to Houghton Main Colliery.

Colin Moore

Colin Moore didn't know all the names of the miners at Darfield Main Colliery – but he knew their faces and their lamp numbers. For more than forty years he worked in the lamp room at the pit, starting in 1936 and retiring as the man in charge in the early 1980s.

I once arranged to see one of our mineworkers who lived

in Lundwood and I was half way there before I realised I didn't know his surname; just his number, 992

said Mr Moore, aged sixty-eight, of Wainwright Place, Wombwell.

When I arrived at Lundwood, I had to find someone who knew everyone at Lundwood and then describe my colleague to him, so I could track him down.
I can still link the lamp numbers with the men. For instance, Edwin Wainwright who worked at the pit and who later became an M.P., had number 25.

Mr Moore had 1,500 lamps to look after and it was his job to make sure they were in good repair and ensure each lamp was handed to the correct miner before he went underground.

When a miner was killed or seriously injured the accident affected us. His lamp on the rack in our room was a constant reminder of the accident. The sadness affected the entire pit. Darfield Main, known as the Valley, was a good pit; it had a friendly atmosphere about it.'

His first boss was Johnny Froggatt from Darfield.

'I remember him wielding his wooden mallet, trying to

'Motties' – the discs placed on coal tubs. *F Burgin*

Darfield Main Colliery, the home of the human nightingale.

loosen a lamp which had become damaged and which would not unscrew. Johnny missed his lamp and struck his leg a mightly blow and he didn't flinch. I thought this man was exceptional; then I realised he had a wooden leg. When the straps broke on his artificial leg, I had to go to his home to collect his spare one... it must have been quite a sight watching Colin Moore cycling down Snape Hill with a wooden leg.

A family of kestrels once nested in the headgear. When one of the birds was injured the men took it to the first aid room and looked after it. We also had a nightingale. But he wasn't a bird.

One of the men used to nip into the grass near the welfare and imitate a nightingale. People came from all over to listen to him, not realising he was a human being.

There were two old ledgers in the time office and when we had a spare moment we would look at them. All the men who had signed on at the pit were in those ledgers. Many years ago the pit took on a joiner who was 89 – he must have been a good craftsman.

The pit had its fair share of characters and jokers. We once asked a man why he had not turned up for work the previous day. On his way to work he had decided to have a cigarette; so he turned his back to the wind, lit up and set off walking... he reached home before he collected his thoughts.

One of the under managers criticised a man for putting the figure 13 in a report. The figure was crossed out and '12 plus one' inserted. Very few men would take a lamp numbered 13. There was a lot of superstition, but I didn't regard 13 as unlucky – I was married on the 13th.

In the Melton Field pit bottom there was a full sized fossilised tree trunk. A part-time photographer, G. Hodgson, took a photograph of the trunk and it won an award in 1940.

Jack Woffenden

Jack Woffenden was the hard man at Dodworth Colliery. He was branch president of the NUM for twenty-four years and delegate for twenty-two.

He ran the union branch and, some said, the pit as well. Very few men crossed him, a few hated him but most of the men had a healthy respect for a man who never lost his idealism and who always had respect for men who kept their word.

Jack came from a mining family. His grandfather was one of the last dependants to draw income from the Oaks Disaster Fund, set up in 1866. His other grandfather, who was six feet four inches and weighed seventeen stone, was brought home dead on a cart following a pit accident at Strafford Main Colliery. The body was dumped on the doorstep and his widow had to drag him indoors.

The body had to remain downstairs until the lads came home from school; then it was carried upstairs to a bedroom, said Jack.

His father started work at fourteen at Rob Royd Colliery, drying the clothes of the shaft sinkers, and afterwards worked underground.

Mr Woffenden recalled many of the influential miners' leaders, including Herbert Smith, 'the man in the cap', and Joe Hall: 'One of the best. He knew what he wanted and he went and fought for it. Management couldn't talk him round.'

On nationalisation, the miners thought the old days had gone forever. No more pit owners, no more bosses. 'But things went from bad to worse,' said Jack. 'All the managers after nationalisation seemed to be college boys.' Jack always believed in Socialism and said:

One day idealism will not be a dirty word. We fought to help people who had been knocked about for generations – I just hope our efforts were not in vain.'

Mr Woffenden died in January, 1989.

173

My Sons
(Written by a Durham woman in 1947)

I am the daughter of a miner. I am a miner's wife. I have four sons in the industry. My earliest recollections are of the frugal life in my father's house. Luxuries were unknown and I can still recall how I and others used to gaze into the shop windows with an intense longing for the many good things that were beyond the family income. Inevitably my brothers followed my father into the pits and that brought my first personal experience of the tragedy of coalmining when my seventeen-year-old brother was killed at his work. The worst period for miners was that between the wars when strikes, lock-outs, short time were the order of the day, highlighted of course by the strike of 1926. By then I had an increasing family of my own and the job of trying to sustain us all on the earnings of one man was almost impossible. Saving for a rainy day was out of the question. No suggestion of a bank book then. No problem of where to go for our holidays in those days. The week the General Strike started my youngest boy was ill with pneumonia and every penny I could scrape up was spent on getting what was needed for him. That meant we started the strike virtually penniless. For the first five weeks we got 22s 6d relief, then that stopped and for the rest of the strike we got nothing. I shall never forget what I lived through then. When my family hear my recounting the events of those days they often laugh. I laugh also now, but in 1926 it was too grim to be humorous. Once I found myself with only sixpence to provide for us all. My father, having died just before, had left a suit which was too large for my husband. I was advised to pawn it and desperation made me agree. Packing the suit into a case I spent sixpence on a single ticket to the nearest pawnshop. When I arrived it was a trades holiday and the shop was closed.

My precious sixpence was gone and I had to walk the six long uphill miles lugging the heavy suitcase. Four weeks later my son Peter was born. Three weeks before his birth my husband and I had nothing to eat from Sunday morning till Tuesday morning – we had to starve to give to our family. It was not uncommon for parents to go to bed with nothing to eat but a piece of raw turnip and to rise to the same for breakfast, this to ensure that their families got what bread and jam was available. What kept most miners' children at school those days was the chance of a meal; porridge for breakfast, soup for dinner, and one and a half slices of bread and cocoa before going home. Then, and for a long time after the strike was over, many miners' children went barefooted and ill-clad to school.

I have nine children and they were all reared during the worst years of the depression. Never was I free from want, nor much above the poverty line until the eldest of them started to work at the expense of their education for the sake of 14s a week. But what a godsend their meagre earnings were to a harassed mother. No family allowances then to help out! How I and many other mothers would have welcomed such a scheme. So far I haven't mentioned housing, not that it isn't important, but because I lived in what was regarded by the standard then prevailing as a good working-class house. I had three rooms – without modern conveniences. Many others, not so fortunate, lived in little better than hovels. You can imagine the scene round my fireside at night with children's clothes hanging across the fireplace and my husband's and sons' wet pit clothes slung across the backs of chairs to dry out for work next morning. No one could get near the fire and the smell of pit water and moleskin filled the house. Nowadays, with the pithead baths, the miners leave their homes clean and return clean.

The nationalisation of the mines has proved a boon to miners and their kin. The five-day week with bonus, guaranteed wage, increased overtime rates, holidays with pay and the paid statutory holidays during the year, and in some cases superannuation schemes, the development of welfare schemes, including pithead baths, canteens, drama guilds and many other physical and cultural pastimes have made something new of mining as a career.

In the midst of all this enlightenment and improvement one thing saddens me very much. After forty-two years in the pits my husband is permanently disabled. Brought home from the pit one night in January last he has been unable to work since. For him there have been the hard times when much effort brought little reward. Today his consolation is watching his sons benefit in the way he and countless others dreamt of but often despaired of seeing.

Joe Harcombe
('My Story' written in 1948)

I come from a mining family. My father worked underground all his life; five of my seven brothers went into the pit as well as me. My father died in 1914 of pneumoconiosis, or 'miner's lung' as we called it in those days. In 1912 one of my brothers was injured. He was carried to our home after working on the night shift, just at the time that I was setting out to work on the morning shift. I could see he was badly hurt; it was a terrible shock to me. My parents, themselves upset, persuaded me to go off to work, and it wasn't until I got back home I found that my brother's arm had been amputated.

Right through the years before 1939 I knew what it was to strike for decent wages and conditions. And I knew also the fear of unemployment and of disablement. But these things didn't worry me very much until I took on responsibility for a family of my own. I married in 1920 and it will show you what life was like when I tell you that my wife and I weren't able to afford a week's holiday together, at Weston-Super-Mare, until 1948, after the industry had been nationalised.

Life was a continual struggle in the old days, particularly in the worst times of the depression. Then six months of unemployment, in which my wife scraped to make ends meet and in which I saw my children having to go without clothes they needed, were followed by a spell of work, during which we tried to get on our feet. After that there would be another six or seven months on the dole. The little money we had managed to save would go and we were back to where we started again.

I was luckier than some of my mates though. Some of them had no work for seven or eight years. The insecurity and the fear of unemployment hung over all of us. I remember being threatened with the sack once because I dared to answer back a manager who insulted me. Luckily he changed his mind and I was allowed to stay at work. The bitterness of the men towards the officials was always strong. I had a spell as an official myself once in the thirties. A few years ago I had studied for a fireman's certificate for a bet. I got the certificate and won the bet. Then later I was offered a job as a fireman – an official. I was expected to do things on behalf of the management that I hated doing (for instance, I had to tell some of my former mates that their pay for a particular job was now to be halved). I put up with it for less than a year, then I went back to my old job.

But we are getting a fair deal since nationalisation. The relations between management and men have certainly improved. There are none of the old insults – we are treated like men instead of animals.

Deputations, which in the past were always met with refusals, now meet the management as equals. And the management is taking the men into its confidence about future plans. Yet, unfortunately, the old spirit of bitterness between officials and the men is not completely dead. Some of my mates find it difficult to forget the long years of struggle behind them. It will be a long time before the old spirit has gone altogether. But it is gradually going. I can tell you what I think about the change in the miner's life since nationalisation. When my two eldest sons were born I swore that they should never work in the pits – I did all I could to keep them out and succeeded.

But the miner now has a new dignity and a hopeful future. My youngest boy is now at the technical school, and I am encouraging him to take up mining as a career. Mining now offers a worthwhile future to my son.

Harry Howley

Mr Harry Howley (seventy-one), Eastfield, Thurgoland, who worked at New Monckton Colliery from the 1930s to the 1960s writes:

I well remember my first encounter with ponies in the mine. I left school at Christmas when I was 14 and started work in the New Year. I remember walking up the dark lane with my older brother to the nearby colliery and going into the pit yard, ablaze with lights. I had earlier been given two metal discs with a number on: the alloy one I handed over at the lamp room window and was issued with an electric lamp.

Some of the men and boys were having their last smoke before they went down. I shall never forget the awful feeling as my stomach seemed to leave me as the cage started to drop at an ever increasing speed. Eventually the cage started to slow down and lights appeared below. As the cage stopped, the gates were opened and we stepped out into what seemed to be a new world.

There were men and boys stood in groups as they waited for instructions from the deputies in charge of the various districts. The deputy in charge of my district asked my name and said: 'Right, lad, go with Charlie Thompson and he will look after you.' So off I went with Charlie, an older boy, and we went through the doors into the stables. The first stall was occupied by the loveliest little black pony I have ever seen and on the board inside was the name 'Wellington'. Next to him was another small pony, 'Sam', followed by 'Midget' and 'Sceptre'. And all four didn't seem to stand any taller than a St. Bernard dog. I couldn't visualize any of these poor little creatures having to haul half ton tubs of coal. As we walked into the stables the ponies got larger. Just inside the entrance on our left was a small office built into the wall of the stables and there sat the man in charge. We were told to take 'Melton'. The pony already had his headgear on – it consisted of a pair of blinkers with a covering over his head to protect him.

We went through two air doors and crossed the main ropeway from the district known commonly as 'Back end'. We then entered the travelling road to the district known as Notton and went through two more air doors. The ponies went ahead of us and two could push open the wooden door with their heads; the third one stood and waited for us to open the door. Charlie said the pony had not been taught to 'trap'. The pony was trained by gently pushing two full tubs of coal against the pony, forcing it to open the door. After a time it got the message. When we were walking along the airway or travelling road, we seemed to be climbing all the way and I thought we would eventually come out at the surface. Eventually we came on to the roperoad and turned right and walked up the 'passby'. This consisted of two separate sets of rails and at the top end set between the rails was the return wheel around which ran the haulage rope which took the full tubs away and brought the empty ones back, 20 at a time.

There were two mangers full of corn for the ponies at the top of the pass-by. Strung up from the girders were several sets of gears which the lads proceeded to put on the ponies to enable them to harness them to the tubs, which were open at one end so they could be emptied with a shovel. These tubs were used by men who had to do repairs and who removed the falls of dirt.

So I got my first taste of life down the mine. When the time came to finish the shift I felt as if I could sleep for a week. But I still had the trek back to the pit bottom to board the cage, to receive our checks through the time office window and be whisked to the surface and hand in our lamps. After meeting my brother, who had been working in another part of the mine, we set off down the little lane to our home and on the way passed our two brothers on their way to start the day shift.

John Burton Threlkeld

John Burton Threlkeld was the son of a Cumbrian farmer who fell on hard times and who had to move with his family to Wombwell to find work during the pre-1914 coal boom.

Arriving in the small mining town at the age of seven, John couldn't come to terms with the dramatic change in the landscape for several months. He had known the fells, the farms and clean rivers of Cumbria; now he had to grow up in what he often described as an ugly smoking bowl, surrounded by pits and pit heaps.

He yearned to return to the fields and rivers of his childhood and often spoke of returning to the Lake District on retirement. Instead he spent fifty years at Mitchell Main and Darfield Main Collieries. His

John Burton Threlkeld

working life spanned the First World War coal boom, the harsh poverty of the 1920s and 1930s and the relative prosperity of the 1950s, during which he earned £20 a week, blue chip earnings in those days.

As a teenager, true to his farming background, he developed a close working relationship with his pit pony.

I suppose I spoilt that pony,' he said, unlike some other handlers who were cruel. Yet despite my kindness, I could never persuade the pony, Boxer, to work beyond the shift. Boxer had his own internal clock. As soon as the shift ended, Boxer moved off and headed for the stables despite my protests.

He always remained in awe of the power of nature and spoke of the interminable battle between man and his underground environment: the roof falls, the gas emissions, the splintering and snapping of wooden props under titanic weights, and the fear that spread among men when the earth trembled.

Mining left its mark. Dust ruined his lungs and left him gasping for breath. And, like thousands of other miners, his back was riddled with blue marks where coal dust had become embedded in cuts. For weeks after his retirement in 1969 coal dust still came out of his pores despite repeated baths.

He often went back to the Lake District for his holidays but he never realised his ambition to spend his retirement at his birthplace, Knipe, near Shap, high on the fells, a couple of miles from the spot where you can find the only pair of breeding eagles in England.

Ken Utley
Ken Utley, Lindhurst Road, Athersley North, worked at Houghton Main, Wharncliffe Woodmoor 1/2/3, North Gawber and Woolley Collieries, where he was senior overman when he took early retirement in 1986.

He was born at Wombwell Main and later lived in Low Valley. At fourteen he started work at Houghton and recalls the Wistow family who were still opening out coal faces with picks and shovels in the 1940s. At eighteen he joined the army and served for two years before returning to the coal industry, at Wharncliffe Woodmoor in 1947.

I was a pony driver when I came out of the army,' he said. 'I had a pony who could open a snap tin better than any man. Another pony called Sam could ride on

a conveyor belt, and enjoyed it. Wharncliffe Woodmoor was an unusual pit in the sense that coal was cut only on the day shift. This may have been as a result of the 1936 pit disaster. Management may have had to make life attractive at the pit to attract miners to work there.

Mr Utley remained at Wharncliffe Woodmoor until its closure in 1966 and then he had six months at North Gawber before starting at Woolley.

Recalling his life in the pits and amusing incidents, Mr Utley said:

I remember Joe Pierrepont being trapped with a large stone on his back. He could move just his lips and eyes. We ran to the scene and asked him if he was all right. 'I can't move a muscle,' he replied. Then someone with a sick sense of humour said: 'You'll have to stay there until we (shot) fire the lot!' Eventually the stone was removed – without the aid of explosives – and Joe was found to be badly bruised, not seriously injured.

When mechanisation was introduced, a coal face could have up to thirty-four men. When he retired, a retreat face employed eight men and an advanced face eleven.

'Ned' Thicket
The disused canal at the Elephant and Castle, Hemingfield, has been restored to its former glory after a generation of neglect. Mr. 'Ned' Thicket (eighty), who lives nearby, can remember the canal in use during the First World War.

Barges lined up near the pub to collect coal from the former Hemingfield Colliery. An overhead gantry brought the coal from the mine to the loading area where the barges were moored. Then the loaded barges moved under the hump-backed bridge into the main canal. He believes the last barge, at the end of the war, was stuck for several days at the Elephant and Castle and cart horses had to be used to free it.

The canal and the railway ran parallel between the Junction at Wombwell and Elsecar Main Colliery, providing transport systems for Cortonwood Hemingfield, Hoyland Silkstone and Elsecar Collieries. Coal from Hoyland Silkstone at Platts Common was transported by endless rope to the canal and railways.

The endless rope ended at four lines of railway track near Hemingfield. The railway wagons were loaded up and then shunted on to the main railway line between Hemingfield and Wath Hump. My uncle was an engine driver and he often hauled 120 empty wagons from the 'hump' to Hemingfield and returned with 100 full wagons. With the closure of Elsecar Main and Cortonwood Collieries, the railway line has been closed.

Anonymous (Written in 1988)
There have been sweeping changes in mining villages over the past forty years. Perhaps they can no longer be described as mining villages. The pits are going and nature is making a comeback, returning the landscape to its former glory. The writer, D H Lawrence, realised what

Hoyland Silkstone Colliery at Platts Common. *F Burgin*

would happen seventy years ago when he said pits were mere accidents in the landscape. Yet in the late 1940s and early 1950s our town was ugly. Ugly pits, ugly buildings, ugly environment.

A pall of smoke hung over us and soot descended on the streets like flakes of black snow and we didn't even notice. Domestic and pit chimneys poured out smoke; our relatives complained they could smell soot as soon as they motored into the Yorkshire coalfield. And then there were the fogs or smogs in the autumn – heavy, dirty fogs that nipped the lungs and left the taste of cinders in the mouth. Autumn still reminds me of those fogs and I can still detect the odour. Streets were blanketed; traffic came to a standstill and adults were driven indoors, leaving children to play in a ghostly world with only the haloes round the gas lamps for company.

Writers always seem to portray mining childhoods as either bleak or sentimental. Mine was neither. It was cosy and rewarding, although it didn't prepare us for adult life in a modern and liberated age. Working class boys are often more spoilt than their middle class cousins who are taught to look after themselves. Even today I have a profound dislike of cooking and housework, for in those days mothers dominated the home, doing all the housework and cooking (and much more), leaving the sons to their own devices. We were the first products of the welfare state. At infants' school, in the early 1950s, we had free milk, orange juice and cod liver oil poured down our throats. We must have been the healthiest children of the twentieth century. The powers that be remembered the hungry 1930s and they were determined that malnutrition would become a thing of the past. Yet there

were still pockets of poverty. I was horrified at the age of seven to hear a middle class teacher ridicule a girl of six, old beyond her years, because she was dirty. The girl couldn't help it.

Some of the lads were hard, very hard. No-one had given them a chance from the day they were born. They were often natural ball players, and intelligent, and they deserved more than a harsh life down the mine.

Sunday school played an important part in community life in those days. I suppose it had something to do with working class snobbery. The child who donned his best clothes and trundled off to Sunday school was more highly respected than the child who didn't. That kind of snobbery didn't mean a thing to a lot of us. We found

Winston Churchill, hated by the miners.

Sunday school embarrassing. The Whit 'Sing', when you paraded through the village on a decorated lorry, in your best clothes, was regarded as girlish. Again it was a sign that mothers dominated many households, and mother demanded that you went to Sunday school. The opiates of my generation, the rough and tumble of football and cricket helped to heal the wounds.

Many of the miners' leaders were the products of Sunday schools. It has not been fully appreciated the role the Sunday School and the church played in the development of the miners' union. John Normansall, the giant of the nineteenth century; A J Cook, the national leader during the 1926 lock-out and Joe Hall, the Yorkshire miners' leader, were all 'educated' at Sunday School. In later life, at public meetings, they sounded like evangelists. I know Arthur Scargill is not a religious man but he adopted the oratory style and delivery of the old fashioned firebrand preacher, if not the philosophy. There were as many churches as pubs in our town. Primitive Methodists, Methodist and Wesleyan Reform were all well represented. By 1954 and 1957 things began to change and Sunday Schools lost their grip on families. I felt sorry for some of those old SS leaders, puritanical, hard working men who didn't understand the world was changing. Children just stopped going to church. Families had more money and the consumer society had been launched. Even cinemas, after controversial opposition from the churches, opened on Sunday evenings, attracting large audiences.

The cinema was a childhood refuge. A magical world in dowdy surroundings. Three weekly visits to the 'Pav', a typical small town cinema, were not unusual. The newsreels provided us with all the news before television became popular. I remember Winston Churchill, the Prime Minister in the first Conservative post war government, being jeered at the local cinema. Miners hated Churchill, mainly because it was alleged he ordered troops to shoot on miners in South Wales before the First World War (this is now disputed by Churchill's biographer) and because of his hysterical editorials during the general strike in 1926. The hatred lasted for two generations.

I think it was Arthur Scargill who said you had to be a member of a mining family to understand the sense of relief that gushed upwards and nearly choked you, half asleep at 10 p.m. when you heard the sound of clogs and the dog barking in the yard, a sign that your father had arrived home safely from the pit. Mining was still a dangerous job in those days. Miners still arrived home covered in dirt and, in some cases, pit baths were still a thing of the future. My cousin, who spent his holidays with us, was shocked the first time he saw my father with his face as black as a minstrel's, the whites of his eyes contrasting with the rest of his face. I have read a biography of D. H. Lawrence, the writer, who spent his bleak childhood at Eastwood, Nottinghamshire. His mother had been a teacher. When she saw her husband on the doorstep, fresh from the pit on the day after their wedding, she thought he was a negro. After my father's pit baths were opened in 1955, some miners still walked home covered in dirt; they were too embarrassed to strip off in front of the young lads.

Miners had a love-hate relationship with coal. They hated the hazardous conditions, the poor pay but some of them seemed to give coal magical qualities. It was sucked to relieve indigestion and I am told it was given to pigs to improve the quality of the pork. It was also hoarded like gold, particularly by old miners who remembered the hard times.

It is often said miners had short and violent lives. Some worked too hard beyond their limitations and were burnt out by their 40s. Others worked in 'dry' pits and suffered from dust on the lungs. You often saw them standing half way up a hill, leaning on a wall fighting for breath. Thankfully, that kind of thing has almost disappeared. Very few new cases are reported these days. But my father lived to be 84 and his brother to 81. Both had muscular bodies. The first time I saw another adult man stripped to the waist I was shocked to see how frail he appeared to be. My father had a strong grip in his late 70s and my uncle could still shovel tons of coal into neighbours' coal cellars at 74. In the 1930s they had only worked two or three days a week (the pit was closed for the rest of the six day week, due to a shortage of orders) and therefore they did not become physical wrecks. Their diet was simple and wholesome and neither drank alcohol, nor could they smoke when working underground. I sometimes think men of their generation were the last real men. Modern men, in comparison, seem soft, effete and over civilised; nature never intended men to be like that.

Elizabeth Levine

Elizabeth Levine, of Peterloo, wrote to her local newspaper:

My eldest brother, who was quite tall and sturdy, went off to work followed by envious mates with a pit cap, much too big water bottles on his shoulders and steel-capped hob nailed boots. A miner at last. He went with his friend in the same gear, but small looking, no more than 12, his mother's one and only son. They went and came back for four days; on the fifth day only my brother walked home- his mate was brought back dead.

My second brother had the same experience. Then when my third brother was about 20, word was brought to him that his best mate had been hewing coal and his pick had hit a detonator that should have been blown, and he was killed. By then I had a son aged 15 and he started at the pit at Easington along with his pal on the bank (top of the pit). They had their bait (food) together and his pal went back to his job, seeing full tubs in a shaft coming to the surface and seeing empty ones back down. He looked over the guard to see if they were coming; they were and he was killed too. My mother and all of us grieved over all these deaths and thanked God He had saved our lads. This may seem far fetched but it is true. My brothers are now about 60, 72 and 74 and my son is 50.

Retired miner

A retired miner who appeared on Channel 4's *Childhood* programme in March, 1989:

It was terrifying going down the shaft when you were a youth. When you got to the bottom you couldn't believe your eyes; yet the conditions at the bottom of the shaft were ten times better than where you worked. You can imagine what a young boy felt – it was a mile to the coal face before you started work.

On your way to work you would knock your head against the roof, knocking you off your feet. You could find yourself in the dark if your lamp went out. The pit still frightens me. Imagine just those pit props between you and all that earth above; I still cannot believe it. I had years as a boy in the pits. You only thought of safety, always looking for danger – the timber cracking, or the roof falling in. Some people don't believe you when you say the floor could rise: the roof came down and the floor came up.

By the time you had walked to your workplace you were worn out. Then you had to pull yourself together. I think the hardest work was carrying the coal to the tubs. I had to wet my fingers to wet my eyes to keep awake. If you were caught asleep you got the sack. The years I spent in the pit were years of exploitation, not just for the boys but for the men as well. I was happy the day I came out of the pit for the last time. I thought 'Thank God'.

John Hunt

John Hunt started work as a pony driver, later became a pit manager and ended his forty-seven year career in the mining industry as a member of the highly skilled management team which supervised the £400 million reconstruction of the Barnsley coalfield. He saw the industry – and the men – from all angles. It is a remarkable story, beginning in the depths of the Depression, when children went to school barefoot, and *'that was the rule rather than the exception,'* and ending in the halcyon, pre-1984/85 miners' strike days when Barnsley pits were among the most modern in the country. His father was a miner from Bolton in Lancashire, who moved to South Kirkby in the 1920s to find work. All John's brothers worked in the industry – three became pit officials and the other remained a miner. Their father died when John was seven and his mother had to bring them up without any National Assistance because the eldest brother was already working. *'It was a harsh life for miners but it was even worse for the mothers,'* he said.

When the lads were working on all three shifts, she did not go to bed until the afternoon shift was completed (11 p.m.). At 4 a.m. she was up again and would not return to bed because she had to cook breakfast for the lad finishing the night shift. This was the average lot of mothers in those days.

In his childhood, there were few toilets – just privy middens, particularly in pit houses – and the family were regarded as lucky when they moved into a new council house in 1925. John left school in December, 1933, but he did not get a job until February, 1934. It was not through lack of trying. Every day at 6 a.m. he set off to walk to South Kirkby Colliery to apply for a job on the surface; then he walked back home, a distance of three miles. At 10 a.m. there was an interview at Brierley, which involved another trek. Then back to South Kirkby at 12.30 to see the under manager, followed by a walk to Frickley Colliery for an interview at 3 p.m. Every day there were long queues of lads with their fathers. If your father worked at the pit, there was a good chance you would get a job.

I was covering between 20 and 30 miles per day. Then one day the under manager said I was always first in the queue, and always smartly dressed, so I got a job as a pony driver to the coal face. I started the following morning but first of all I had to buy a snap tin – it was so big it rattled my ankles.

He still remembers his first descent in the cage – *'I nearly lost my breakfast. When the cage came to a standstill the pit bottom looked like an illuminated cave.'* Coal mining in those days was highly skilled work and sometimes the men who did the most work did not necessarily receive the most pay. If the coal was soft, a miner would produce a lot of coal; if the coal was hard, or 'wooden', then a miner had a difficult job on his hands. Invariably men working hard coal would be on the 'mini' (their pay would be made up to the minimum wage).

The skills of mining were many – a lot depended on the 'cleavage' of the coal. The skilled miner by advancing the 'cutting side' would enable the rest of the face to be more easily worked for his mates. It was a gruelling task requiring changing pick blades, often using ten to 15 blades per shift. The blades were carried on a ring from the 'pick hole,' where the blades were sharpened each day by the colliery blacksmith's department. 'Shafting' of the pick was done at home where the steel socket was fitted to the wooden shaft, by heating the socket in the open fire until it was red hot. Once fitted the socket was immersed in cold water to give a tight fit. The shaft would be cut to size using a sharp knife and smoothed to the miner's satisfaction by shaving it with broken glass.

Men who worked in thin seams sometimes did not like being transferred to thick seams and vice versa. Kneeling down in a thin seam meant that the strain was taken on the stomach muscles; in thick seams, such as the Barnsley Bed, the back took the strain. In the thinner seams in the north east men had to shovel coal on their sides. Some men filled coal tubs with garden forks because they did not want small coal or slack. Their wages depended on the amount of coal produced and the owners said small coal had no commercial value. At South Kirkby the chargeman of the stall (work place) drew the money for all the work done in the stall that week. This would be divided by the number of shifts worked and the men paid out. Spare coppers were given to pony drivers and rope runners as 'tip money,' and in some cases tip money exceeded the drivers' wages.

My first wage as a pony driver was 2s.10d. These were hard times. I have seen men go to work in extreme pain, with four or five boils on their bodies, because they could not afford to take time off work. But there was a camaraderie that had to be seen to be believed – no-one locked his door, for instance, because there was little crime. You could walk in and out of every house in the village.

Life revolved round the pit buzzer: in the 30s pits were on short time and when the buzzer split the silence at 7.30 the miners knew there would be no work the following day at the pit. When there was a fatal accident the buzzer went on and on. The men also relied on the bell man who went round the village announcing there would be no work at such and such a pit. In a village like South Kirkby the men worked at a number of pits. He was at South Kirkby Colliery in 1935 when an explosion killed eleven men in the Barnsley Bed. That afternoon he was working in the Haigh Moor seam when there was a message to clear the mine. Mr. Hunt knew there had been a 'gob' fire in the Barnsley Bed but at that time he didn't realise there had been an explosion. When they saw the pit yard full of people, they soon realised what had happened. For thirteen years he worked on the face at Frickley Colliery. In the late 40s he broke his leg – and to occupy his mind he did papers on a mining course his friend was taking. Then he obtained his deputy's certificate. Returning to South Kirkby Colliery in 1949, he offered himself on a month's trial – to give management a chance to gauge his capabilities. It was agreed that at the end of the trial he would get an official's job, or he would return to Frickley. Later he was given a shotfiring job, the first step on the managerial ladder. The decision to pursue a career in management was prompted by the need for greater job security. He remembered the pre-war, three day working week, when miners turned up at the pit for work and then had to return home because there was a shortage of wagons.

This was particularly disconcerting if you were on nights and you had spent, as before, most of the day in bed. During the severe winter of 1947 men were sent home, not just on the odd day, but for a week or more. But pit officials had greater security of employment and guaranteed work.

In 1963 he was appointed manager of Ferrymoor, followed by similar posts at Wharncliffe Silkstone, Tankersley, which had a long and distinguished history and which had been one of the first pits to have baths, Smithywood, Dearne Valley and Wentworth Silkstone, Stainborough. Experience teaches managers man management techniques, not text books.

You meet many types of men and firmness, fairness and good communications are required. There were men who did not need supervision, practical pit men who only required to know what you wanted. Then you let them get on with the job. These men were the salt of the earth and without them few pits would work successfully. At the other end of the scale you had the awkward squads, men who were hell bent on forcing their will on others, very often to the detriment of the other men. You had to deal with them with firmness and without compromise.

Man management techniques varied from pit to pit, depending on the size of the catchment area. The larger the catchment area the more difficult and militant the men appeared to be, probably because there were so many divided opinions among them. On the other hand, the small catchment areas produced the family pit, where the men were drawn from nearby villages and many of them were closely related. Industrial relations problems were rare at these pits. There were exceptions. Wentworth Silkstone, with its pine forest, was a family pit with good men, although most of them came from Dodworth. Yet the Dodworth pit was very militant. Before I arrived at Wentworth, the pit had a poor safety record but we got the men safety motivated and we twice reached the national finals of the NCB competitions, at Drury Lane and at the Opera House, Blackpool. We had our own pit newspaper with stories from the safety officer, and even horse racing and gardening tips supplied by Gordon Totty of Dodworth.

When the colliery closed in the late 70s, the NCB, out of respect to the men, transferred them to Houghton Main Colliery, where part of the Dunsil seam was earmarked for the men. This kept them together as a team. Some men were nervous about the transfer: they had always worked in a drift mine and the thought of descending a shaft frightened them.

Mr Hunt went on to be a manager in the management team which rebuilt the Barnsley coalfield, working on the Grimethorpe drift as well as the shaft deepening at pits which were linked underground to Grimethorpe, retiring in 1981. He came up the hard way – valuable experience when dealing with miners.

You are either a pit man or not. That goes a long way towards getting the men's respect. Respect is very important. You may not be at the top of the popularity polls but then popularity is the cheapest commodity you can buy. The years have brought affluence and a tragedy. Today we have a selfish society, a society that has lost that old camaraderie which has been replaced with greed and envy and a disregard for others or their property.

Chapter 9

Scrapbook

No it's not the monster from the deep lagoon. A pit official appears to be testing new (1909) rescue equipment. *Yorkshire Mining Museum/Leeds City Museum*

Woolham Colliery and Hickleton Main, circa 1920. *F Burgin*

"The Holocaust and Martyrdom of the Mine."

DEDICATED TO HUMANITY BY
EDWARD A. RYMER, Monk Bretton, near Barnsley, 1903.

Deep beneath the solid earth,
Where volcanoes have their birth,
There engraved on leaves of stone,
Pictured ages past and gone.

Where natures vast and boundless store
Enrich the earth from shore to shore,
And countless ages leave behind,
A sublime record for mankind.

The nations speak with lightning power,
Engines eternal space devour;
And art has wrought a mighty scroll,
From energy stored up in coal.

In searching out this boundless worth,
From east to west, from south to north,
The mining toiler wins the coal,
And commerce sends from pole to pole.

Bold science with a stern command
In triumph conquors every land,
Her mandates rush across the line,
With blood and treasure from the mine.

From British Isle to Austral plains,
Britain still her power maintains.
From India to Canadian shores,
The miner o'er the world explores.

At his grim toil, faced with death,
Inhaling poison with each breath,
While every impulse of his soul,
Reminds him of the funeral pall.

The fiery demon lurks around,
In sunless regions underground,
And subtle gases fill the air,
Menacing destruction everywhere.

Lo! the pit has fired and flames arise,
The mine fiend mocks its victims cries,
While thundering echoes shake the ground,
And shrieks are heard for miles around.

The aged father groans with fear,
The loving mother tears her hair,
And children fly amidst the gloom,
To yonder pit—their father's tomb.

The stricken widow faints with grief,
Convulsed amidst a scene of death;
And children clutch her struggling form,
And wail at every parting groan.

Behold! the volunteers descend:
As pilots in the gulf of death;
With love and hope their spirits blend,
While choke damp poisons every breath.

With fire and smoke and dead around,
Those heroes of the burning mine
A ransom give till all is found,
And makes a record so sublime.

There's none to help them in their need,
None to cheer them in their deed,
Doves of hope to those beneath,
And pilots in the gulf of death.

'Tis natures last and only stay,
Oh aid them angels on their way,
And bless them for their noble deed,
To help the miner in his need.

If danger be by fire or flood,
The sons of Britain know the word;
Help and rescue, brings warriors forth,
To bless the land that gave them birth.

Let justice plead and mercy crave
For England's noble sons, and brave,
Whose deeds enshrined on scroll of fame
Makes hallowed grand Old England's name.

Oh England! shall thy sons so brave,
Sink helpless to a pauper's grave?
For statesmen shudder at the scene
Lamented by the nation's Queen!

Go see within yon gloomy cot
The crowning risk of the miner's lot,
And measure the sorrow of that devoted wife
Then grasp the struggle of the miner's life.

Arrest, oh Britain this saddening tale,
Nor waft it o'er the morning gale,
That hapless victims find a tomb,
In struggling with the miners' doom.

Miners processions... above 1987 and below Barnsley, 1975. *British Coal*

A deputy at Royston Drift,
a few days before the
closure in 1989. *Anton Want*

Maltby Colliery. *F Burgin*

The Mitchell and Darfield Main Miners' Welfare Club in Netherwood Road, Wombwell, was opened in June 1930 by Mr Robert Claytor and Coun. J Hall, of Wombwell Urban Council. Also pictured: G. Kilner (chairman), G E Crowther (secretary), J R Brittan, H Copeland, J Ellis, W Stubbs, T H Spooner, J Wainwright and S Blackwell.

The end is in sight for Wombwell Main. An engine room attendant contemplates his future in 1969. *M Firth*

The last shift finishes at Wombwell Main, 23 May 1969. Wombwell Wood is in the background. *M Firth*

What the well dressed miner was wearing in 1981. The two men were 'modelling' working clothes for publicity purposes at Barrow Colliery. *British Coal*

The entrance to Grimethorpe Colliery, 1992. *Barnsley Chronicle*

Houghton Main announced a new drivage record in 1992. These men – and the fearsome looking machine – were photographed for publicity purposes. *British Coal*

Index